super
salads

super
salads

More than 250 fresh recipes
from classic to contemporary

3 1571 00257 3783

Published by The Reader's Digest Association Limited
Sydney • London • New York • Montreal

super salads

Project Editor Lynn Lewis

Senior Designer and Design Concept Donna Heldon

Project Designer Joanne Buckley

Translator Angela Armstrong

Publishing Coordinator Françoise Toman

Photographers Christiane Kruger, Ian Hoffstetter

Illustrator Merrilee Fleeting

Proofreader Susan McCreery

Indexer Diane Harriman

Production Manager General Books Janelle Garside

READER'S DIGEST GENERAL BOOKS

Editorial Director Elaine Russell

Managing Editor Rosemary McDonald

Art Director Carole Orbell

We are interested in receiving your comments
on the contents of this book. Write to: The Editor,
General Books Editorial, Reader's Digest (Australia)
Pty Limited, GPO Box 4353, Sydney, NSW 2001, or
email us at bookeditors.au@readersdigest.com

Super Salads is published by
Reader's Digest (Australia) Pty Limited
80 Bay Street, Ultimo, NSW 2007
www.readersdigest.com.au; www.readersdigest.co.nz;
www.readersdigeststore.co.za, www.rd.com, www.rd.ca,
www.readersdigest.co.uk

First published 2008
Copyright © Reader's Digest (Australia) Pty Limited 2008
Copyright © Reader's Digest Association Far East
Limited 2008 Philippines Copyright © Reader's Digest
Association Far East Limited 2008

This book was adapted from *Tolle Salate* published
by Reader's Digest, Germany, 2005

National Library of Australia Cataloguing-in-Publication data:

Super salads : more than 250 fresh recipes from classic
to contemporary

ISBN 978 192107788 3

ISBN 978-0-7621-0926-5 (US and Canada)

1. Salads. I. Reader's Digest Association.

641.83

Prepress by Sinnott Bros, Sydney
Printed and bound by Leo Paper Products Ltd, China

Front cover Warm grilled mixed vegetable salad (p 107).
Back cover (left to right); Grilled tomato salad (p 108);
Chicken kebab salad with peanut sauce (p 228); Mixed
fruit salad in melon halves (p 284). **Page 2** Warm summer
fruit salad with sabayon (p 294). **Page 3** Spinach, roasted
garlic and parmesan (p 32); Prawn and mango salad
(p 262); Chef's salad (p 29). **Contents** Gado gado (p 62).

introduction

Salads are for all seasons. Year-round, there's a great variety of fresh vegetables and salad greens available. Putting together combinations of flavours, colours and textures that taste delicious, look attractive and are good for you is a surprisingly easy and rewarding thing to do.

With salad making, you can travel the world. Many countries have their own signature salads that highlight particular salad greens, herbs or other seasonings. Some include rice, pasta, beans or grains while others use bread as a way to add valuable nutrients and to help make a little go a long way.

This compilation of more than 250 recipes includes all the classic salads as well as contemporary ideas for inexpensive everyday family meals and for special occasions. There are main-course and side-dish recipes for meat, seafood and poultry lovers as well as many options for vegetarians. For a sweet finale, dessert fruit salads are the perfect showcase for top-quality seasonal produce.

We hope you enjoy using these recipes and are inspired to create some of your own. And, if you're in a hurry, don't forget that a salad is fast food at its very best!

The Editors

contents

the art of making salads 9

* salad days 10 * buying equipment 11 * the nature of
herbs 12 * salad greens at a glance 14 * oils 18 * vinegars 19
* herb dressings 20 * creamy sauce classics 22

the classics 24

salad greens and vegetable salads 64

rice, pasta, bean and grain salads 146

meat and poultry salads 198

fish and seafood salads 239

dessert fruit salads 276

index 306

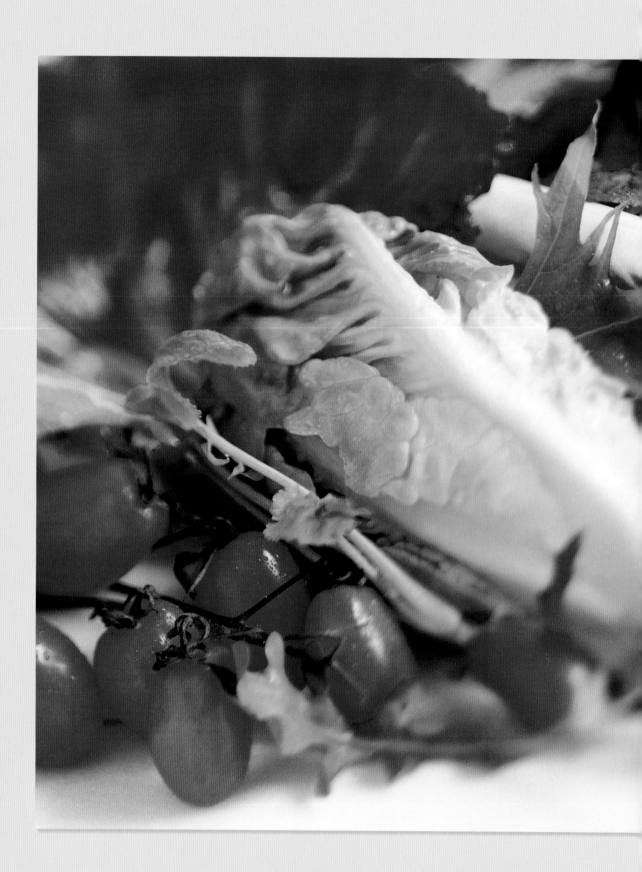

the art of making salads

Making salads is one of the easiest things to do and basic cooking skills will see you through. One of the keys to a great salad is using top quality ingredients. Learn more about the many salad ingredients and seasonings now available and your palate and your health will be sure to reap rewards.

salad days

Salad making is one of the easiest forms of meal preparation and one of the most versatile. It provides scope for a great deal of creativity and imagination, drawing on a wide range of ingredients. Gone are the days when a salad was little more than an afterthought, a plain little affair comprised of a few sad lettuce leaves, canned beetroot (beets) and a sliced tomato. Today's salads are full of flavour and beneficial nutrients.

reap the benefits

A salad you've made yourself has the big advantage in that you know exactly what's in it, right down to the last grain of salt. Salad greens, raw or cooked vegetables, crunchy grains, different types of pasta, fresh berries, citrus fruits, hard-boiled eggs, nuts, rice, soft and hard cheeses, meat, poultry and fresh or canned fish — you can draw on all these to make a salad. A flavoursome dressing provides the perfect finishing touch. This could be as simple as a mixture of good-quality olive oil and balsamic vinegar or as sophisticated as a rich Roquefort cheese dressing. Research indicates that eating at least five servings of vegetables and fruit each day provides a wide range of nutrients required for general health and daily function. Regularly incorporating salads into your diet is a simple way to achieve that goal and obtain sufficient vitamins, phytochemicals, fibre and minerals. The ideal is to choose servings according to the traffic light principle. What this means in practice is that every day you should eat at least one serving of red fruit or vegetables (such as capsicums (bell peppers), radishes, tomatoes and strawberries), at least one of yellow or orange (carrots, yellow squash or zucchini, melon, pineapple or oranges), as well as at least one of green (broccoli, beans, spinach, salad greens, peas, watercress, apples, pears or kiwifruit). Follow this formula and you will include the broadest possible range of nutrients in your diet.

eat your greens. . . they're good for you

* Some types of lettuces and other salad greens contain beta carotene, folate, vitamin C, iron and potassium. Dark green or other deeply coloured leaves have more beta carotene and vitamin C than pale ones. Cos (romaine) lettuce has five times as much vitamin C and more beta carotene and folate than iceberg.

* Deeply coloured lettuces and greens are also high in bioflavonoids, plant pigment known to work with vitamin C to prevent cancer-causing cell damage.

* Rocket (arugula), a member of the same plant family as broccoli, is one of the most nutritious of all salad greens, with more calcium than most others.

buying equipment

A sharp knife, a cutting board, a large strainer and a bowl: everyone has the basic equipment to make a simple salad. But if you make salads often and value variety, you'll want to acquire more utensils. First to add to the list should be a salad spinner, which makes drying washed salad greens a quick and easy task. But whether you buy a mezzaluna, an eggslice or a mezzaluna for chopping herbs, always buy the best quality you can afford. Your rewards? A product that works well and that's made to last.

for cutting and cleaning

Mandoline slicer (1) is perfect for cutting firm vegetables such as carrots into even slices. It is also useful for grating cabbage leaves finely for coleslaw. Some have multiple blades of different widths. Mezzaluna (2) has a sharp, curved blade for finely chopping fresh herbs. Its name means half-moon in Italian. Vegetable brush (3) is for cleaning vegetables such as mushrooms that do not need washing but do have some surface dirt that requires gentle removal. Fruit zester (4) makes it easy to pare very fine strips of peel from citrus fruits.

for shaping, pitting and slicing

Melon baller (1) is useful for scooping even rounds from melons or other soft fruit. Eggslice (2) cuts hard-boiled eggs, cooked potatoes, mushrooms, mozzarella and other firm to soft ingredients into even slices. Cherry pitter (3) makes the removal of cherry and olive pits easy. Vegetable peelers (4) come in numerous different styles, all equally efficient. Choose whichever type fits comfortably in the palm of your hand. Apart from using them to peel fruit or vegetables, vegetable peelers are good for shaving thin slices or decorative curls from hard cheeses, vegetables and chocolate.

the nature of herbs

A handful of finely chopped fresh parsley, a tablespoon of chopped chives or a scattering of tarragon leaves gives salads that extra layer of flavour. Ideally, use fresh herbs in salads. They're best purchased as and when needed because they do not keep well for more than a few days. If you have the space, it's very rewarding to grow your own. When a recipe calls for dried herbs, remember that they are much stronger in flavour than fresh. They will keep their flavour for longer if stored in cool, dark, tightly sealed containers.

1 basil

Basil is synonymous with Mediterranean cooking. Sweet basil, the most commonly known, has a warm, aniseed flavour that complements tomatoes. Thai and purple Greek basil are more pungent. Basil goes well with fish and seafood salads and pasta and rice salads. It is used to make pesto, which in turn can be used in salad dressings.

2 chives

Chives are the mildest member of the onion family. They are often used in salads, particularly ones containing hard-boiled eggs or potatoes. They team well with other herbs such as parsley, dill or chervil (with its subtle parsley/aniseed flavour).

3 coriander (cilantro)

This is a love-it-or-hate-it herb with an assertive taste containing an undercurrent of heat. Often used with other strongly flavoured ingredients which can stand up to it, such as lime juice and chilies, it features in Middle Eastern, Asian, South American, Mexican and Mediterranean dishes.

4 dill

Dill's caraway-seed taste enhances egg, cucumber, potato, beetroot (beets) or fish. It can be mistaken for fennel leaves (which have an aniseed flavour).

5 lemon grass

The tough outer leaves of this slender, tall herb are stripped away and the bases of the lemon-scented and lemon-flavoured internal stems are used. Lemon grass features in Thai and South-East Asian salads, especially those containing meat or fish.

6 marjoram

Traditionally used in Mediterranean and Mexican cooking, marjoram is a good complement to darker

green salad leaves or tomato salads and warm salads of zucchini (courgettes) and eggplant (aubergine). It has a strong, spicy flavour. Use it sparingly. Marjoram is closely related to and similar in taste to oregano.

7 mint

This refreshing herb enlivens many types of salads and dessert fruit salads. Steep the leaves in olive oil or white wine vinegar to make flavoured vinaigrettes. There are many varieties, the different flavours and aromas ranging from spearmint to apple and lemon.

8 parsley

Parsley is available all year. It comes in curly-leaf and flat-leaf (Italian) varieties. They are interchangeable, although flat-leaf is generally thought to have the finer flavour. Parsley is ideal in potato, mushroom or grain salads, among many others, and is often used simply as a garnish. Parsley is said to stimulate the appetite and to be good for rheumatism.

9 rocket (arugula)

Interchangeable as a salad green and herb, rocket has a peppery taste that becomes more pungent with age. Older leaves also tend to be coarser in texture.

10 rosemary

The long, narrow leaves (needles) of rosemary have an intense, slightly resinous, earthy taste. Popular in Mediterranean cooking, rosemary teams well with other herbs such as thyme, marjoram and parsley in herb vinaigrettes, oils and marinades. Very finely chopped, it can also be used in mushroom salads or salads that include meat or poultry.

'rosemary . . . it is sacred to remembrance and to friendship . . .'

Sir Thomas More, English writer, statesman and philosopher (1478-1535)

11 tarragon

Tarragon, one of the classic French *fines herbes,* is used extensively in French cuisine. Its aniseed flavour works well in green salads as well as carrot, seafood, chicken or egg salads. Tarragon is also used to flavour vinegars, oils and mustards.

12 thyme

It is impossible to imagine the cooking of Provence and Italy without this herb. With its robust, spicy flavour, thyme complements a mix of salad greens as well as carrot, potato, mushroom, bean or pasta salads. A key ingredient, with parsley and bay, in a bouquet garni, it is also used to flavour oils and vinegars for marinades, vinaigrettes and dressings. Lemon thyme is another common variety. Lesser known, but also suitable for culinary use, are orange thyme and caraway thyme.

13 watercress

Rich in vitamin C, watercress has a hot, peppery taste. Sprigs can be used as a garnish or the leaves used in a variety of salads. Watercress is, in fact, a member of the high-nutrition cruciferous vegetable family to which broccoli and brussels sprouts belong.

salad greens at a glance

There is a large variety of lettuce types and salad greens to choose from all year round, with new varieties appearing regularly in the marketplace. Visit your local farmers' market to look for new ones that your supermarket or vegetable shop may not yet stock. Butter or butterhead lettuces are soft and loose-hearted, while icebergs are dense and crunchy. Cos (romaine) lettuces have crisp, upright leaves. Loose-leaf lettuces don't form hearts. They are harvested as dense heads and, with no central core, individual leaves are easily separated.

shopping

Freshness is the key to buying salad greens. Packaged, pre-washed salad green mixtures can be a useful, quick option at times, but putting together your own combination of leaves is by far the more flavoursome and creative way to go.

✳ Regardless of variety, lettuces, herbs and other salad greens should look clean and fresh with no wilted or slimy leaves.

✳ Avoid any produce that has yellowing leaves or rust-coloured or dark spots.

✳ Avoid lettuces with a lot of tough outer leaves that will have to be discarded.

washing

All lettuces and salad greens need to be washed, even if they are labelled 'organic'. Packaged salad mixes should also be rinsed and the 'use-by' date noted. One of the best ways to wash and dry salad greens is to separate the leaves and then wash them in a sink full of cold water. Any very muddy or gritty leaves can be washed individually under cold, running water. Drain the leaves, shaking off excess water and place them in a salad spinner and spin dry. If the leaves still seem a little wet, pat them dry with paper towels.

storing

The delicate varieties such as cos, oak leaf and lamb's lettuce (mâche), in particular, wilt within a couple of days of harvesting and lose their vitamin content. Iceberg lettuce, curly endive (frisée), witlof (Belgian endive/chicory) and radicchio are more robust and last longer.

✳ Salad greens are best kept in a cool, dark place, preferably in a sealed plastic container or in the vegetable crisper in the refrigerator.

✳ Do not add dressings or vinaigrettes until close to serving time because acid that they contain will make the leaves wilt.

salads for health

Salads provide an easy, delicious way to enjoy a wide variety of foods and a wide variety of essential nutrients. All kinds of fruits and vegetables can be included and, because they are mostly used raw, or are only briefly cooked, they retain the maximum amount of vitamins and minerals. For example, the vitamin C content of raw vegetables and fruit is higher than that of cooked. An added benefit is that raw foods take longer to chew and also take longer for the system to digest, which can help to curb the urge to overeat. Starchy carbohydrates, such as rice, potatoes, pasta, grains and bread are important to a healthy diet and are easy to incorporate into salads. Also, by adding moderate amounts of protein-rich food, such as meat, chicken, fish, nuts or eggs, a salad can be turned into a well-balanced main dish. If weight watching is an issue, it's important to be mindful of the choice and amount of dressing used. There are many low-fat options that taste good and are good for you.

baby spinach

Glossy green spinach leaves have a slight metallic taste because of their iron content. The iron is not all absorbed by the body, however, due to the leaf's oxalic acid content. Spinach does contain many other valuable nutrients, especially antioxidants and bioflavonoids that may help block cancer-causing substances and processes. Use raw baby spinach leaves in salads for the best flavour.

Dressing A simple olive oil and vinegar dressing containing a few drops of walnut oil.

bok choy

This leafy, dark green vegetable is a variety of Chinese cabbage, which it resembles in taste. For salads, add raw chopped leaves and stems cut into thin strips.

Dressing An Asian-style dressing including hot and spicy ingredients such as chilies and soy sauce, as well as crushed garlic and finely chopped fresh ginger.

butter lettuce

Green and also red butter (butterhead) lettuces are among the most popular varieties. They form small heads with soft, tender leaves. The heart is tender and the leaves have a mild flavour. Do not cut the large, floppy outside leaves; just tear them into bite-sized pieces.

Dressing A light herb vinaigrette or a yogurt or sour cream dressing.

cos lettuce (romaine)

This long, oval head of fairly tightly packed leaves has sturdy, rich green outer leaves and crisp white ribs. It has a mild, tangy flavour. Cos lettuce contains carotenoids and is rich in potassium.

Dressing A vinaigrette containing finely chopped hard-boiled eggs or crumbled feta cheese.

cress and sprouts

Mustard cress (top) is a mixture of seedlings of garden cress and white mustard (or sometimes rape). It is commonly grown and used in the UK. The very delicate shoots taste peppery. They, like alfalfa or mung bean sprouts (bottom), are often used as a garnish, and also add plenty of texture to salads.

Dressing A classic vinaigrette with a few drops of hazelnut or sesame oil.

curly endive

This is also known as frisée lettuce. The large, slightly flattened round head has thin, light green leaves with wavy edges tapering to fine points. They have a bitter taste. The paler, greenish-yellow leaves at the centre form a compact heart. They are milder and more tender than the outer ones.

Dressing Thousand Island dressing and cream or sour cream dressings.

iceberg lettuce

A large, round, tightly packed lettuce that looks like a type of cabbage, iceberg has pale green leaves with a bland but refreshing taste. This lettuce is useful more for its crunch than its taste.
Dressing The mild taste works with all types.

lamb's lettuce

Also known as mâche, corn salad or field salad, this lettuce is comprised of small rosettes of pretty, delicate, mid-green leaves. They have a velvety texture and a mild flavour. Young leaves are the sweetest. Lamb's lettuce is high in beta carotene, which is thought to help fight heart disease and certain types of cancers.
Dressing Classic vinaigrettes using fruit vinegars, such as raspberry vinegar, and a few drops of walnut oil combined with olive oil.

lollo rossa and lollo bionda

These two Italian relatives of the butter (butterhead) lettuce form compact leaf rosettes without a firm head. They look very frilly because the ends of the reddish dark copper or light green leaves are finely crinkled, with lacy edges. The crisp aromatic leaves are more robust than those of butter lettuce and will last a little longer.
Dressing A classic vinaigrette of good-quality olive oil and balsamic vinegar.

mignonette

A loose-head lettuce, the mignonette has small, soft, mild-tasting leaves with ruffled edges. It is available in red and green varieties which look attractive mixed together in a salad. Because it is a loose-head lettuce with no firm core, the leaves are easy to pick individually.
Dressing Cream dressing with herbs.

nasturtiums

This plant with its bright orange, red and yellow blossoms looks attractive in mixed green salads and fruit salads. Other small, pretty flowers, such as pansies, violets or daisies or the flowers of edible herbs such as borage can be used. Be sure to wash flowers carefully and avoid any that have been sprayed with herbicides. Flowers vary greatly in taste from peppery to virtually tasteless and are valued more for their appearance than for their flavour.
Dressing All types of dressings.

oak leaf lettuce

The leaf shape gives this lettuce its name. Oak leaf is a loose-head lettuce with thin, tender reddish-brown or green scalloped leaves. They have a mild nutty flavour that teams well with mushroom or meat salads.
Dressing Stronger vinaigrettes with red wine vinegar or specialty vinegars such as cassis vinegar.

radicchio

A member of the endive (chicory) family, radicchio is a tight head of crisp leaves that are a vibrant red or reddish-purple with white veins. They have a bitter, nutty taste that teams particularly well with citrus fruits. Treviso is a variety of radicchio with long, elongated leaves and a slightly milder flavour. Radicchio is high in beta carotene and other cancer-fighting phytochemicals.
Dressing A robust dressing, such as one containing mustard or blue cheese.

rocket

Also known as arugula, rocket (which is also termed a herb) is made up of clumps of rounded and spiked tender leaves that jut out from slender stems. Their distinctive peppery taste becomes more pronounced as the plant ages. Rocket goes well with tomatoes, feta, Parmesan, olives and roasted, marinated vegetables.
Dressing Classic vinaigrette containing balsamic vinegar and a little lemon juice.

sorrel

The elongated dark green leaves of sorrel resemble those of spinach but are more oval or spear-shaped. They have a pronounced sharp, lemony taste. Slice leaves into thin strips and use sparingly in combination with milder salad greens or other wild herbs or the taste can be overpowering. Use in white fish or salmon salads.
Dressing A mild dressing made with cream cheese or a more robust blue cheese.

witlof

Also known as Belgian endive or chicory, this is a bullet-shaped head of smooth, compact, white to pale yellow leaves. The pale tones are the result of the plant not being exposed to sunlight during its growth. Crisp and succulent, witlof leaves have a bitter taste that works well in egg salads or ones that contain citrus fruits or celery.
Dressing A garlicky or herb dressing.

'you don't have to cook fancy or complicated masterpieces. . .just good food from fresh ingredients.'

Julia Child, American cookbook author (1912-2004)

oils

Oil, be it a fruity olive oil, an aromatic sesame or walnut oil or a mild safflower, peanut or canola oil, gives each type of salad its characteristic aroma and flavour. It also complements or accentuates the taste of the individual ingredients. For the best results and maximum flavour, always buy the best oil that you can afford. Store oils in tightly sealed bottles in a dark, cool place, but not in the refrigerator. Nut oils have an intense flavour and should be used sparingly. They are much more susceptible to spoilage and quickly turn rancid in hot conditions, so buy them in small quantities and use them as quickly as possible.

canola (rapeseed) oil

A mildly nutty monounsaturated oil that is good in salads and for use as a general cooking oil.

grapeseed oil

This oil varies in taste from delicately dry to mild and fruity. It is rich in the antioxidant vitamin E.

peanut (groundnut) oil

The mild flavour is good for lighter salad dressings. It is a very good cooking oil for stir-frying as it does not intrude on the other flavours.

olive oil

Olive oil is the classic for most vinaigrettes. Different varieties of olive and a different growing region will give the oil its own special properties, and it can be peppery, salty, fruity, creamy, mild and so on. Ideally, have at least one basic mild extra virgin olive oil in your pantry and experiment with other types. Olive oil, used in moderation, is considered one of the healthiest vegetable oils available, because it is high in monounsaturated fatty acids, which seem to help to lower blood cholesterol. Olive oil is also rich in phytochemicals and vitamin E.

safflower oil

One of the very mild, virtually flavourless oils, like sunflower, peanut or canola oil.

sesame oil

This is pressed from unroasted or roasted sesame seeds and ranges from mild to strong and darkly coloured. Use just a few drops combined with a more neutral-tasting oil. Use the darker type in Asian-style salads with chilies and soy sauce.

walnut and hazelnut oils

Only a few drops are needed, as with sesame oil. Use combined with another mild oil such as peanut to impart just a hint of their flavour. The nutty taste and aroma go well with salads that include cheese, chicken, celery, spinach, apples and green beans.

vinegars

Vinegar has been used for many centuries to flavour and preserve food. Apple cider and wine are the common basic ingredients, but almost any product that can produce alcoholic fermentation can be used to make vinegar, as evidenced by the range used in this book. Create your own varieties by adding fresh herbs, chilies or fruit to cider or wine vinegars. Store in tightly sealed bottles in a dark place. The acetic acid will keep the herbs or fruit from spoiling.

apple cider vinegar

Sharp and refreshing, this golden-coloured vinegar is good in dressings for cheese and ham salads.

'to make a good salad is to be a brilliant diplomatist; the problem is entirely the same. . . to know exactly how much oil one must put with one's vinegar.'

Oscar Wilde, Irish poet, novelist, dramatist and critic (1854-1900)

balsamic vinegar

Dark, richly complex in flavour, balsamic vinegar has a mild sweetness and a slight acidity. It originated in Modena, Italy, and is considered by many to be the best quality vinegar available. It is produced from a type of red wine and the most prized, and expensive, varieties are aged for from 15 to 50 years in wood barrels. Prices vary accordingly. Buy the best you can afford. It goes well with tomato or berry salads.

champagne vinegar

A mild, light vinegar fermented from champagne. Rice vinegar can be used in its place (see below). Champagne vinegar goes well in vinaigrettes and dressings for chicken, veal, fish or vegetable salads.

red wine and white wine vinegar

The classics, with red the slightly more robust, the taste depends on the wines used and their maturity. Sherry vinegar has an even fuller flavour. It goes with rice, grain, meat or fish salads. Cassis vinegar is a specialty vinegar made of blackcurrants and red wine. The bitter fruity vinegar goes well with oak leaf lettuce as well as mushrooms, beef or tuna.

rice vinegar

Used in Asian cooking, spicy, aromatic rice vinegars are sweeter and milder than Western ones because of a lower acid content. Use with rice or grain salads.

herb dressings

Herb dressings look attractive and go well with many types of salads such as green or vegetable salads and also with pasta or rice, fish or meat salads. To maximise their flavour, it's a good idea to make them in advance and store them in the refrigerator for a day or two. Taste and add more chopped fresh herbs just before serving. Make your own herb vinegars or oils and the results will be even better.

raspberry nut herb vinaigrette

This complements bitter radicchio or peppery rocket (arugula) leaves.

2 teaspoons hazelnut oil

3 tablespoons canola or peanut oil

2 tablespoons raspberry or other fruit vinegar

1 tablespoon Dijon mustard

salt and ground white pepper

2 spring onions (scallions), finely chopped

4 sprigs each parsley, tarragon, basil and dill

Whisk the two oils with the vinegar, mustard, salt and pepper. Add spring onions and finely chopped leaves of all the herbs. Note: Vary the types and amounts of herbs to suit different salad ingredients.

raspberry vinegar

Crush 500 g (1 lb) fresh or frozen raspberries. Add 2 cups (500 ml/16 fl oz) white wine vinegar. Leave overnight. Press through a sieve into a sterilised jar. Add 1½ cups (375 g/12 oz) caster (superfine) sugar; stir until the sugar has completely dissolved. Refrigerate or store in a cool, dark place for up to 2 weeks.

classic herb vinaigrette

Good with green salads and vegetable salads as well as grain or rice salads.

3 tablespoons white wine, sherry,
   or herb vinegar, or lemon juice
1 teaspoon Dijon or herb mustard
salt or herb salt and ground white pepper
4 tablespoons good-quality olive oil
5 small sprigs each parsley and dill
small bunch of chives
2 sprigs each marjoram and basil
pinch of sugar

Whisk vinegar, mustard, salt and white pepper in a bowl until salt has dissolved. Add olive oil, whisking until vinaigrette is slightly creamy. Chop herb leaves finely and stir into vinaigrette. Add sugar and more salt and pepper, to taste.

lemon thyme vinaigrette

Use with green and vegetable salads, chicken, beef or seafood salads.

4 tablespoons olive oil
2 tablespoons lemon juice
1 teaspoon Dijon mustard
4 lemon segments, peel and pith removed
salt and ground white pepper
pinch of sugar
$\frac{1}{2}$ teaspoon grated lemon rind
$\frac{1}{2}$ teaspoon chopped fresh lemon thyme leaves

Combine olive oil, lemon juice and mustard in a bowl. Beat vigorously with a whisk. Chop lemon segments coarsely; whisk into vinaigrette. Season with salt, white pepper and sugar. Stir in lemon peel and lemon thyme.

creamy sauce classics

Mayonnaise-style sauces that form a coating over salad ingredients are suitable for potato or pasta salads. Thin them with a little yogurt or milk for delicate green or vegetable salads. Some of these sauces are based on an egg yolk and oil combination. The eggs should be very fresh. (If you do not want to use raw eggs, buy good-quality mayonnaise in a jar.) The oil can be a neutral-tasting one such as canola or peanut oil or a full-bodied olive oil. For the best result, use ingredients at room temperature.

roquefort dressing

This tangy dressing goes well with mixed bean, green or vegetable salads.

50 g (2 oz) Roquefort or Gorgonzola cheese
½ cup (125 g/4 oz) crème fraîche or light sour cream
2 tablespoons white wine vinegar
3 tablespoons fresh orange juice
1 tablespoon walnut oil
salt and freshly ground black pepper, to taste
generous pinch of sugar
3 tablespoons coarsely chopped walnuts, optional

Mash cheese finely with a fork in a bowl. Add crème fraîche and stir to make a smooth, creamy mixture. Add vinegar, orange juice and walnut oil and mix well. Add salt, pepper and sugar, to taste. Stir in chopped walnuts, if using.

garlic sauce (aïoli)

Goes with potato, meat or salmon or white fish salads.

1 large slice white bread, crust removed
2 to 3 tablespoons milk
3 cloves garlic, roughly chopped
1 teaspoon salt
2 medium very fresh egg yolks
1 cup (250 ml/8 fl oz) olive oil
1 tablespoon lemon juice
freshly ground black pepper
4 tablespoons yogurt, optional

Tear bread into small pieces; drizzle with milk. Mix to a fine paste with garlic and salt. Using an electric whisk, add egg yolks and 2 tablespoons oil. Whisk in lemon juice, then another 2 tablespoons oil, drop by drop. Add remaining oil in a thin, steady stream; stir constantly. Add salt and pepper. Add yogurt, if using.

thousand island dressing

Particularly good with fish and seafood salads. This is a very easy, quick recipe.

1 cup good-quality mayonnaise
½ cup (125 ml/4 fl oz) chili sauce or
    tomato sauce (ketchup)
few drops Tabasco (optional)
2 tablespoons chopped pimiento-stuffed olives
2 tablespoons finely chopped green capsicum
    (bell pepper)
1 tablespoon finely chopped white onion
1 teaspoon finely chopped pimiento
salt and freshly ground black pepper

Combine the ingredients and refrigerate. Add salt and pepper, to taste, just before serving.

classic mayonnaise

Perfect for potato salads. Spices or herbs can be added to the recipe.

2 medium very fresh egg yolks
1 teaspoon Dijon mustard
2 tablespoons white wine vinegar or lemon juice
1 cup (250 ml/8 fl oz) olive oil
salt and freshly ground white pepper

Whisk egg yolks, mustard and vinegar in a medium bowl. Using an electric whisk, add oil, first drop by drop, then in a slow, steady stream. (If mixture curdles or splits, add a little hot water and beat vigorously.) Add salt and white pepper to taste. Refrigerate 1 to 2 days.

middle eastern bread salad (page 56)

the classics

Many salad recipes have stood the test of time, earning their position as 'classics' in the repertoire of restaurant chefs and home cooks alike. Salads are an international favourite and these globetrotting recipes take us from the USA to Russia, from the Middle East to Asia and from Europe to Africa.

caesar salad

In 1924 in Tijuana, Mexico, Caesar Cardini first mixed cos lettuce, Parmesan and croutons, dressed with garlic, lemon, egg, olive oil and Worcestershire sauce.

2 small heads cos (romaine) lettuce

4 large leaves iceberg lettuce

50 g (2 oz) Parmesan, in a piece

2 slices sourdough bread, crusts removed

2 tablespoons olive oil

anchovy dressing

4 anchovy fillets

1 clove garlic, roughly chopped

5 tablespoons olive oil

1 very fresh large egg yolk

2 tablespoons lemon juice

2 tablespoons Dijon mustard

1 tablespoon Worcestershire sauce

pinch of sugar

salt and freshly ground black pepper

serves 4

preparation 30 minutes

----

per serving 1758 kilojoules/420 calories, 10 g protein, 38 g total fat, 8 g saturated fat, 60 mg cholesterol, 10 g carbohydrate, 3 g fibre

1 Cut cos and iceberg lettuce leaves into bite-sized pieces. Use a vegetable peeler or cheese grater to shave Parmesan into thin slivers.

2 To make anchovy dressing, place anchovy fillets and garlic in a bowl and mash to a paste. Whisk in olive oil, egg yolk, lemon juice, mustard, Worcestershire sauce and sugar. Add salt and freshly ground black pepper, to taste.

3 To make croutons, cut bread into small cubes. Heat olive oil in a large nonstick pan over medium heat. Add bread cubes; cook until golden brown on all sides, taking care they do not burn. Set aside; keep warm.

4 Arrange lettuce leaves and shaved Parmesan on individual serving plates. Drizzle dressing over salad and sprinkle on bread cubes.

mix and match

✳ Omit olive oil and egg yolk from the anchovy dressing. Use 1 cup (250 g/8 oz) good-quality, mayonnaise instead.

✳ Add 2 cooked skinless chicken breasts (about 300 g/10 oz in total) or chicken tenderloins cut into strips to the salad.

waldorf salad

500 g (1 lb) celery or celeriac
  (celery root)
2 medium tart apples
  (about 300 g/10 oz)
3 tablespoons lemon juice
1 cup (150 g/5 oz) red grapes
100 g (4 oz) walnuts
½ cup (125 g/4 oz) mayonnaise
pinch of sugar
salt and freshly ground black pepper
mint sprigs, for garnish

serves 4
preparation 25 minutes

---

per serving *1478 kilojoules/353 calories, 5 g protein,*
27 g total fat, 2 g saturated fat, 8 mg cholesterol,
24 g carbohydrate, 5 g fibre

1 Cut celery into fine matchsticks. Halve and core apples and cut or grate into fine strips. Place celery and apples in a bowl; stir in 2 tablespoons lemon juice to prevent discolouration.

2 Reserve a few grapes for garnish; halve and seed the rest. Reserve a few walnuts for garnish; coarsely chop the rest. Add halved grapes and chopped walnuts to bowl.

3 To make dressing, whisk mayonnaise with remaining 1 tablespoon lemon juice in a small bowl. Add sugar and salt and pepper to taste.

4 Stir dressing into salad. Garnish with reserved grapes and walnuts and top with mint sprigs.

chef's salad

2 skinless chicken breast fillets
    (about 300 g/10 oz in total)
oil, for brushing
1 large head cos (romaine) lettuce
4 roma (plum) tomatoes, cut into wedges
150 g (5 oz) thinly sliced ham
125 g (4 oz) thinly sliced Swiss-style cheese
3 medium eggs, hard-boiled, thinly sliced

white wine vinaigrette

3 tablespoons olive oil
2 tablespoons white wine vinegar
1 teaspoon Dijon mustard
½ teaspoon sugar
salt and freshly ground black pepper

serves 4
preparation 10 minutes
cooking 15 minutes

per serving 2115 kilojoules/505 calories, 46 g protein,
33 g total fat, 11 g saturated fat, 273 mg cholesterol,
4 g carbohydrate, 3 g fibre

1 Preheat grill (broiler) or barbecue to medium-hot.
Brush chicken with oil; cook about 5 minutes each side or
until cooked through. Let stand 5 minutes; slice thinly.

3 Tear lettuce leaves into small pieces. Arrange on a large
platter. Top with chicken, tomatoes, ham, cheese and eggs.

4 To make vinaigrette, whisk oil, vinegar, mustard and
sugar until combined. Drizzle salad with vinaigrette and
season with black pepper.

a bite of history

This salad is so named because it's a flexible
way to use ingredients that you may have in
your pantry: it can include combinations of
cold meats, cheeses, eggs and salad greens.

cobb salad

This substantial salad of chicken, bacon, eggs, lettuce, tomatoes, avocado and blue cheese is a meal in itself.

2 cups (500 ml/16 fl oz) chicken stock

½ cup (125 ml/4 fl oz) dry white wine

1 small lemon, chopped

4 skinless chicken breast fillets
   (about 600 g/1 lb 8 oz in total)

4 rashers (slices) bacon, chopped

3 medium eggs, hard-boiled, chopped

1 small head red mignonette (bibb) lettuce

2 cups trimmed watercress

3 medium tomatoes (about 500 g/1 lb),
   chopped

1 large avocado, diced

150 g (5 oz) blue cheese, crumbled

vinaigrette

3 tablespoons olive oil

2 tablespoons white wine vinegar

2 teaspoons finely chopped tarragon

1 teaspoon Dijon mustard

1 teaspoon honey

1 clove garlic, crushed

salt and freshly ground black pepper

serves 6

preparation 20 minutes

cooking 15 minutes

----

per serving 2121 kilojoules/507 calories, 43 g protein,
35 g total fat, 11 g saturated fat, 219 mg cholesterol,
4 g carbohydrate, 3 g fibre

1 Combine stock, wine and lemon in a medium saucepan; bring to a boil. Reuce heat; add chicken. Simmer, covered, about 15 minutes or until cooked through. Drain chicken; cut into bite-size pieces. Leave to cool.

2 Cook bacon in a frying pan over high heat until crisp. Drain on paper towels.

3 Tear lettuce leaves into small pieces. Arrange lettuce and watercress on individual serving plates and top with chicken, bacon, eggs, tomatoes, avocado and cheese.

4 To make vinaigrette, whisk oil, vinegar, tarragon, mustard, honey and garlic until combined. Add salt and pepper to taste. Drizzle salad with vinaigrette.

a bite of history

This salad was created in 1926 by Bob Cobb at the Brown Derby in Los Angeles. The story is that he wanted a snack and put together leftovers from the restaurant kitchen.

cook's tip

Mignonette (bibb) lettuces have soft, floppy leaves. To add crunch to this salad, use cos (romaine) lettuce or iceberg lettuce.

spinach, roasted garlic and parmesan

8 small cloves garlic, unpeeled
3 tablespoons olive oil
50 g (2 oz) Parmesan, in a piece
300 g (10 oz) baby spinach leaves
3 tablespoons pine nuts, roasted
90 g (3 oz) drained sun-dried tomatoes
2 tablespoons balsamic vinegar
salt and freshly ground black pepper

serves 4
preparation 5 minutes
cooking 20 minutes

----

per serving *1340 kilojoules/320 calories, 10 g protein,*
27 g total fat, 5 g saturated fat, 12 mg cholesterol,
10 g carbohydrate, 5 g fibre

1 Preheat oven to 180°C/350°F. Place garlic in a small roasting pan; drizzle with 1 tablespoon of the oil. Roast about 20 minutes or until soft. Peel garlic.

2 Using a vegetable peeler, slice Parmesan into large, thin shavings.

3 Place garlic and Parmesan in a serving bowl with remaining ingredients. Add salt and pepper to taste. Toss gently to combine.

stuffed avocado salad

2 spring onions (scallions)
1 large lemon
1 tablespoon canola oil
1 tablespoon sherry vinegar
salt and freshly ground black pepper
175 g (6 oz) cooked, peeled prawns (shrimp)
4 medium ripe avocados
1 cup (50 g/2 oz) trimmed watercress

dill dressing

½ cup (125 g/4 oz) sour cream
2 tablespoons crème fraîche (optional)
3 tablespoons finely chopped fresh dill
salt and freshly ground black pepper

serves 4
preparation 20 minutes

per serving *3002 kilojoules/717 calories, 15 g protein, 72 g total fat, 21 g saturated fat, 124 mg cholesterol, 3 g carbohydrate, 4 g fibre*

1 Finely dice spring onions. Cut lemon in half. Cut one half into thin slices and squeeze juice from other half.

2 Whisk oil and vinegar until combined; add salt and pepper to taste. Add spring onions and prawns. Marinate while making dressing.

3 To make dill dressing, whisk sour cream, crème fraîche (if using) and 1 teaspoon lemon juice in a bowl until creamy. Add salt and pepper to taste. Stir in dill.

4 Cut avocados in half and remove stones. Remove flesh, leaving a rim about 5 mm (¼ inch) wide. Dice flesh finely and mix with 1 tablespoon lemon juice and a little salt.

5 Combine avocado, watercress, prawns and spring onions and spoon into avocado shells. Spoon dill dressing on the top. Garnish with lemon slices.

three bean salad tuscan-style

This classic Tuscan salad uses cannellini beans, red kidney beans and fresh green beans. Combinations of different beans can be used.

300 g (10 oz) green beans, trimmed, halved

1 can (400 g/14 oz) red kidney beans, rinsed and drained

1 can (400 g/14 oz) cannellini or lima beans, rinsed and drained

1 small red onion, finely chopped

2 large tomatoes (about 350 g/12 oz), seeded, chopped

3 tablespoons chopped fresh flat-leaf parsley

3 tablespoons olive oil

2 tablespoons lemon juice

1 clove garlic, crushed

salt and freshly ground black pepper

serves 4
preparation 10 minutes
cooking 7 minutes

per serving 1046 kilojoules/250 calories, 10 g protein, 15 g total fat, 2 g saturated fat, 0 mg cholesterol, 19 g carbohydrate, 11 g fibre

1 Half fill a medium saucepan with water and bring to a boil. Add green beans; cook 5 to 7 minutes or until just tender. Drain; rinse with cold water.

2 Combine green beans, kidney beans, cannellini beans, onion, tomatoes and parsley in a serving bowl. Mix oil, lemon juice and garlic. Add salt and pepper to taste. Stir into salad.

red kidney beans

A good source of fibre, protein, vitamin B6 and vitamin C and containing many important minerals, these beans have a full flavour that complements fresh green beans.

mix and match

✳ Add 1 small green or red capsicum (bell pepper), finely diced. Add a generous pinch of sugar to the oil, lemon juice and garlic and season with salt and pepper to taste. Toss to combine.

✳ Use 1 can (400 g/14 oz) borlotti beans, rinsed and drained, in place of fresh green beans. Add 3 tablespoons chopped fresh coriander (cilantro).

american potato salad

1 kg (2 lb) potatoes, peeled, cut into
   small pieces
2 tablespoons apple cider vinegar
3 medium eggs, hard-boiled, chopped
1 medium red onion, chopped finely
2 celery stalks, chopped finely
¼ cup (50 g/2 oz) chopped dill pickles
   (cucumbers)
4 tablespoons chopped fresh parsley
1 cup (250 g/8 oz) good-quality mayonnaise
2 teaspoons Dijon mustard
½ teaspoon celery seeds
salt and freshly ground black pepper
3 spring onions (scallions), sliced thinly

serves 4
preparation 15 minutes
cooking 12 minutes

----

per serving *1802 kilojoules/430 calories, 12 g protein,
24 g total fat, 4 g saturated fat, 178 mg cholesterol,
43 g carbohydrate, 6 g fibre*

1 Half fill a large saucepan with water; add potatoes
and bring to a boil. Reduce heat to a simmer, cook 10 to
12 minutes or until just tender. Drain.

2 Place warm potatoes in a large serving bowl; add vinegar
and toss to combine. Add eggs, red onion, celery, pickles and
parsley; toss gently.

3 Combine mayonnaise, mustard and celery seeds in a
small bowl. Add salt and pepper to taste. Stir gently into
salad. Top with spring onions.

why warm?

Potatoes are used warm in these two salads
because they will absorb the flavours of the
dressings. Dressings added to cold potatoes
tend to 'sit' on them rather than soak in.

bacon and potato salad

1 kg (2 lb) small new potatoes (chats)

5 rashers (slices) bacon, chopped

4 medium eggs, hard-boiled, quartered

¼ cup (50 g/2 oz) chopped pickled cucumbers

3 tablespoons chopped fresh flat-leaf parsley

⅔ cup (150 g/5 oz) good-quality mayonnaise

4 tablespoons sour cream

1 tablespoon lemon juice

1 teaspoon ground sweet paprika

2 tablespoons chopped fresh dill

serves 4
preparation 10 minutes
cooking 15 minutes

per serving *2327 kilojoules/556 calories, 25 g protein,*
32 g total fat, 10 g saturated fat, 283 mg cholesterol,
43 g carbohydrate, 7 g fibre

1 Half fill a large saucepan with water; add potatoes and bring to a boil. Reduce heat to a simmer, cook 10 to 12 minutes or until just tender. Drain and cut in half.

2 Cook bacon in a lightly oiled frying pan over high heat until crisp. Drain on paper towels.

3 Place warm potatoes in a large serving bowl; add eggs, cucumbers and parsley; toss gently.

4 Combine mayonnaise, sour cream, lemon juice and paprika in a small bowl. Add to salad and toss gently. Sprinkle bacon and dill on top.

cook's tip

Both the bacon and eggs can be cooked ahead of time and used cold. It is only the potatoes that must be used warm.

coleslaw

From the Dutch koolsla, coleslaw is a salad
of shredded cabbage mixed with mayonnaise.
It is the archetypical picnic and barbecue salad.

½ head medium savoy (green) cabbage
    (about 500 g/1 lb)
1 large carrot, grated
½ small onion, finely chopped
3 spring onions (scallions), thinly sliced
2 celery stalks, thinly sliced
3 tablespoons chopped fresh flat-leaf
    parsley
½ cup (125 g/4 oz) good-quality
    mayonnaise
2 teaspoons lemon juice
1 teaspoon Dijon mustard
salt and freshly ground black pepper

serves 4
preparation 10 minutes

*per serving 595 kilojoules/142 calories, 3 g protein,
10 g total fat, 1 g saturated fat, 8 mg cholesterol,
12 g carbohydrate, 6 g fibre*

1 Finely shred the cabbage using a sharp knife or a mandoline slicer (see page 11).

2 Place cabbage in a large bowl with carrot, onion, spring onions, celery and parsley; toss to combine. Whisk mayonnaise, lemon juice and mustard in a small bowl until well combined. Add salt and pepper to taste. Add dressing to salad; toss gently to combine.

mix and match

❋ Mixed cabbage coleslaw Replace half the green cabbage with red cabbage and add 1 tablespoon toasted caraway seeds.

❋ Fruity coleslaw Add 1 large green apple cut into matchsticks and 3 tablespoons sultanas (golden raisins) to basic coleslaw salad.

❋ Crunchy nut coleslaw Replace onion with 6 red radishes cut into matchsticks; add 4 tablespoons toasted slivered almonds.

coleslaw

Coleslaw is one of the most versatile of salads. Ideal in winter when salad greens may not be in great supply, it is inexpensive and the perfect choice when catering for a crowd.

cucumbers with dill and sour cream dressing

In this German-style salad, the fresh flavour of dill complements tangy, raw red onion and mild-tasting cool cucumbers.

2 large telegraph (English) cucumbers
   (about 550g/1 lb 4 oz)
1 teaspoon salt
1 small red onion, thinly sliced
3 tablespoons chopped fresh dill

sour cream dressing

½ cup (125 g/4 oz) sour cream
2 tablespoons white wine vinegar
1 teaspoon sugar
2 teaspoons Dijon mustard
salt and freshly ground black pepper

serves 4
preparation + chilling 50 minutes

----

per serving 604 kilojoules/144 calories, 3 g protein,
13 g total fat, 8 g saturated fat, 41 mg cholesterol,
5 g carbohydrate, 2 g fibre

1 Cut cucumbers in half lengthwise and scoop out seeds with a small spoon. Slice flesh thinly. Place cucumbers in a colander and sprinkle with salt. Let stand 15 minutes.

2 Rinse under cold water to remove excess salt; drain. Place cucumbers, onion and dill in a large bowl. Cover and refrigerate at least 30 minutes.

3 To make sour cream dressing, whisk sour cream, vinegar, sugar and mustard until combined. Add salt and pepper to taste. Spoon over cucumbers, onion and dill; toss gently to coat.

tzatziki

❋ Peel 4 large telegraph (English) cucumbers (about 1 kg/2 lb in total). Remove seeds and chop flesh finely. Place cucumbers in a colander; sprinkle with 2 teaspoons coarse salt. Let stand for 15 minutes. Rinse under cold water to remove excess salt; drain.

❋ Place 2 cups (500 g/1 lb) Greek-style yogurt in a serving bowl; add the cucumber and 1 clove garlic, crushed. Season with salt and freshly ground black pepper. Serve well chilled as a dressing or as a side salad.

cucumbers with dill and sour cream dressing

tex mex salad

Pico de gallo (Spanish for 'rooster's beak') is
a fresh salsa made from chopped tomatoes, onion
and chilies (usually jalapeños or serranos).

2 skinless chicken breast fillets
(about 400 g/14 oz in total)
1 tablespoon vegetable oil
3 tablespoons enchilada sauce from a jar
4 large corn tortillas
1 large head cos (romaine) lettuce
1 can (400 g/14 oz) red kidney beans,
rinsed and drained
1 large avocado, diced
2 tablespoons chopped pickled jalapeños
(hot chilies)
2 sprigs flat-leaf parsley, for garnish

pico de gallo

2 large tomatoes (about 350 g/12 oz),
seeded, chopped
1 small red onion, finely chopped
1 fresh small red chili, finely chopped
3 tablespoons chopped fresh coriander
(cilantro)
3 tablespoons vegetable oil
2 tablespoons lime juice
1 clove garlic, crushed

serves 4
preparation 20 minutes
cooking 15 minutes

per serving 2613 kilojoules/624 calories, 41 g protein,
37 g total fat, 6 g saturated fat, 85 mg cholesterol,
29 g carbohydrate, 10 g fibre

1 Preheat grill (broiler) or barbecue to medium hot.

2 Brush chicken with half the oil; cook 5 minutes each side
or until cooked through. Leave 5 minutes; slice thinly.

3 Bring enchilada sauce to a boil in a medium saucepan;
add chicken and toss to coat. Remove from heat and cover
to keep warm.

4 Brush tortillas with remaining oil; cook on barbecue
grill plate (rack) about 2 minutes each side or until browned
lightly and crisp. Break into large pieces.

5 To make pico de gallo, combine tomatoes, onion, chili
and coriander in a small bowl; add combined oil, lime juice
and garlic and toss to combine.

6 Chop or tear lettuce leaves into small pieces. Arrange
lettuce on a large serving platter. Top with beans, avocado,
pickled jalapeños and pico de gallo. Arrange chicken on top
and sprinkle with tortilla pieces. Garnish with parsley.

cook's tip

*Replace chicken with homemade
chili, using the quantity of red
kidney beans used in this recipe.
Use tortilla chips instead of fresh
corn tortillas. Top with sour cream.*

salad with camembert

100 g (4 oz) rocket (arugula)

50 g (2 oz) dandelion leaves or extra rocket

½ head batavia lettuce or curly endive (frisée)

1 small wheel camembert (about 125 g/4 oz)

1 medium egg

salt and freshly ground black pepper

¾ cup (100 g/4 oz) dried breadcrumbs

2 tablespoons sunflower oil

50 g (2 oz) fresh cranberries
   or precooked frozen cranberries

vinaigrette

2 tablespoons sunflower oil

2 tablespoons raspberry vinegar

2 teaspoons preserved cranberries

1 shallot, finely diced

salt and freshly ground black pepper

serves 4

preparation 15 minutes

cooking 10 minutes

----

per serving *1624 kilojoules/388 calories, 12 g protein,
29 g total fat, 8 g saturated fat, 83 mg cholesterol,
19 g carbohydrate, 3 g fibre*

1 Place rocket, dandelion and lettuce in a serving bowl, tearing any large leaves into small pieces.

2 Cut camembert into quarters. In a shallow bowl, beat egg with salt and pepper. Place breadcrumbs on a plate.

3 To make vinaigrette, whisk oil, raspberry vinegar, preserved cranberries and shallot until combined; add salt and pepper to taste. Drizzle over salad.

4 Heat 2 tablespoons oil in a nonstick pan. Coat cheese in egg, then in breadcrumbs. Cook cheese over high heat, turning once, until golden brown. Drain on paper towels. Add cheese and cranberries to salad.

cook's tip

To cook frozen cranberries, cover with water; add a little sugar. Bring to a boil. Simmer just until they pop or they'll turn mushy. Add a little butter to stop pan from boiling over.

salad niçoise

150 g (5 oz) fresh or frozen green beans

1 medium orange capsicum (bell pepper)

2 potatoes, boiled the previous day
    and left unpeeled

1 medium head cos (romaine) lettuce

1 large tomato, cut into wedges

1 can (185 g/7 oz) tuna, in oil or
    water-packed, drained

1 medium red onion, thinly sliced

4 medium eggs, hard-boiled, quartered

1/3 cup (50 g/2 oz) black olives

vinaigrette

4 tablespoons olive oil

3 tablespoons red wine vinegar

1 clove garlic, crushed

salt and freshly ground black pepper

serves 4

preparation 15 minutes

cooking 5 minutes

per serving 1745 kilojoules/417 calories, 20 g protein,
30 g total fat, 5 g saturated fat, 230 mg cholesterol,
17 g carbohydrate, 6 g fibre

1 Cook beans in lightly salted water about 5 minutes or
until crisp-tender. Drain and leave to cool. Cut into pieces.

2 Halve capsicum and cut into strips. Peel potatoes; slice
thinly. Tear lettuce leaves into strips. Mix beans, capsicum,
potatoes, lettuce and tomato in a large bowl.

3 To make vinaigrette, whisk oil, vinegar and garlic until
combined; add salt and pepper to taste. Pour over salad.

4 Break tuna into pieces with a fork. Place tuna, onion,
eggs and olives on salad.

a bite of history

Salad niçoise, from Nice, France, is one
of many classics open to interpretation, with
olives, potatoes, green beans and a vinaigrette
dressing regarded as essential. Some say
that the salad should be served on a bed of
lettuce; others favour tomatoes as the base.
Some simply toss all the ingredients together.

bocconcini, basil and tomatoes

Bocconcini are bite-sized balls of fresh
mozzarella. Bocconcini is Italian for 'mouthful'.
The cheese is milky-white with a mild taste.

300 g (10 oz) drained baby bocconcini
(baby mozzarella balls), cut in half

500 g (1 lb) cherry tomatoes, cut in half

½ cup (80 g/3 oz) black olives

2 tablespoons chopped fresh
flat-leaf parsley

12 fresh basil leaves

2 teaspoons olive oil

salt and freshly ground black pepper

serves 4

preparation 15 minutes

----

per serving 878 kilojoules/210 calories, 14 g protein,
14 g total fat, 8 g saturated fat, 26 mg cholesterol,
7 g carbohydrate, 2 g fibre

1 Place bocconcini, tomatoes and olives in a serving bowl.

2 Sprinkle on parsley and basil. Drizzle salad with olive oil
and add salt and pepper to taste. Toss gently to combine.

a bite of history

The green, white and red ingredients in this
salad reflect its Italian origins and represent
the colours of the Italian flag. The combination
of mild bocconcini, aromatic basil and full-
flavoured ripe tomatoes is a summer classic.

tuscan white bean salad with tuna

2 cans (400 g/14 oz each) white beans, drained and rinsed

1 can (425 g/15 oz) tuna, in oil or water-packed, drained

1 medium red onion, sliced

3 tablespoons olive oil

3 teaspoons lemon juice

a few fresh sage leaves

1 tablespoon chopped fresh parsley

serves 6

preparation 5 minutes

---

per serving *1312 kilojoules/313 calories, 17 g protein, 23 g total fat, 3 g saturated fat, 19 mg cholesterol, 9 g carbohydrate, 5 g fibre*

1 Toss beans, tuna, onion, oil, lemon juice and sage leaves together in a large serving bowl.

2 Sprinkle with chopped parsley just before serving.

cook's tip

Cannellini beans are traditionally used in this recipe, but any type of small white bean can be used. Sage is popular in Italian cooking and is a good complement to cheese.

italian bread salad

300 g (10 oz) day-old ciabatta

1 large red onion, diced

2 medium tomatoes, diced

2 stalks celery, diced

2 Lebanese (Mediterranean)
   cucumbers, diced

3 sprigs oregano

4 tablespoons finely chopped fresh
   basil leaves

4 tablespoons olive oil

salt and coarsely ground black pepper

3 tablespoons good-quality red wine
   vinegar

serves 4

preparation + chilling 1 hour 10 minutes

----

per serving 1572 kilojoules/375 calories, 8 g protein,
20 g total fat, 3 g saturated fat, 0 mg cholesterol,
39 g carbohydrate, 5 g fibre

1 Cut bread into large pieces and moisten with a little water. Soak briefly, squeeze to remove liquid, then tear into small pieces. Mix bread, onion, tomatoes, celery and cucumbers in a serving bowl.

2 Finely chop oregano leaves. Mix with basil, oil, salt and pepper. Pour over bread and vegetables. Chill, covered, about 1 hour. Stir in red wine vinegar. Season to taste.

ciabatta

Ciabatta, an oval, flattish yeast bread with an open texture and crisp crust, is ideal for this salad. Many frugal peasant dishes use day-old crusty bread as an ingredient.

bread salad with roasted capsicums

4 large red capsicums (bell peppers), cut in half

1 tablespoon olive oil

300 g (10 oz) crusty Italian or French bread, cubed

1 large tomato, diced

1 medium cucumber, diced

100 g (4 oz) feta cheese, crumbled

½ cup (80 g/3 oz) black olives

serves 4

preparation 2 hours + 15 minutes

cooking 10 minutes

per serving 1529 kilojoules/365 calories, 15 g protein, 13 g total fat, 5 g saturated fat, 17 mg cholesterol, 47 g carbohydrate, 5 g fibre

1 Grill (broil) capsicums (instructions page 111). Peel skin; cut flesh into thin strips. Drizzle with oil. (Allow 2 hours.)

2 Preheat oven to 190°C/375°F). Spread bread cubes on a baking tray and bake, tossing occasionally, 5 minutes or until lightly crisped but not browned.

3 Combine capsicums, toasted bread, tomato, cucumber, feta and olives in a large bowl, tossing well to combine. Serve at room temperature or chilled.

health guide

All cheeses contain casein, which provides a natural tooth protectant. The calcium and phosphorus in cheese helps remineralise tooth enamel. Many cheeses are high in salt and saturated fat, so eat them in moderation.

russian salad

In Russia, beetroot (beets) are on just about every menu.
To preserve their colour and nutrients, do not peel or cut
them before cooking; just scrub them gently.

500 g (1 lb) beetroot (beets), trimmed

500 g (1 lb) potatoes, peeled, cut into
    wedges

½ cup (60 g/2 oz) frozen peas

3 tablespoons sliced dill pickles
    (cucumbers)

1 small red onion, finely sliced

3 tablespoons good-quality mayonnaise

3 tablespoons sour cream

2 teaspoons white wine vinegar

1 teaspoon Dijon mustard

serves 4

preparation 15 minutes

cooking 30 to 35 minutes

----

*per serving 913 kilojoules/218 calories, 5 g protein,
11 g total fat, 4 g saturated fat, 24 mg cholesterol,
25 g carbohydrate, 5 g fibre*

1 Half fill a large saucepan with water; add beetroot and
bring to a boil. Cook 20 to 25 minutes or until just tender.
Drain and cool. Peel; cut into wedges.

2 Half fill a medium saucepan with water; add potatoes
and bring to a boil. Cook 8 minutes; add peas. Cook another
2 minutes or until vegetables are tender. Drain.

3 Combine beetroot, potatoes and peas in a large bowl;
add pickles and onion. Whisk mayonnaise, sour cream,
vinegar and mustard in a small bowl until smooth. Add to
salad; toss gently to combine.

mix and match

✳ Poach or pan-fry 2 skinless chicken breast
fillets (about 300 g/10 oz in total). Cut into
strips and add to salad.

✳ Thinly slice 300 g/10 oz cold roast duck or
other game bird and add to salad.

cook's tip

*Ideally, cook beetroot
(beets) a day ahead.
Chill, covered, until
ready to use. If fresh
beetroot is unavailable,
use canned whole baby
beetroot, drained.*

herring and dill salad with potatoes

250 g (8 oz) matjes herring fillets (or other pickled herring) in oil, drained

2 medium white onions

2 large dill pickles (cucumbers)

4 potatoes, cooked the previous day and left unpeeled

herb cream

½ cup (125 g/4 oz) yogurt

100 g (4 oz) whipping cream

1 teaspoon grated horseradish paste

1 to 2 teaspoons lemon juice

3 tablespoons finely chopped fresh chervil

4 tablespoons finely chopped fresh dill

3 tablespoons finely chopped fresh flat-leaf parsley

salt and ground white pepper

serves 4

preparation + chilling 2 hours 25 minutes

----

per serving *1640 kilojoules/391 calories, 13 g protein, 22 g total fat, 8 g saturated fat, 77 mg cholesterol, 34 g carbohydrate, 5 g fibre*

1 Pat matjes fillets dry and cut into small pieces. Thinly slice onions and cucumbers. Peel potatoes and slice.

2 Arrange potatoes on a platter. Place matjes pieces on top. Place one third of the onion rings and cucumber slices on top of matjes herrings.

3 To make herb cream, combine yogurt and cream. Stir in horseradish, lemon juice and all the herbs; season with salt and pepper. Spoon over salad.

4 Refrigerate, covered, at least 2 hours. Let salad reach room temperature before serving. Garnish with remaining onion rings and sliced cucumbers.

cook's tip

Salty matjes fillets become milder if soaked in buttermilk overnight. Other types of pickled herring may be used in this recipe. Smoked fish can also be used.

herring salad with radish and rocket

❋ Peel 1 white radish (daikon) and cut into thin sticks. Halve 250 g (8 oz) cherry tomatoes. Peel 1 medium red onion and cut into thin rings. Remove stalks from 125 g (4 oz) rocket (arugula). Cut 250 g (8 oz) ready-to-eat matjes fillets into small pieces and arrange on top of salad ingredients.

❋ Whisk 3 tablespoons corn oil with 2 tablespoons lemon juice. Season with salt and pepper and drizzle over salad.

herring and dill salad with potatoes

middle eastern bread salad

1 telegraph (English) cucumber, seeded and diced

3 medium tomatoes, seeded and diced (cubes should be about the same size as the cucumber)

6 spring onions (scallions), finely chopped

salt and freshly ground black pepper

1 small iceberg lettuce, roughly chopped

3 small rounds pita bread

2 tablespoons olive oil

dressing

4 tablespoons olive oil

grated peel and juice of 1 lemon

2 cloves garlic, crushed

2 tablespoons roughly chopped fresh flat-leaf parsley

2 tablespoons roughly chopped fresh mint leaves

2 tablespoons roughly chopped fresh coriander (cilantro) leaves

serves 6

preparation 20 minutes

cooking 5 minutes

per serving 945 kilojoules/226 calories, 4 g protein, 16 g total fat, 2 g saturated fat, 0 mg cholesterol, 16 g carbohydrate, 4 g fibre

1 Combine cucumber, tomatoes and spring onions in a colander and sprinkle with salt. Leave 10 minutes to drain. Place in a serving bowl with lettuce.

2 Roughly tear pita bread into small pieces. Heat oil in a frying pan. Fry bread over medium heat until golden brown. Drain on paper towels to remove excess oil.

3 To make dressing, whisk all ingredients together until combined. Drizzle over salad; toss well to coat. Season with salt and pepper. Top with pieces of fried pita bread.

a bite of history

In Lebanon, this salad is called fattoush. For a traditional touch, sprinkle the salad with a teaspoon of sumac, a purplish-red ground spice with a slightly sour, lime taste.

cook's tip

Pita bread can be toasted instead of fried. Separate each round into layers. Spray each one lightly with oil. Place on a baking tray; toast in a preheated 180°C/350°F oven for about 8 minutes or until golden. Break into small pieces.

tabouleh

This is a colourful, flavoursome Lebanese salad.
For added health benefits, use twice the amount
of parsley in place of the lettuce strips.

1 cup (180 g/7 oz) instant burghul (bulgur
    wheat) or couscous

2 medium tomatoes, finely diced

3 Lebanese (Mediterranean) cucumbers,
    finely diced

4 spring onions (scallions), sliced

2 cups (about 125 g/4 oz) finely chopped
    fresh flat-leaf parsley

1½ cups (about 75 g/3 oz) finely chopped
    fresh mint

4 tablespoons olive oil

6 tablespoons lemon juice

salt and freshly ground black pepper

cos (romaine) lettuce leaves, for serving

1 heart cos (romaine) lettuce, cut into strips

mint and coriander sprigs, for garnish

1 large tomato, cut into wedges, for garnish

serves 4
preparation + standing 45 minutes

----

per serving *1485 kilojoules/355 calories, 9 g protein,*
20 g total fat, 3 g saturated fat, 0 mg cholesterol,
34 g carbohydrate, 12 g fibre

1 Place burghul in a pan with 2 cups (500 ml/16 fl oz)
water. Bring to a boil. Remove from heat; leave 20 minutes
to absorb liquid. Fluff with a fork.

2 Combine burghul, tomatoes, cucumbers, spring onions,
parsley and mint in a bowl. Whisk oil and 4 tablespoons
lemon juice; add salt and pepper to taste. Pour over salad
and toss to combine; leave 30 minutes.

3 Arrange lettuce leaves on a large platter. Season
tabouleh to taste with salt and remaining 2 tablespoons
lemon juice; fold in lettuce strips. Arrange on lettuce leaves.
Garnish with herb sprigs and tomato wedges.

health guide

This is a nutritious salad, containing plenty
of fibre. Consumed in portions of at least
30 g (1 oz), fresh parsley contains useful
amounts of vitamin C, iron and calcium.

cook's tip

Instant or quick-cooking couscous
will give a quicker result. It needs
about 10 minutes standing time
after boiling.

asian chicken salad

1 tablespoon peanut or sunflower oil

1 tablespoon grated fresh ginger root

1 stalk lemon grass, chopped

2 fresh red chilies, chopped

2 cloves garlic, chopped

500 g/1 lb chicken mince

3 tablespoons fresh lime juice

1 tablespoon Asian fish sauce

1 teaspoon soft brown sugar

1 medium red onion, thinly sliced

2 tablespoons shredded fresh mint

1 cup (60 g/2 oz) coriander (cilantro) leaves

1 small head cos (romaine) or ½ small head
    iceberg lettuce, leaves separated

serves 4

preparation 10 minutes

cooking 6 minutes

----

per serving *1070 kilojoules/255 calories, 26 g protein,*
14 g total fat, 3 g saturated fat, 89 mg cholesterol,
5 g carbohydrate, 2 g fibre

1 Heat oil in a large nonstick frying pan over medium heat. Add ginger, lemon grass, chilies and garlic. Cook 1 minute, stirring. Add chicken and cook, stirring, 5 minutes or until chicken is cooked.

2 Remove from heat and allow to cool slightly. Combine lime juice, fish sauce and sugar; pour over chicken.

3 Add onion, mint and coriander, reserving a few leaves for garnish. Toss gently. Place salad in individual bowls, garnish with remaining coriander. Scoop portions of salad onto lettuce leaves to form parcels or cups for eating.

cook's tip

For a quick version of this salad, buy a cooked chicken. Remove the skin and bones, then finely chop the chicken breast meat or shred it with a fork.

greek salad

This popular salad has many variations. It can also include rice-stuffed vine leaves and anchovies. Traditionally, it does not include lettuce.

3 medium tomatoes

3 small Lebanese (Mediterranean) cucumbers

2 large red onions

2 medium green capsicums (bell peppers)

⅔ cup (100 g/4 oz) black olives

100 g (4 oz) pickled mild or hot chilies

4 tablespoons olive oil

2 tablespoons red wine vinegar

salt and freshly ground black pepper

300 g (10 oz) feta cheese

1 teaspoon dried oregano or 2 teaspoons fresh oregano leaves

serves 4
preparation 20 minutes

----

per serving 2018 kilojoules/482 calories, 17 g protein, 36 g total fat, 14 g saturated fat, 52 mg cholesterol, 22 g carbohydrate, 5 g fibre

1 Cut tomatoes into wedges. Cut cucumbers into thick slices. Slice onions, not too thinly. Cut capsicums into strips.

2 Place all the vegetables in a bowl. Top with olives and pickled chilies. To make vinaigrette, whisk 3 tablespoons oil and all the vinegar until combined; add salt and pepper to taste. Drizzle over salad.

3 Cut feta into thick cubes or crumble coarsely; add to salad. Sprinkle oregano on top and drizzle with remaining 1 tablespoon oil.

cook's tip

In Mediterranean cooking, oregano and marjoram are interchangeable. They have a warm, slightly sharp taste with an underlying spiciness. Oregano often has a lemony taste.

thai beef salad with peanuts

3-cm (1-inch) piece fresh ginger root

4 sprigs coriander (cilantro)

500 g (1 lb) beef fillet

4 tablespoons sunflower oil

3 tablespoons lime juice

2 tablespoons soy sauce

1/2 teaspoon ground ginger

1/3 cup (50 g/2 oz) unsalted peanuts

2 medium red onions, thinly sliced

salt

2 spring onions (scallions)

1 fresh red chili

1 Lebanese (Mediterranean) cucumber,
   thinly sliced, for garnish

few mint sprigs, for garnish

serves 4

preparation 20 minutes

cooking 10 minutes

----

*per serving 1759 kilojoules/420 calories, 29 g protein,
31 g total fat, 6 g saturated fat, 66 mg cholesterol,
7 g carbohydrate, 2 g fibre*

1 Peel ginger and chop finely. Chop coriander leaves finely. Cut beef into very thin strips.

2 Heat oil in a wok or deep frying pan. Sear meat on all sides over high heat, stirring, until no more juice escapes. Place in a bowl. Mix lime juice, soy sauce, ground ginger and fresh ginger and add to meat, stirring to combine.

3 Wipe wok or pan with paper towels. Dry-roast peanuts lightly over medium heat; add to meat. Stir red onions and coriander into meat. Season with salt.

4 Slice pale green and white parts of spring onions on the diagonal. Cut chili in half, remove seeds. Cut into fine strips.

5 Spoon salad onto individual plates. Sprinkle with spring onions and chili strips. Garnish with cucumber slices and mint leaves.

spicy beef salad with capsicum and corn

✳ Cut 500 g (1 lb) beef fillet into strips and fry as described in main recipe. Place in a bowl and mix with 2 tablespoons lime juice, 1 tablespoon red wine vinegar, 1 teaspoon ground cumin and 1 crushed garlic clove.

✳ Finely slice 2 red onions. Cut 2 red capsicums (bell peppers) into strips. Dice 3 tomatoes. Add 150 g (5 oz) canned corn kernels, onions, capsicums and tomatoes to beef, mix in and season with salt and pepper.

✳ Halve 2 red chilies and chop finely. Heat 2 tablespoons sunflower oil in a wok until very hot and briefly sauté chilies, stirring. Spoon salad onto plates. Top with chilies and 2 tablespoons chopped fresh coriander (cilantro).

thai beef salad with peanuts

gado gado

Gado means 'mixed'. This traditional Indonesian specialty is a combination of raw and lightly cooked vegetables served with spicy peanut sauce.

1 small head iceberg lettuce, leaves separated

2 large potatoes, boiled and sliced

200 g (7 oz) green beans, sliced, blanched

¾ cup (80 g/3 oz) bean sprouts, blanched

1½ cups (125 g/4 oz) shredded Chinese (napa) cabbage, blanched

2 medium tomatoes, cut into wedges

1 medium red onion, sliced

3 spring onions (scallions), cut in short lengths

1 Lebanese (Mediterranean) cucumber, thinly sliced

2 fresh red chilies, seeded and thinly sliced

4 medium hard-boiled eggs, sliced

125 g (4 oz) fried tofu (bean curd), cut into cubes

peanut sauce

½ cup (125 ml/4 fl oz)) vegetable oil

1¼ cups (200 g/7 oz) raw unsalted peanuts

2 cloves garlic, chopped

4 spring onions (scallions), chopped

salt

½ teaspoon chili powder

1 teaspoon soft brown sugar

1 tablespoon dark soy sauce

2 cups (500 ml/16 fl oz) water

juice of 1 lemon

serves 6

preparation 30 minutes

cooking 15 minutes

----

per serving 1597 kilojoules/382 calories, 18 g protein, 27 g total fat, 4 g saturated fat, 143 mg cholesterol, 17 g carbohydrate, 9 g fibre

1 Arrange lettuce leaves on a large plate. Add all the remaining salad ingredients in small groups (for people to help themselves). Serve peanut sauce separately.

2 To make peanut sauce, heat oil in a wok or frying pan over high heat. Stir-fry peanuts until light golden brown, about 4 minutes. Remove with a slotted spoon and place on paper towel to cool. Pound or process peanuts until finely ground. Discard oil from pan, reserving 1 tablespoon.

3 Crush garlic and spring onions in a mortar and pestle with a little salt. Fry in reserved oil, about 1 minute. Add chili powder, sugar, soy sauce and water. Bring to a boil; add ground peanuts. Simmer, stirring occasionally, until sauce is thick, about 10 minutes. Add lemon juice and more salt, if needed. Cool. (Sauce can be made ahead and stored in a jar in the refrigerator for up to 1 week.)

a bite of history

Gado gado ingredients vary from region to region. Other additions are spinach, snow peas or cauliflower. Firm vegetables can be served raw, blanched or steamed. Whatever method is used, they must remain crunchy. Serve the salad cold or at room temperature.

grilled tomato salad (page 108)

salad greens and vegetable salads

Different types of lettuces and vegetables form the basis of a limitless number of attractive and nutritious side dish and main meal salads. Choose from the freshest and best seasonal ingredients and add complementary or contrasting flavours with a variety of dressings and vinaigrettes.

green salad with creamy chive yogurt

3 heads cos (romaine) lettuce

2 spring onions (scallions), thinly sliced

vinaigrette

1 tablespoon olive oil

1 tablespoon white wine vinegar

1 tablespoon lemon juice

1 teaspoon Dijon mustard

salt and freshly ground black pepper

creamy chive yogurt

$\frac{2}{3}$ cup (170 g/6 oz) light sour cream

3 tablespoons yogurt

$\frac{1}{2}$ cup (30 g/1 oz) chopped chives

salt and freshly ground black pepper

croutons

3 thick slices of bread

2 tablespoons butter mashed with

　1 teaspoon finely chopped fresh basil

serves 4

preparation 15 minutes

cooking 3 to 4 minutes

per serving 1405 kilojoules/336 calories, 9 g protein, 23 g total fat, 12 g saturated fat, 54 mg cholesterol, 22 g carbohydrate, 8 g fibre

1　Chop lettuces into wide strips. Place in a serving bowl.

2　To make vinaigrette, whisk oil, vinegar, lemon juice and mustard until combined; add salt and pepper to taste. To make creamy chive yogurt, combine sour cream, yogurt and chives; add salt and pepper to taste.

3　To make croutons, cut bread into small cubes. Melt herb butter in nonstick pan over medium heat. Add bread cubes; cook until golden brown on all sides, taking care butter does not burn. Set aside; keep warm.

4　Drizzle vinaigrette over lettuce. Toss to coat. Sprinkle with spring onions. Spoon on dressing; top with croutons.

cook's tip

Herb butters for cooking croutons are easy to make. Mash a little finely chopped garlic or chives into the butter as an alternative, or another fresh seasonal herb.

green salad with creamy herb yogurt

✳ Combine a mixture of salad greens, such as rocket (arugula), oak leaf and iceberg, in a bowl. Make vinaigrette and croutons as for main recipe.

✳ To make creamy herb yogurt, combine 2 tablespoons each chopped fresh dill, chives, tarragon, parsley and watercress with sour cream and yogurt, salt and pepper, as for main recipe. Drizzle vinaigrette over salad leaves; toss to coat. Spoon creamy herb yogurt over the top. Add croutons.

green salad with creamy chive yogurt

curly lettuce salad with eggs and crisp bacon

1 large head curly endive (frisée) lettuce

5 spring onions (scallions), finely sliced

4 tablespoons vegetable oil

4 thin slices bacon, sliced lengthwise

4 medium eggs

mustard horseradish vinaigrette

5 tablespoons tarragon or other
   herb vinegar

generous pinch of hot mustard powder

1 teaspoon horseradish sauce, or to taste

salt and freshly ground black pepper

serves 4

preparation 15 minutes

cooking 10 minutes

per serving 1383 kilojoules/330 calories, 17 g protein,
28 g total fat, 6 g saturated fat, 239 mg cholesterol,
2 g carbohydrate, 3 g fibre

1 Tear or chop lettuce into small pieces. Divide among serving plates. Sprinkle evenly with spring onions.

2 To make vinaigrette, whisk 2 tablespoons of the oil, 2 tablespoons of the vinegar, mustard and horseradish until combined. Add salt and pepper to taste. Drizzle over salad ingredients.

3 Hall-fill a large saucepan with water. Add remaining 3 tablespoons vinegar; bring to a boil. Heat remaining 2 tablespoons oil in a frying pan. Add bacon; fry until crisp. Keep warm.

4 One at a time, break eggs onto a plate and slide them into the boiling water. Reduce heat to a simmer. Poach eggs 4 to 5 minutes, or until cooked as desired. Remove with a slotted spoon and drain. Trim ragged edges. (Alternatively, hard-boil the eggs; peel and slice when cooled.) Place 1 egg on each serving of salad. Top with bacon. Serve immediately.

salad with egg vinaigrette

1 large head cos (romaine) or iceberg lettuce

4 medium tomatoes

1 small red onion, thinly sliced into rings

egg vinaigrette

2 medium eggs, hard-boiled

½ cup (30 g/1 oz) each finely chopped
  fresh basil and fresh flat-leaf parsley

½ cup (30 g/1 oz) chopped chives

2 leaves fresh lemon balm, chopped

2 sprigs marjoram, leaves finely chopped

3 tablespoons olive oil

1 tablespoon white wine vinegar

1 tablespoon lemon juice

pinch of sugar

salt and freshly ground black pepper

serves 4

preparation 20 minutes

per serving 867 kilojoules/207 calories, 7 g protein,
17 g total fat, 3 g saturated fat, 108 mg cholesterol,
6 g carbohydrate, 5 g fibre

1 Tear or chop lettuce into small pieces. Divide among
serving plates. Halve and core tomatoes; cut into eighths.
Arrange around lettuce. Top with onion rings.

2 To make egg vinaigrette, peel eggs and dice very finely.
Combine all the chopped herbs.

3 Whisk oil, vinegar and lemon juice in a medium bowl
until combined. Stir in chopped eggs and herbs. Add sugar
and salt and pepper to taste. Drizzle over salad ingredients.

mushroom salad

1 head red or green oak leaf lettuce,
　or a mixture of both
250 g (8 oz) brown cap or chanterelle
　mushrooms
2 sprigs rosemary
4 sprigs thyme
3 tablespoons olive oil
3 shallots, finely chopped
2 tablespoons red wine vinegar
2 tablespoons port wine
salt and freshly ground black pepper
2 tablespoons crème fraîche or
　light sour cream
3 tablespoons dried cranberries

serves 4
preparation 10 minutes
cooking 12 minutes

per serving *918 kilojoules/219 calories, 3 g protein,*
18 g total fat, 5 g saturated fat, 12 mg cholesterol,
9 g carbohydrate, 3 g fibre

1 Tear lettuce into small pieces. Use to line a serving bowl. Wipe mushrooms with paper towel. Trim and cut large ones in half. Finely chop rosemary and thyme leaves.

2 Heat oil in a large frying pan. Sauté shallots until transparent. Add mushrooms and cook until golden brown, stirring occasionally. Add chopped herbs, saving a little for garnish; sauté briefly.

3 Add vinegar and port wine to mushroom mixture. Cook, uncovered, until mixture is slightly reduced, about 2 minutes. Add salt and pepper to taste. Spoon over prepared salad. Spoon a little crème fraîche or light sour cream onto each portion. Sprinkle with dried cranberries.

lettuce, carrot and fennel salad with vinaigrette

4 tablespoons sunflower seeds

1 head red lettuce, such as oak leaf or red coral

1 small head radicchio

2 medium carrots (about 250 g/8 oz)

1 medium fennel bulb (about 500 g/1 lb), with leafy fronds

fresh lemon balm leaves, for garnish

lemon and sherry vinaigrette

2 tablespoons lemon-flavoured olive oil (available from specialty food stores)

1 tablespoon sherry vinegar

1 tablespoon lemon juice

3 tablespoons tomato juice

salt and freshly ground black pepper

serves 4

preparation + cooking 25 minutes

----

per serving *795 kilojoules/190 calories, 5 g protein, 16 g total fat, 2 g saturated fat, 0 mg cholesterol, 8 g carbohydrate, 6 g fibre*

1 Toast sunflower seeds in a frying pan over medium heat until golden, stirring occasionally. Transfer to a plate; set aside to cool. Tear or chop lettuce and radicchio into small pieces; arrange on a serving platter.

2 Coarsely grate carrots. Cut fennel bulb into thin slices. Place carrots and fennel on top of lettuce. Finely chop a few fennel fronds; set aside.

3 To make lemon and sherry vinaigrette, whisk oil, vinegar, lemon juice and tomato juice until combined. Add salt and pepper to taste. Add to salad and toss. Add sunflower seeds, fennel fronds and lemon balm leaves.

cook's tip

Some people find that raw fennel is difficult to digest. To solve this problem, first cook the fennel bulb in lightly salted boiling water for 3 to 4 minutes. Cool in iced water.

turkish carrot salad with garlic yogurt

Cooked or raw carrots were first used in salads in north-western Africa. This salad is good served with warmed pita bread.

2 cups (500 g/1 lb) Greek-style yogurt

3 tablespoons olive oil

4 medium carrots (about 500 g/1 lb), coarsely grated

2 cloves garlic, crushed

2 to 3 tablespoons lemon juice (or more, as liked)

salt and freshly ground black pepper

flat-leaf parsley sprigs, for garnish

serves 4

preparation + chilling 1 hour 30 minutes

cooking 10 minutes

----

per serving *1230 kilojoules/294 calories, 9 g protein,
22 g total fat, 7 g saturated fat, 30 mg cholesterol,
15 g carbohydrate, 3 g fibre*

1 Line a large sieve with coffee filter paper or muslin (cheesecloth); place over a large bowl. Spoon yogurt into sieve. Strain 20 minutes.

2 Heat oil in a nonstick pan over medium heat. Add carrots, cook, stirring occasionally, 10 minutes, or until almost soft. Remove from heat; leave to cool.

3 Combine strained yogurt and carrots in a serving bowl. Add garlic and 2 tablespoons lemon juice; toss. Add more lemon juice, if needed, and salt and pepper to taste.

4 Cover salad and chill for at least 1 hour. Taste again just before serving, adding lemon juice, salt and pepper, as liked. Spoon into serving bowls; garnish with parsley.

cook's tip

If you choose to use low-fat yogurt, it will stay runny after straining. Ideally, use a thick, Greek-style, full-fat yogurt to achieve the right consistency.

turkish carrot salad with garlic yogurt

fresh beetroot salad with yogurt

✳ Wash 500 g (1 lb) fresh beetroot (beets). Boil in a saucepan with plenty of water for 1 to 1 hour 30 minutes until soft. Drain and rinse under cold running water. Allow to cool before peeling. Grate beetroot coarsely. (Take care; the juice stains clothing.)

✳ Prepare yogurt as described in main recipe and combine with grated beetroots. Season as described. Add 1 tablespoon olive oil just before serving. Serve garnished with parsley sprigs.

carrot salad

4 medium carrots (about 500 g/1 lb),
   peeled, cut into matchsticks
¾ cup (60 g/2 oz) flat-leaf parsley leaves
4 tablespoons shredded coconut, toasted
3 tablespoons hazelnuts, toasted, chopped
3 tablespoons sultanas
3 tablespoons olive oil
2 tablespoons orange juice
1 teaspoon ground cumin, toasted

serves 4
preparation 15 minutes

----

per serving 1151 kilojoules/275 calories, 3 g protein,
23 g total fat, 6 g saturated fat, 0 mg cholesterol,
15 g carbohydrate, 6 g fibre

1 Place carrots, parsley, coconut, hazelnuts and sultanas in a medium serving bowl.

2 Combine oil, juice and cumin and stir into salad. Divide salad among individual serving bowls.

cook's tip

Most nuts benefit from toasting before being used in a recipe. The process brings out the flavour and reduces any bitter taste. Toast nuts just before you need to use them.

moroccan-style carrot salad

4 medium carrots (about 500 g/1 lb), thickly sliced

2 teaspoons vegetable oil

1 teaspoon ground coriander

1 teaspoon ground cumin

¼ teaspoon ground ginger

pinch of salt

2 teaspoons honey

2 tablespoons lemon juice

1 tablespoon orange juice

4 tablespoons finely chopped fresh coriander (cilantro) leaves

serves 4

preparation + standing 25 minutes

cooking 8 minutes

1 Cook carrots in boiling water for 5 minutes, or until slightly softened. Place in a food processor with a little of the cooking liquid; process just until roughly chopped. Transfer to a serving dish.

2 Heat oil in a nonstick frying pan over medium heat. Add ground coriander, cumin, ginger and salt. Cook 2 to 3 minutes, or until aromatic. Add spice mixture to carrots; toss to coat. Add honey; toss again.

3 Combine lemon juice, orange juice and chopped coriander. Pour over salad. Leave for 10 minutes to allow the flavours to develop.

per serving *277 kilojoules/66 calories, 1 g protein, 3 g total fat, 0.5 g saturated fat, 0 mg cholesterol, 10 g carbohydrate, 3 g fibre*

red and green salad with champagne vinaigrette

1 head red lettuce, such as lollo rossa
  (red coral)
1 heart pale lettuce, such as light yellow
  butter (butterhead)
4 small eggs, hard-boiled
4 large radishes, thinly sliced
1 tablespoon mayonnaise
1 tablespoon red or black caviar (optional)
watercress sprigs, for garnish

champagne vinaigrette

3 tablespoons olive oil
2 tablespoons champagne vinegar
1 tablespoon Dijon mustard
pinch of sugar
salt and freshly ground black pepper

serves 4
preparation 20 minutes

per serving 909 kilojoules/217 calories, 7 g protein,
20 g total fat, 3 g saturated fat, 177 mg cholesterol,
3 g carbohydrate, 2 g fibre

1 Tear or chop both lettuces into small pieces. Arrange on a serving platter. Peel eggs and cut in half.

2 To make champagne vinaigrette, whisk oil, vinegar and mustard until combined. Add sugar and salt and pepper to taste. Drizzle vinaigrette over salad greens. Add radishes. Toss to combine.

3 Place a little mayonnaise on each egg half. Top with caviar, if using. Place egg halves on top of salad greens. Garnish with watercress.

heirloom varieties

Check out your local farmers' market for unusual types of lettuces. Heirloom varieties feature leaves in shades of red, green or yellow. Try contrasting the various colours.

mixed salad greens with avocado

1 tablespoon olive oil

1 tablespoon lemon juice

1 teaspoon Dijon mustard

pinch of salt

350 g (12 oz) mixed salad greens, such as iceberg, radicchio and rocket (arugula)

1 medium red onion, thinly sliced

1 large avocado, peeled and diced

serves 4

preparation 5 minutes

per serving *810 kilojoules/194 calories, 3 g protein,*
19 g total fat, 4 g saturated fat, 0 mg cholesterol,
5 g carbohydrate, 3 g fibre

1 Whisk oil, lemon juice, mustard and salt in a serving bowl until combined.

2 Add salad greens and red onion. Toss well to coat with dressing. Add avocado; toss to combine.

health guide

Although creamy tasting avocados are high in fat, it is mostly monounsaturated. This type of fat helps to lower blood levels of low-density lipoprotein — the bad cholesterol.

snow pea and lettuce salad with crunchy croutons

500 g (1 lb) snow peas (mange-tout)

crisp hearts of 2 green lettuces

3 spring onions (scallions), finely sliced

2 tablespoons vegetable oil

2 tablespoons white wine vinegar

salt and freshly ground black pepper

trimmed alfalfa or mung bean sprouts or
    mustard cress, for garnish

2 thick slices whole-grain bread

1 tablespoon butter

1 clove garlic, peeled, sliced lengthwise

serves 4

preparation 20 minutes

cooking 5 minutes

----

per serving *991 kilojoules/238 calories, 7 g protein,*
16 g total fat, 4 g saturated fat, 12 mg cholesterol,
16 g carbohydrate, 6 g fibre

1 Blanch snow peas in lightly salted boiling water 1 minute. Immerse in iced water; drain. (*See step-by-step instructions.*)

2 Tear lettuce into pieces. Distribute among serving bowls. Add snow peas; sprinkle with spring onions.

3 To make vinaigrette, whisk oil, vinegar and a generous seasoning of salt and pepper. Drizzle over salad greens. Sprinkle with sprouts.

4 To make croutons, cut bread into small cubes. Heat butter in a nonstick frying pan over medium heat. Add garlic, cut surfaces face down. Fry 30 seconds; remove from pan and discard. Place bread cubes in garlic butter; cook until golden brown on all sides, taking care butter does not burn. Serve salad topped with hot croutons.

to blanch snow peas

1 Snow peas require minimal cooking. Blanching is ideal for brief cooking and retains the fresh colour of the vegetable. Trim tips from snow peas and remove any strings.

2 Place trimmed snow peas in lightly salted boiling water. Cook over high heat 1 minute.

3 Remove from boiling water with a slotted spoon. Immerse in iced water to cool and retain their colour. Drain.

multi-layered salad with yogurt mayonnaise

Layered salads are very versatile. You can vary the type of beans or try chicken instead of ham or a firm blue cheese instead of gouda.

1 cup (180 g/7 oz) drained canned corn

1½ cups (275 g/10 oz) drained canned white beans

1 head iceberg lettuce

1 red and 1 yellow capsicum (bell pepper)

250 g (8 oz) ham, in one piece

200 g (7 oz) gouda, in one piece

20 medium radishes

4 medium sweet and sour cucumbers

2 slices pumpernickel bread (optional)

yogurt mayonnaise

1 cup (250 g/8 oz) yogurt

¾ cup (175 g/6 oz) mayonnaise

2 tablespoons milk

½ teaspoon English (hot) mustard

2 tablespoons sunflower or olive oil

1 tablespoon white wine vinegar

1 tablespoon lemon juice

½ teaspoon ground sweet paprika

salt and freshly ground black pepper

1 cup (80 g/3 oz) finely chopped fresh parsley

½ cup (30 g/1 oz) finely chopped fresh dill

1 cup (60 g/2 oz) finely chopped chives

leaves of 3 sprigs thyme, chopped

serves 6

preparation + chilling 1 hour 40 minutes

- -

per serving 2028 kilojoules/485 calories, 24 g protein, 30 g total fat, 10 g saturated fat, 67 mg cholesterol, 28 g carbohydrate, 8 g fibre

1 RInse corn and beans. Chop lettuce into strips. Cut capsicums in half, discard seeds and chop into dice.

2 Trim ham of excess fat. Dice finely. Cut cheese into narrow strips. Chop radishes into quarters. Chop cucumbers into rounds.

3 Layer salad ingredients in a tall glass serving bowl in the following order: lettuce, radishes, corn, ham, cucumbers, capsicums, cheese, beans.

4 To make yogurt mayonnaise, place yogurt, mayonnaise and milk in a bowl. Whisk in mustard, oil, vinegar and lemon juice. Add sweet paprika and salt and pepper to taste. Be generous with the seasonings. Fold in herbs. Pour dressing over salad. Chill, covered, 1 hour. Crumble pumpernickel bread, if using, over salad just before serving.

health guide

Sunflower oil is an all-purpose cooking oil with a mild taste. It is low in saturated fat. Use mild-tasting peanut (groundnut) oil or a richer flavoured olive oil, if preferred, both of which are good for your health.

multi-layered salad
with yogurt mayonnaise

italian-style layered salad

* In a glass serving bowl, layer 4 roma (plum) tomatoes, chopped, 150 g (5 oz) torn rocket (arugula), 2 red capsicums (bell peppers), seeded and chopped, 250 g (8 oz) sliced mozzarella, 2 cos (romaine) lettuce hearts, torn into small pieces, 1 cup (120 g/4 oz) black olives, 250 g (8 oz) artichoke hearts, chopped, and 1 small cucumber, diced.

* Mix 3 tablespoons homemade or store-bought pesto, 3 tablespoons olive oil, 2 tablespoons lemon juice and 4 tablespoons chicken or vegetable stock (broth). Add salt and pepper to taste. Pour over salad. Chill, covered, 1 hour. Serve with toasted ciabatta or sourdough bread.

marinated vegetable salad

This simple salad can be varied according to what's in season. Mix textures, flavours and cheerful colours. Blanch broccoli and squash briefly, if you prefer.

1 cup (100 g/4 oz) sliced broccoli
   and/or cauliflower florets

150 g (5 oz) cherry tomatoes, halved

1 large carrot, cut into matchsticks

2 small yellow squash or 1 small zucchini
   (courgette), thinly sliced

1/4 cup (30 g/1 oz) finely sliced celery

marinade

1/2 cup (125 ml/4 fl oz) balsamic vinegar

1/2 cup (125 ml/4 fl oz) olive oil

3 tablespoons chopped fresh parsley
   or fresh coriander (cilantro) leaves

1 tablespoon sugar

2 tablespoons finely chopped fresh dill
   or 2 teaspoons dried dill

1/2 teaspoon salt

1/4 teaspoon freshly ground black pepper

serves 4
preparation 25 minutes
marinating 8 hours or overnight

---

per serving 892 kilojoules/213 calories, 3 g protein,
19 g total fat, 3 g saturated fat, 0 mg cholesterol,
8 g carbohydrate, 4 g fibre

1 Place vegetables in a large, heavy-duty plastic bag. To make marinade, place all ingredients in a screw-top jar and shake well to combine.

2 Pour marinade over vegetables and seal top of bag. Store in refrigerator 8 hours or overnight, turning the bag occasionally to ensure vegetables absorb the maximum flavours from the marinade.

3 Use a slotted spoon to transfer the vegetables to a serving bowl. Serve at room temperature.

cauliflower

We're all used to seeing cauliflowers with heads of creamy white curd. Now, lime green as well as purple and orange varieties are also available. Use a mixture in this recipe to create a very attractive salad.

cook's tip

Always store tomatoes at room temperature. Refrigeration spoils their taste and texture. Slightly underripe tomatoes will ripen in a brown paper bag.

marinated vegetable salad

salad with celery and mint dressing

✳ Slice 6 large red radishes into rounds and add to salad ingredients in main recipe. Replace celery with 1 small finely sliced cucumber.

✳ For the marinade, add 1 tablespoon finely chopped celery leaves. Use finely chopped fresh mint in place of dill and celery salt in place of salt. Celery salt and celery leaves accentuate the taste of tomatoes.

russian salad with potato and capers

500 g (1 lb) waxy potatoes

200 g (7 oz) carrots

1 large red capsicum (bell pepper)

1 cup (250 ml/9 fl oz) salt-reduced
  vegetable stock (broth)

150 g (5 oz) green beans

1 cup (120 g/4 oz) frozen peas

2 medium eggs, hard-boiled

3 tablespoons chopped fresh parsley

mayonnaise

1 medium egg yolk

pinch of mustard powder

generous pinch of salt

freshly ground black pepper

½ cup (125 ml/4 fl oz) vegetable oil

1 to 2 tablespoons lemon juice

2 tablespoons small capers plus
  2 to 3 tablespoons brine from the jar

serves 4

preparation + chilling 1 hour 30 minutes

cooking 15 minutes

per serving 1802 kilojoules/430 calories, 10 g protein,
34 g total fat, 4 g saturated fat, 161 mg cholesterol,
22 g carbohydrate, 7 g fibre

1 Peel potatoes and cut into small cubes. Cut carrots and capsicum into small cubes.

2 Bring stock to a boil in a large saucepan. Add potatoes, carrots and beans. Cook, covered, over medium heat, 5 minutes. Add capsicum and peas. Cook, covered, another 5 minutes. Transfer vegetables to a sieve; leave to cool.

3 To make mayonnaise, make sure all the ingredients and the bowl are at room temperature to prevent curdling. Whisk egg yolk, mustard powder and a generous pinch of salt until creamy. Add oil in a thin stream, whisking until mixture thickens. Add 1 tablespoon lemon juice and salt and pepper to taste. Add 2 tablespoons caper brine. Taste, adding more brine, if liked.

4 Place vegetables and capers in a serving bowl. Spoon on mayonnaise, stirring to coat. Place in refrigerator 1 hour.

5 Just before serving, add more salt, pepper and lemon juice to taste. Peel eggs; slice into wedges. Add to salad. Sprinkle with parsley.

cook's tip

It's worth making double the quantity of this salad because it keeps very well and the flavours intensify. Cover and store in the refrigerator for up to 3 days.

russian salad with potato and capers

potato salad with cucumber

✳ Cook 800 g (1 lb 12 oz) waxy potatoes in boiling water until just cooked. Drain, rinse under cold water. Cool, peel and slice. Finely slice 1 small red onion and 1 small cucumber, seeds removed. Place in a serving bowl.

✳ To make vinaigrette, whisk 3 tablespoons white wine vinegar, 4 tablespoons olive oil, $\frac{1}{2}$ teaspoon hot mustard and 4 tablespoons vegetable stock (broth) until combined. Add salt and pepper to taste. Mix with salad. Cover and refrigerate for 30 minutes.

✳ Just before serving, add salt, pepper, vinegar and stock to taste. Sprinkle with chopped chives.

root vegetable salad with spicy vinaigrette

Beetroot tastes sweet because it is richer in natural sugar than any other vegetable. Small beetroot with their greens still attached have the most flavour.

600 g (1 lb 8 oz) beetroot (beets)

500 g (1 lb) waxy potatoes

3 medium tomatoes

2 spring onions (scallions), finely chopped

2 cloves garlic, finely chopped

½ cup (40 g/2 oz) finely chopped
    fresh flat-leaf parsley

3 sprigs coriander (cilantro),
    leaves finely chopped

⅔ cup (100 g/4 oz) black olives, for garnish

spicy vinaigrette

5 tablespoons white wine vinegar

6 tablespoons olive oil

½ teaspoon salt

pinch of freshly ground black pepper

pinch of cayenne pepper

serves 4

preparation + chilling 1 hour

cooking 1 hour 30 minutes

----

per serving *1594 kilojoules/381 calories, 5 g protein, 28 g total fat, 4 g saturated fat, 0 mg cholesterol, 27 g carbohydrate, 6 g fibre*

1 Place beetroot in a large saucepan, cover with water and bring to a boil. Cook 1 hour 30 minutes, or until a fork is easily inserted. Drain, reserving 4 tablespoons cooking water. Refresh under cold running water; leave to cool.

2 Cook potatoes in boiling water 20 to 30 minutes, or until just cooked. Drain, refresh under cold running water; leave to cool. Peel beetroot and potatoes, halve and slice thinly. Place in separate bowls.

3 Plunge tomatoes into boiling water 1 minute. Transfer to bowl of iced water. Peel tomatoes, cut in halves, remove seeds and dice flesh. Combine tomatoes and spring onions with beetroot. Add garlic, parsley, coriander and reserved cooking water.

4 To make spicy vinaigrette, whisk vinegar, oil, salt, pepper and cayenne pepper until combined. Stir two thirds vinaigrette into beetroot mixture and remainder into potatoes. Cover and refrigerate 30 minutes.

5 Just before serving, add salt, pepper and more vinegar to taste. Spoon beetroot salad onto a platter and arrange potato salad around it. Garnish with olives.

mixed salad with caperberries

800 g (1 lb 12 oz) waxy potatoes

150 g (5 oz) rocket (arugula),
  roughly chopped

2 medium red onions, finely sliced into rings

200 g (7 oz) cherry tomatoes, halved

½ cup (60 g/2 oz) each pitted green and
  black olives

caperberry vinaigrette

2 to 3 tablespoons sherry vinegar

¼ cup (50 g/2 oz) caperberries or capers
  plus 1 to 2 tablespoons brine from the jar

1 teaspoon Dijon mustard

4 tablespoons olive oil

salt and freshly ground black pepper

serves 4

preparation + chilling 40 minutes

cooking 20 minutes

----

*per serving 1389 kilojoules/332 calories, 6 g protein,
19 g total fat, 3 g saturated fat, 0 mg cholesterol,
34 g carbohydrate, 6 g fibre*

1 Cook potatoes in boiling salted water for 20 minutes, or until just cooked. Rinse under cold running water. Peel and dice when cool enough to handle. Place potatoes, rocket, onions, tomatoes and olives in a serving bowl.

2 To make caperberry vinaigrette, whisk vinegar, 1 to 2 tablespoons caperberry brine, mustard and oil until combined. Add salt and pepper to taste. Pour vinaigrette over salad and toss gently to combine.

3 Leave salad, covered, in a cool place 30 minutes. Add more salt, pepper and vinegar to taste. Slice caperberries in half and add to salad.

cook's tip

If the potato salad becomes a little dry while standing, add 2 tablespoons or so of hot stock (broth). Let stand 5 minutes before serving.

caperberries

Caperberries are the fruit of the caper bush. They are about 2 cm (1 inch) long and are pickled in brine with their stems intact. They are available from delicatessens and some supermarkets. Eat whole as part of an antipasto plate. Alternatively, slice for use as a garnish.

mixed salad with caperberries

light potato salad with baby spinach

✳ Cook and peel 800 g (1 lb 12 oz) potatoes as described in the main recipe; cut into rounds instead of dice.

✳ Finely slice 3 spring onions (scallions). Tear 150 g (5 oz) baby spinach leaves into small pieces. Place salad in a bowl. Whisk ½ cup (125 g/4 oz) low-fat yogurt, ½ cup (125 g/4 oz) light sour cream, 1 tablespoon white wine vinegar, 1 tablespoon lemon juice and 2 tablespoons olive oil until combined. Pour over and toss through salad. Add salt and pepper to taste.

artichoke and herb salad with white beans

4 large globe artichoke hearts
   (in oil and vinegar, from a jar)

100 g (4 oz) ham, in one piece

4 tablespoons olive oil

2 cloves garlic, finely chopped

4 tablespoons dry white wine

4 sprigs thyme, leaves finely chopped

2 sprigs marjoram, leaves finely chopped

1 sprig rosemary, leaves finely chopped

½ cup (40 g/2 oz) finely chopped fresh
   flat-leaf parsley

1⅓ cups (250 g/8 oz) drained and rinsed
   canned white beans

2 roma (plum) tomatoes, sliced

150 g (5 oz) rocket (arugula), torn
   into small pieces

salt and freshly ground black pepper

2 to 3 tablespoons lemon juice

serves 4

preparation 10 minutes

cooking 5 minutes

----

per serving *1370 kilojoules/327 calories, 11 g protein,*
25 g total fat, 4 g saturated fat, 13 mg cholesterol,
13 g carbohydrate, 6 g fibre

1 Cut artichoke hearts into even pieces. Cut ham into dice, discarding any excess fat.

2 Heat 2 tablespoons oil in a nonstick pan. Add garlic, cook, stirring, just until transparent. Add artichoke pieces and wine. Cook over high heat, covered, 2 minutes. Add ham and herbs; heat briefly. Set pan aside and let mixture cool to lukewarm. Transfer to a serving bowl.

3 Add beans, tomatoes and rocket to artichoke mixture. Add salt, pepper and remaining lemon juice and oil to taste.

globe artichokes

The globe artichoke is the large flower bud of a bushy thistle plant. Its edible portions are the buttery heart and the earthy-tasting fleshy part at the base of the outer leaves. Steaming, boiling or baking are the best cooking methods. To prepare for cooking, see page 112.

bean salad
with paprika vinaigrette

bean salad with paprika vinaigrette

4 1/4 cups (600 g/1 lb 8 oz) frozen
   or shelled fresh broad (fava) beans

1 small cucumber

2 shallots, finely diced

3 roma (plum) tomatoes, sliced

1 small red and 1 yellow capsicum (bell
   pepper), seeded and diced

1/2 cup (40 g/2 oz) finely chopped
   fresh flat-leaf parsley

paprika vinaigrette

4 tablespoons olive oil

2 tablespoons balsamic vinegar

1 tablespoon lemon juice

1 teaspoon ground cumin

1/2 teaspoon ground sweet paprika

pinch of cayenne pepper

pinch of freshly ground black pepper

serves 4

preparation 15 minutes

cooking 15 minutes

per serving *1171 kilojoules/280 calories, 12 g protein,*
19 g total fat, 3 g saturated fat, 0 mg cholesterol,
14 g carbohydrate, 8 g fibre

1 Place beans in a saucepan. Cover with lightly salted water; bring to a boil. Cook 15 minutes or until crisp-tender. Drain and leave to cool.

2 Cut cucumber in half lengthwise and remove seeds with a teaspoon. Slice cucumber thinly. Combine broad beans, cucumber, shallots and tomatoes in a serving bowl.

3 To make paprika vinaigrette, whisk ingredients until combined. Stir in diced capsicums.

4 Arrange salad on individual plates. Stir diced capsicums into vinaigrette. Drizzle on salad. Sprinkle with parsley.

cook's tip

Flat-leaf or Italian parsley tends to have more flavour than curly parsley. Avoid using dried parsley as it has little flavour and none of the true parsley taste.

bean salad with cream dressing

* Cook broad (fava) beans as described in main recipe and allow to cool. Peel and finely dice 2 shallots and place in a bowl with the broad beans.

* To make dressing, whisk 2 tablespoons white wine vinegar, 1 tablespoon olive oil, 3 tablespoons whipping cream, 2 tablespoons crème fraîche or light sour cream and salt and freshly ground black pepper to taste. Stir dressing into salad. Cover and refrigerate 30 minutes. Serve with whole-grain bread.

mixed bean salad with spicy cream dressing

Crème fraîche is a thick soured cream with a velvety texture. It is available from specialty food stores and delicatessens. Light sour cream may be used instead.

250 g (8 oz) green beans

250 g (8 oz) butter (yellow wax) beans

$^3/_4$ cup (140 g/5 oz) drained and rinsed canned red kidney beans

200 g (7 oz) cherry tomatoes, sliced

1 large red onion, finely sliced

1 cup (80 g/3 oz) finely chopped fresh flat-leaf parsley

salt and freshly ground black pepper

spicy cream dressing

1 clove garlic, roughly chopped

$^1/_4$ teaspoon salt

4 tablespoons crème fraîche or light sour cream

2 teaspoons tomato paste

1 tablespoon olive oil

2 tablespoons balsamic vinegar

freshly ground black pepper

pinch of sugar

1 to 2 pinches of cayenne pepper

serves 4

preparation 10 minutes

cooking 15 minutes

per serving 835 kilojoules/199 calories, 6 g protein, 14 g total fat, 7 g saturated fat, 25 mg cholesterol, 13 g carbohydrate, 8 g fibre

1 Chop green and butter beans into short lengths. Place in a steamer basket over pan of simmering water. Cover pan; steam beans for 12 to 15 minutes until crisp-tender. Remove from pan; leave to cool.

2 To make spicy cream dressing, place garlic in a mortar with $^1/_4$ teaspoon salt; grind to a fine paste. Mix with remaining dressing ingredients.

3 Combine salad ingredients in a serving bowl, adding salt and pepper to taste. Serve dressing separately.

health tip

Steaming is one of the cooking methods that best preserves the nutritional value, taste and texture of vegetables. Water and stock (broth) are both suitable steaming liquids.

mixed bean salad
with spicy cream dressing

golden yellow salad with crisp bacon

✻ Prepare 1 kg (2 lb) butter (yellow wax) beans, as for main recipe. Cook
15 to 18 minutes in lightly salted boiling water. Drain and let cool.

✻ Finely dice 2 shallots. Place in a bowl with the beans.

✻ Combine 4 tablespoons olive oil, 2 tablespoons tarragon vinegar, salt and
pepper and pour over bean mixture. Leave in a cool place 2 hours, then
season to taste. Grill or pan-fry 4 slices bacon until crisp. Chop and sprinkle
over salad while still warm. Sprinkle with chopped fresh parsley.

fennel and green bean salad

Many kinds of canned beans will work well in this recipe. Or, try a combination of small and large canned beans of different colours.

grated rind and juice of 1 small orange

1 teaspoon whole-grain mustard

1½ tablespoons olive oil

1 clove garlic, crushed

1 can (400 g/14 oz) flageolet
or navy beans, drained and rinsed

⅔ cup (80 g/3 oz) pitted green olives

salt and freshly ground black pepper

1 medium fennel bulb, about
500 g (1 lb), sliced

150 g (5 oz) green beans, halved

2 zucchini (courgettes), about 200 g (7 oz)
in total, sliced

6 slices Parma ham or other prosciutto,
about 90 g (3 oz) in total, fat removed
and slices halved

serves 4
preparation 10 minutes
cooking 5 to 10 minutes

----

per serving *809 kilojoules/193 calories, 9 g protein,
9 g total fat, 1 g saturated fat, 11 mg cholesterol,
20 g carbohydrate, 8 g fibre*

1 Combine orange rind and juice, mustard, olive oil, garlic, flageolet beans and olives in a shallow baking dish. Season with salt and pepper to taste.

2 Bring a pan of salted water to a boil. Add fennel and green beans; simmer 1 minute. Add zucchini; cook another 4 minutes or until vegetables are just tender. Meanwhile, preheat grill (broiler) to high.

3 Drain vegetables and combine with mixture in baking dish. Scrunch up Parma ham slices and arrange on top. Place dish under grill 1 to 2 minutes, sufficient to warm ham.

health guide

Recipes that use fennel sometimes list celery as an alternative. Although they are similar in texture, the nutritional differences between the two are significant. Fennel provides more potassium, vitamin C and folate than celery and has much more fibre.

cook's tip

Parma ham is the best known and one of the most expensive of the Italian salted, air-dried prosciutto. Pancetta (salt-cured bacon) or coppa (salted, spiced dry-cured ham) may also be used in this recipe.

eggplant salad with tahini

This Mediterranean dish has a deliciously smoky and nutty taste and a creamy texture. Serve it with wedges of warm pita bread.

2 large eggplants (aubergines)
  (about 600 g/1 lb 8 oz))

7 tablespoons lemon juice

3 tablespoons tahini (sesame seed paste)
  from a jar plus 1 tablespoon oil from jar

3 cloves garlic, crushed

salt

2 tablespoons pomegranate seeds,
  for garnish (optional)

chopped fresh parsley, for garnish

serves 4

preparation + chilling 1 hour 20 minutes

cooking 25 to 30 minutes

----

*per serving 714 kilojoules/171 calories, 5 g protein,
14 g total fat, 2 g saturated fat, 0 mg cholesterol,
5 g carbohydrate, 6 g fibre*

1 Preheat oven to 240°C/475°F. Line a baking tray with cooking (aluminum) foil. Wash eggplants; place wet on foil. Bake 25 to 30 minutes, turning occasionally.

2 Rinse eggplants under cold running water. Cut in half, scoop flesh into a bowl and drizzle with 3 tablespoons lemon juice to prevent discolouration.

3 Mash eggplants in a bowl. Mix in tahini and 1 tablespoon oil from the jar, 3 tablespoons lemon juice and the garlic. Cover and refrigerate at least 1 hour.

4 Just before serving, add remaining 1 tablespoon lemon juice and salt to taste. Garnish with pomegranate seeds, if using, and parsley.

cook's tip

Buy large eggplants to get the maximum amount of flesh. Store them in a cool place but not in the refrigerator because eggplants tend to soften and become bitter. Cook them within a couple of days of purchase.

tahini

Tahini is a paste made from ground sesame seeds. It is a key ingredient in hummus and other Middle Eastern recipes. Tahini is available from delicatessens and health food stores and is sold both salted and unsalted. Once opened, it will keep in a sealed jar in the refrigerator for several weeks.

eggplant salad with tahini

eggplant salad with chilies and cumin

❋ Cut 2 large eggplants (aubergines) into large dice. Place in a bowl; stir in 2 teaspoons salt. (Eggplants can be bitter; salting helps rid them of the taste.) Set aside for 20 minutes. Wash eggplants; pat dry with paper towels.

❋ Heat 6 tablespoons olive oil in a pan. Add eggplants; fry until golden brown. Add more oil, if necessary. Remove from heat. Leave to cool. Place in a serving bowl.

❋ Place eggplants in a serving bowl. Slice 2 mild green chilies into strips and add to bowl. Combine 3 tablespoons lemon juice, 1 teaspoon ground cumin, salt and pepper. Stir into salad. Serve with pita bread and tomatoes.

mixing mayonnaise

1 Place egg yolk, garlic paste and half the lemon juice in a mixing bowl. Whisk vigorously for about 1 minute.

2 Beat oil into mixture a drop at a time at first. The mixture will gradually thicken.

3 Whisk in remaining oil in a thin, steady stream until well combined. Add yogurt and remaining lemon juice; whisk briefly. Season to taste.

asparagus salad with lemon and garlic mayonnaise

1 kg (2 lb) medium-thick white asparagus

1 teaspoon sugar

generous pinch of salt

200 g (7 oz) smoked ham, trimmed
   of excess fat

fresh parsley, for garnish

lemon and garlic mayonnaise

1 clove garlic, roughly chopped

$\frac{1}{2}$ teaspoon salt

1 medium egg yolk

1 tablespoon lemon juice

3 tablespoons olive oil

2 tablespoons lemon-flavoured olive oil

$\frac{1}{2}$ cup (125 g/4 oz) yogurt

salt and ground white pepper

serves 4

preparation 15 minutes

cooking 20 minutes

----

per serving *1411 kilojoules/337 calories, 16 g protein,*
28 g total fat, 5 g saturated fat, 76 mg cholesterol,
5 g carbohydrate, 3 g fibre

1 Remove woody ends from asparagus. Peel stalks thinly. Half fill a large saucepan with water, add sugar and salt and bring to a boil. Add asparagus, cook 18 to 20 minutes, depending on thickness, or until crisp-tender. Remove asparagus from pan. Drain; keep warm until serving.

2 Cut ham into wide strips and arrange over base of serving dish.

3 To make lemon and garlic mayonnaise, pound garlic and salt to a fine paste in a medium bowl. Add egg yolk and $\frac{1}{2}$ tablespoon lemon juice. Whisk vigorously until thickened.

4 Whisk both olive oils into the mixture, drop by drop, until it starts to thicken. Add remainder in a thin, steady stream until well combined. Add yogurt and remaining lemon juice. Season to taste with salt and white pepper.

5 Place asparagus on top of ham, coat with a little mayonnaise and sprinkle with parsley leaves. Serve remaining mayonnaise in a separate bowl.

cook's tip

White asparagus is thicker than green asparagus. If using green asparagus, halve the cooking time. The mayonnaise uses white pepper, not black, because a dressing for white asparagus ideally is uniformly pale, with no dark speckles visible to spoil the appearance.

radish and cucumber salad

1 large white (daikon) radish, peeled
salt
1 medium cucumber
16 medium red radishes, thinly sliced
½ cup (40 g/2 oz) chopped fresh parsley
½ cup (30 g/1 oz) chopped chives
mung bean sprouts, for garnish

vinaigrette

1 tablespoon white wine vinegar
1 tablespoon lemon juice
3 tablespoons canola or peanut oil
salt and freshly ground black pepper

serves 4
preparation 25 minutes

---

per serving *622 kilojoules/149 calories, 2 g protein,*
14 g total fat, 1 g saturated fat, 0 mg cholesterol,
4 g carbohydrate, 3 g fibre

1 Using a vegetable peeler or sharp knife, cut white radish into very thin curls. Place in a colander, sprinkle with salt and leave to drain for 15 minutes. Rinse and pat dry with paper towel.

2 Peel away thin strips the length of the cucumber to create a striped effect. Slice cucumber very thinly; arrange on individual plates or a serving platter. Place red and white radishes on top of cucumber slices.

3 To make vinaigrette, whisk vinegar, lemon juice, oil and salt and pepper to taste in a bowl. Drizzle over radishes. Top with chives and mung bean sprouts.

cucumber salad

1 medium cucumber

¼ teaspoon salt

2 large spring onions (scallions) with green
   stems, finely sliced

4 medium red radishes, thinly sliced

sour cream dressing

½ cup (125 g/4 oz) sour cream

2 tablespoons tarragon vinegar or white
   wine vinegar

1 tablespoon finely chopped fresh dill
   or 1 teaspoon dried dill

1 teaspoon sugar

1 teaspoon Dijon mustard

¼ teaspoon freshly ground black pepper

serves 4

preparation 40 minutes

chilling 1 hour

*per serving 569 kilojoules/136 calories, 1 g protein,
13 g total fat, 8 g saturated fat, 41 mg cholesterol,
4 g carbohydrate, 1 g fibre*

1 Slice cucumber in half lengthwise and scoop out seeds
with a teaspoon. Slice cucumber thinly. Place in a bowl,
sprinkle with salt and let stand 30 minutes. Drain, pat dry.
Place cucumber, spring onions and radishes in a large bowl.

2 To make sour cream dressing, whisk sour cream, vinegar,
dill, sugar, mustard and pepper until combined. Spoon over
cucumber mixture. Toss to coat. Cover and refrigerate 1 hour.

cook's tip

*The process of salting cucumbers
removes some of the liquid so that
the flavour of a dressing is not
heavily diluted. Also, it helps to
remove any bitter taste that the
cucumbers may have.*

egg and radish salad

Both of the salad greens used in this recipe have a slightly bitter taste that is complemented by the peppery heat of the radishes.

2 medium eggs, hard-boiled

8 large curly endive (frisée) lettuce leaves

2 medium heads witlof (Belgian endive/chicory)

2 spring onions (scallions)

16 medium red radishes

cream cheese dressing

100 g (4 oz) cream cheese with herbs or plain cream cheese

3 tablespoons yogurt

2 tablespoons herb vinegar

2 tablespoons canola oil

2 tablespoons finely chopped fresh herbs such as a mixture of parsley, chives, dill, chervil or sorrel

salt and freshly ground black pepper

serves 4

preparation 25 minutes

----

per serving *958 kilojoules/229 calories, 7 g protein, 21 g total fat, 7 g saturated fat, 134 mg cholesterol, 2 g carbohydrate, 1 g fibre*

1 Slice eggs into thin rounds. Divide endive among serving plates. Place witlof leaves on top, open sides upwards.

2 Finely chop white part of spring onions; slice green part into thin rounds. Finely dice radishes. Mix with white part of spring onions.

3 To make cream cheese dressing, combine cream cheese, yogurt, vinegar and oil. Add herbs, reserving a little for garnish. Season with salt and pepper.

4 Sprinkle radish/spring onion mixture evenly over the witlof. Top with dressing. Add egg slices. Sprinkle with remaining herbs and green parts of spring onions.

health guide

Rapeseed oil (marketed as canola oil) is one of the world's major oil crops. Canola (which was originally and curiously called Canadian oilseed, low-acid versatile) is a neutral-tasting oil that is very low in saturated fat. Use safflower or peanut oil as alternatives.

warm grilled mixed vegetable salad

500 g (1 lb) green capsicums (bell peppers), seeded and sliced thickly

500 g (1 lb) red capsicums (bell peppers), seeded and thickly sliced

500 g (1 lb) zucchini (courgettes), thinly sliced lengthwise

1 large red onion, cut into wedges

6 baby eggplants (aubergines), thinly sliced lengthwise

150 g (5 oz) portobello or large Swiss brown mushrooms, thickly sliced

3 tablespoons olive oil

1 medium head treviso or round radicchio

1 cup (120 g/4 oz) pitted black olives

2 tablespoons balsamic vinegar

1 tablespoon finely chopped fresh oregano

serves 4
preparation 20 minutes
cooking 15 minutes

*per serving 1098 kilojoules/262 calories, 9 g protein,
15 g total fat, 2 g saturated fat, 0 mg cholesterol,
23 g carbohydrate, 8 g fibre*

1 Preheat grill (broiler) or barbecue until medium-hot.

2 Mix capsicums, zucchini, onion, eggplants, mushrooms and 1 tablespoon oil in a large bowl. Cook vegetables on barbecue grill plate until browned and tender, turning occasionally to cook evenly.

3 Place warm vegetables in a serving bowl. Add treviso, olives, vinegar, oregano and remaining 2 tablespoons oil. Toss gently to combine.

cook's tip

Grill (broil) or barbecue an extra quantity of vegetables. Cool; place in a glass container. Pour in olive oil to cover. Seal jar and store in a cool place away from direct light. Serve as part of an antipasto plate.

health guide

Mushrooms contain very few kilojoules (calories) and are virtually fat-free. To get the maximum nutrients, store mushrooms for no more than five days in the refrigerator.

grilled tomato salad

Grilling or broiling tomatoes intensifies their flavour. Buy ripe but firm tomatoes that will keep their shape during cooking.

10 roma (plum) tomatoes,
  halved lengthwise
2 cloves garlic, finely sliced
150 g (5 oz) rocket (arugula)
¾ cup (90 g/3 oz) pitted green olives

croutons

4 thick slices baguette
3 tablespoons olive oil

vinaigrette

2 tablespoons olive oil
1 tablespoon balsamic vinegar
1 tablespoon lemon juice
salt and freshly ground black pepper

serves 4
preparation 10 minutes
cooking 10 minutes

----

per serving 1388 kilojoules/332 calories, 5 g protein,
24 g total fat, 3 g saturated fat, 0 mg cholesterol,
23 g carbohydrate, 4 g fibre

1 Preheat grill (broiler) or barbecue to medium-hot. To grill (broil) tomatoes, place cut-side up on a baking tray. Sprinkle with garlic. Place under grill 2 to 3 minutes. Turn and cook another 2 minutes. To barbecue, place tomatoes cut-side down on a piece of cooking (aluminum) foil. Cook over fire 2 to 3 minutes. Turn; cook another 2 minutes. Tomatoes should still hold their shape.

2 To make croutons, slice bread into small cubes. Heat 3 tablespoons of the olive oil in a nonstick frying pan over medium heat. Add bread cubes; cook until crisp on all sides. Set aside.

3 Tear rocket into small pieces. Arrange on serving plates. To make vinaigrette, whisk balsamic vinegar, lemon juice, salt, pepper and remaining oil until combined.

4 Place grilled tomatoes on top of rocket. Drizzle with vinaigrette. Add olives and croutons.

health guide

Tomatoes are a wonder food. One medium tomato contains more than half the daily requirement for vitamin C. Tomatoes also contain a phytochemical called lycopene that protects against prostate cancer and is known to slow damage to human cells caused by ageing and disease.

grilled tomato salad

grilled tomato salad with cheese

✳ Thickly slice 600 g (1 lb 8 oz) large tomatoes or use cherry tomatoes and cut in half. Grill (broil) or barbecue as for the main recipe, but for 2 or 3 minutes only. Place in a serving bowl with 1 medium red onion sliced into thin rings.

✳ To make vinaigrette, whisk 4 tablespoons olive oil, 2 tablespoons red wine vinegar, salt, freshly ground black pepper and 2 tablespoons chopped fresh mixed herbs until combined. Stir into salad.

✳ Cut 250 g (8 oz) feta or baked ricotta into cubes. Sprinkle over salad. Add chopped fresh basil leaves. Serve with ciabatta.

green summer salad

Select capsicums with firm, glossy skin that feel heavy for their size. Red, yellow or orange varieties may be used. They taste sweeter than green.

1 kg (2 lb) green capsicums (bell peppers),
   cut in half lengthwise
4 tablespoons olive oil
2 tablespoons red wine vinegar
salt and freshly ground black pepper

serves 4
preparation + chilling 1 hour 15 minutes
cooking 15 minutes

per serving *822 kilojoules/196 calories, 3 g protein,*
18 g total fat, 3 g saturated fat, 0 mg cholesterol,
5 g carbohydrate, 2 g fibre

1 Preheat grill (broiler) or barbecue until hot. Or, preheat oven to 240ºC/475ºF. If grilling (broiling) or cooking in the oven, place capsicums on cooking (aluminum) foil on a baking tray. If barbecuing, omit baking tray and place on foil directly onto grill. Cook 15 minutes, turning halfway through, or until blackened and blistered. Remove from heat. Place cloth towel soaked in cold water on top. Leave 5 minutes. Peel away skin with a small knife.

2 Cut flesh into thin strips. Place on a platter. Drizzle with combined oil and vinegar. Refrigerate, covered, 1 hour. Add salt and pepper to taste before serving.

to prepare capsicums

1 Place capsicums on a baking tray lined with cooking (aluinum) foil. Using a hot grill (broiler), barbecue or oven, cook about 20 minutes, turning halfway, or until the skin has blackened and bubbled.

2 Place cloth towel soaked in cold water on top of capsicums. Leave for 5 minutes. Peel away skin with a small knife.

3 Or, remove capsicums from heat and immediately place in a large freezer bag. Seal bag. Place in a bowl of iced water. Leave 2 minutes before peeling.

artichoke and radicchio salad

4 small globe artichokes

1 clove garlic, thinly sliced

4 tablespoons olive oil

100 ml (4 fl oz) dry white wine

salt and freshly ground black pepper

2 tablespoons balsamic vinegar

3 tablespoons finely chopped fresh
flat-leaf parsley

few sprigs lemon thyme, leaves
finely chopped

2 medium heads treviso or round radicchio

80 g (3 oz) pecorino

lemon wedges, to serve

serves 4

preparation 10 minutes

cooking 12 minutes

----

*per serving 1154 kilojoules/276 calories, 10 g protein,
24 g total fat, 6 g saturated fat, 18 mg cholesterol,
4 g carbohydrate, 2 g fibre*

1 Use kitchen scissors to trim tips of artichoke leaves. Cut artichokes in half. Scrape out fibrous inner part with a teaspoon. Rinse well to remove any remaining fibre. Cut artichokes into four pieces.

2 Heat oil in a nonstick frying pan with a lid over medium heat. Add artichoke pieces and garlic. Cook, stirring, about 5 minutes. Add wine; season with salt and pepper. Cover pan and cook for about 6 minutes, or until artichokes are crisp-tender.

3 Using a slotted spoon, transfer artichokes to a plate. Leave to cool. Stir vinegar and herbs into pan juices. Cut radicchio into large pieces. Combine raddichio and pan juices and distribute among serving plates.

4 Using a vegetable peeler, slice pecorino into large, thin shavings. Arrange artichokes on top of radicchio. Scatter on pecorino. Serve with lemon wedges.

to trim artichokes

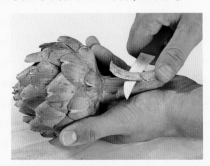

1 Cut off stalk, leaving a small length. Thinly slice skin from remaining stalk.

2 Trim tips of leaves with kitchen scissors. Remove the papery internal leaves.

3 Scrape out fibrous matter at base with a teaspoon. Wash artichoke bases to completely remove fibres.

roast pumpkin and parmesan salad

300 g (10 oz) butternut pumpkin (squash),
   peeled and thinly sliced
5 tablespoons olive oil
1 tablespoon balsamic vinegar
salt and freshly ground black pepper
250 g (8 oz) rocket (arugula)
50 g (2 oz) Parmesan

serves 4
preparation 15 minutes
cooking 30 minutes

- -

per serving *1185 kilojoules/283 calories, 7 g protein,*
27 g total fat, 6 g saturated fat, 12 mg cholesterol,
3 g carbohydrate, 2 g fibre

1 Preheat oven to 180°C/350°F. Toss pumpkin with
1 tablespoon of the oil in a shallow baking dish. Cook
30 minutes, turning occasionally, or until golden brown.
Set aside to cool a little.

2 Whisk vinegar and remaining 4 tablespoons oil until
combined; season with salt and pepper to taste. Using a
vegetable peeler, slice Parmesan into large, thin shavings.

3 Combine rocket and warm pumpkin in a serving bowl.
Add vinaigrette and toss well. Top with Parmesan.

rocket and radicchio salad with tomatoes

250 g (8 oz) cherry tomatoes
1 small onion
200 g (7 oz) rocket (arugula)
1 head treviso or round radicchio
4 tablespoons olive oil
3 tablespoons balsamic vinegar
1 clove garlic, crushed
salt and freshly ground black pepper
50 g (2 oz) Parmesan

serves 4
preparation 20 minutes

----

per serving *1063 kilojoules/254 calories, 7 g protein,*
23 g total fat, 5 g saturated fat, 12 mg cholesterol,
5 g carbohydrate, 2 g fibre

1 Cut tomatoes in half. Slice onion into thin rings. Layer rocket, radicchio, tomatoes and onion rings on a platter.

2 Whisk oil, vinegar and garlic until combined. Add salt and pepper to taste. Using a vegetable peeler, slice Parmesan into large, thin shavings.

3 Drizzle dressing over salad. Top with Parmesan.

treviso radicchio

Treviso is a type of radicchio that has long, narrow, pointed leaves, resembling witlof (Belgian endive/chicory). It has a slightly milder bitter taste than round radicchio.

bavarian cabbage salad

1 kg (2 lb) tender green cabbage

salt

1 tablespoon caraway seeds

100 g (4 oz) piece of speck or bacon,
  rind removed, finely diced

3 tablespoons vegetable oil

3 to 4 tablespoons white wine vinegar

freshly ground black pepper

1 teaspoon sugar

3 tablespoons chopped chives and
  a few whole chives, for garnish

serves 4

preparation + chilling 1 hour

cooking 10 minutes

- -

per serving 910 kilojoules/217 calories, 8 g protein,
17 g total fat, 3 g saturated fat, 16 mg cholesterol,
7 g carbohydrate, 8 g fibre

1 Remove core from cabbage. Shred leaves finely with a knife or grate with a cheese grater.

2 Place 2 litres (3½ pints) water in a large saucepan with 1 teaspoon salt and the caraway seeds. Bring to a boil. Add shredded cabbage; cook 2 minutes. Pour cabbage into a colander; refresh under cold running water. Leave to drain and cool completely.

3 Heat 1 tablespoon oil in a heavy-based pan over high heat. Add speck and cook on all sides until crisp. Combine speck and cabbage in a serving bowl.

4 Whisk remaining 2 tablespoons oil, vinegar, a little salt, pepper and the sugar in a bowl until well combined. Stir vinaigrette into salad. Place in refrigerator, covered, 45 minutes to allow flavours to develop.

5 Just before serving, taste salad and adjust seasonings. Serve garnished with chopped and whole chives.

fresh tomato salad

3 medium tomatoes (about 500 g/1 lb)

4 spring onions (scallions), finely sliced

½ cup (30 g/1 oz) chopped fresh coriander (cilantro) leaves

3 tablespoons chopped fresh mint leaves

2 small red chilies, seeds removed, finely chopped

½ teaspoon ground coriander

½ teaspoon ground cumin

¼ cup lime juice

salt and freshly ground black pepper

serves 4

preparation + standing 40 minutes

per serving *124 kilojoules/30 calories, 2 g protein,*
0.5 g total fat, 0 g saturated fat, 0 mg cholesterol,
4 g carbohydrate, 3 g fibre

1 Cut tomatoes in half, remove seeds and dice flesh. Place in a serving bowl with spring onions, coriander, mint, chilies, ground coriander, cumin and lime juice. Stir to combine.

2 Leave for 30 minutes to allow the flavours to develop. Taste just before serving, adding salt and freshly ground black pepper to taste.

watercress and baby spinach with goat cheese

The peppery mustard-like taste of watercress and the sharpness of the goat cheese give this attractive salad a full, bold flavour.

3 slices light rye bread, crusts removed
2 tablespoons butter
1 large clove garlic, halved lengthwise
100 g (4 oz) firm goat cheese
100 g (4 oz) watercress
100 g (4 oz) baby spinach leaves
1 shallot, finely chopped
2 tablespoons olive oil
2 tablespoons balsamic vinegar
$\frac{1}{2}$ teaspoon Dijon mustard
salt and freshly ground black pepper

serves 4
preparation 15 minutes
cooking 15 minutes

per serving *1204 kilojoules/288 calories, 7 g protein,*
22 g total fat, 9 g saturated fat, 35 mg cholesterol,
15 g carbohydrate, 3 g fibre

1 To make croutons, cut bread into small cubes. Melt about $1\frac{1}{2}$ tablespoons butter in a nonstick frying pan over medium heat. Add garlic, sauté 2 minutes; discard. Add bread cubes; cook until golden brown on all sides, taking care butter does not burn. Set aside; keep warm.

2 Slice goat cheese into four equal pieces. Heat remaining butter in a pan over medium heat. Add cheese; cook until it begins to melt and develops a golden-brown crust, about 4 minutes each side.

3 Divide watercress, spinach and shallot among serving plates. Whisk oil, vinegar, mustard, salt and pepper until combined. Drizzle over salad greens. Place a piece of cheese on each plate and top with croutons.

cook's tip

Goat cheese is made from pure goat milk or a combination of goat and cow milk. Fresh goat cheese has a creamy consistency and a mild, slightly tangy flavour. As it ages, goat cheese hardens and becomes sharper in taste.

health guide

Spinach contains many valuable nutrients such as antioxidants and bioflavonoids that help to block cancer-causing substances and processes.

bok choy with pan-fried tofu and peanuts

Bok choy is a type of Chinese cabbage that looks like a leafy green vegetable rather than a cabbage. It is richer in beta carotene and calcium than green cabbage.

2 small heads baby bok choy

2 medium carrots

4 spring onions (scallions)

200 g (7 oz) firm tofu
(smoked variety, if available)

2 small red chilies, or to taste

3 tablespoons peanut oil

2 tablespoons lime juice

2 tablespoons soy sauce

¼ teaspoon ground ginger

¼ teaspoon grated lemon peel

pinch of soft brown sugar

salt

3 tablespoons roasted peanuts

1 tablespoon finely chopped fresh coriander
(cilantro) leaves, for garnish

serves 4

preparation 20 minutes

cooking 5 minutes

----

per serving 1022 kilojoules/244 calories, 9 g protein,
20 g total fat, 3 g saturated fat, 0 mg cholesterol,
6 g carbohydrate, 4 g fibre

1 Cut bok choy into thin strips. Score five narrow grooves lengthwise along each carrot. Slice carrots into thin rounds to create flower-shaped disks.

2 Finely dice white parts of spring onions. Cut green parts into thin rings. Distribute bok choy, carrots and spring onions among serving plates.

3 Cut tofu into small cubes. Halve chilies lengthwise and discard seeds. Dice chilies finely.

4 Whisk 2 tablespoons of the peanut oil, all the lime juice, soy sauce, ground ginger, lemon peel, sugar and a little salt in a bowl until combined. Stir in chilies. Drizzle over salad.

5 Heat remaining 1 tablespoon oil in a nonstick frying pan over medium heat. Add tofu and fry until golden brown on all sides. Add peanuts and cook briefly, stirring. Add tofu and peanuts at once to salad. Sprinkle with coriander and serve.

health guide

Tofu, or bean curd, is made from soy beans. It is high in protein and is a good source of B vitamins. Tofu is available in firm, soft or silken textures and a variety of flavours.

asian bean sprout salad

Mung bean sprouts and peanuts add crunch to this salad. Mung beans have a hint of sweetness. In Chinese medicine, they are considered a yin or cooling food.

150 g (5 oz) mung bean sprouts

2 spring onions (scallions), sliced into rounds

4 medium celery stalks, thinly sliced

1 medium mango or 2 small nectarines

½ small fresh pineapple (about 500 g/1 lb)

4 to 6 large Chinese (napa) cabbage leaves

4 tablespoons coarsely chopped roasted, salted peanuts

spicy fruit dressing

2 tablespoons raspberry vinegar

3 tablespoons olive oil

4 tablespoons orange juice

¼ to ½ teaspoon sambal oelek (available in jars from Asian food shops)

½ teaspoon ground ginger

¼ teaspoon finely grated lemon peel

serves 4

preparation 25 minutes

---

per serving 1140 kilojoules/272 calories, 6 g protein, 19 g total fat, 3 g saturated fat, 0 mg cholesterol, 19 g carbohydrate, 6 g fibre

1 Combine sprouts, spring onions and celery in a large bowl. Peel mango and slice flesh thinly. Peel pineapple and cut into small chunks. Add to bowl.

2 To make spicy fruit dressing, whisk all the ingredients in a small bowl until combined. Stir into salad.

3 Cut Chinese cabbage leaves into wide strips. Distribute among serving plates. Add bean sprout salad and sprinkle with peanuts.

sambal oelek

A sambal is a fresh or cooked relish. Sambal oelek is a spicy relish which is often used in conjunction with other sambal ingredients. It is made from ground chilies, salt and vinegar or tamarind. Tamarind is a very acidic fruit which gives sambals a particularly sharp taste. In a traditional oelek, the chilies are not seeded, adding more heat.

asian bean sprout salad

sprouts salad with mushrooms and celery

✳ Slice 250 g (8 oz) button mushrooms. Slice 2 spring onions (scallions) and 4 medium celery stalks as in the main recipe. Trim 150 g (5 oz) mung bean sprouts. Finely chop 1 clove garlic.

✳ In a wok, heat 2 tablespoons oil over medium heat. Cook mushrooms, spring onions and celery, stirring, 2 minutes. Add sprouts and garlic. Toss over high heat, 1 minute. Add 2 tablespoons each of rice vinegar and soy sauce. Remove from heat. Season with salt to taste. Serve warm.

mixed mushroom salad

about 700 g (1 lb 8 oz) button mushrooms, halved

150 g (5 oz) portobello or Swiss brown mushrooms, thickly sliced

150 g (5 oz) oyster mushrooms, chopped

2 cloves garlic, crushed

1 tablespoon fresh thyme leaves

3 tablespoons olive oil

150 g (5 oz) enoki mushrooms

1 medium red onion, sliced thinly

¾ cup (60 g/2 oz) chopped fresh parsley leaves

½ cup (30 g/1 oz) chopped chives

2 tablespoons red wine vinegar

salt and freshly ground black pepper

serves 4

preparation 10 minutes

cooking 25 minutes

per serving 853 kilojoules/204 calories, 11 g protein, 15 g total fat, 2 g saturated fat, 0 mg cholesterol, 8 g carbohydrate, 10 g fibre

1 Preheat oven to 200°C/400°F. Mix button, Swiss brown and oyster mushrooms with garlic and thyme in a roasting pan; drizzle with oil. Roast about 20 minutes or until tender. Add enoki mushrooms; roast another 5 minutes.

3 Place warm mushrooms in a large serving bowl; add onion, parsley, chives and vinegar. Add a little salt and a generous amount of pepper. Toss to combine.

mushrooms

Button mushrooms have a very subtle flavour while oyster mushrooms have a very slight oyster taste that is enhanced with cooking. Enokis have a long, thin stem and a tiny button cup. They have a unique crunchy texture when eaten raw.

cook's tip

When cooking several varieties of mushrooms together, always add enoki last because they need very little cooking. Freshly ground black pepper brings out the flavour of mushrooms, as does fresh thyme.

tossed salad with pears and blue cheese

The sweet taste of pears is complemented by the sharp, rich taste of blue cheese. Choose a variety of blue cheese that crumbles easily, such as Roquefort or Stilton.

2 pears, halved, cored and thinly sliced
³/₄ cup (185 ml/6 ½ fl oz) buttermilk
1 tablespoon white wine vinegar
salt and freshly ground black pepper
2 tablespoons chives, cut into short pieces
1 head butter (butterhead) lettuce
1 head radicchio or other red lettuce
2 cups (75 g/3 oz) watercress leaves
1 small cucumber, thinly sliced
2 tablespoons crumbled blue cheese

serves 6
preparation 20 minutes

- -

per serving 394 kilojoules/94 calories, 4 g protein, 3 g total fat, 2 g saturated fat, 10 mg cholesterol, 12 g carbohydrate, 3 g fibre

1 In a small bowl, toss pears with 2 tablespoons of the buttermilk to prevent flesh browning. Whisk the remaining buttermilk, the vinegar and a pinch each of salt and pepper in another small bowl until combined. Add chives.

2 Tear or chop leaves of both lettuces. Mix with watercress and cucumber. Arrange on serving plates and top with blue cheese and sliced pears. Drizzle a little buttermilk dressing over the top, serving the remainder separately.

cook's tip

Mesclun, also called field greens, is a mixture of young salad leaves. The petals of edible flowers such as nasturtiums are sometimes included. Mesclun is sold loose or in packets from greengrocers and supermarkets. It's an easy, quick option when making a salad.

health guide

The darker the greens, the more nutritious the salad. Watercress and rocket (arugula), for instance, contain more beta carotene and vitamin C than the pale leaves of iceberg and butterhead lettuces.

orange and asparagus salad

2 large oranges

about 250 g (8 oz) thin asparagus spears

150 g (5 oz) mixed salad greens

2 medium avocados, halved and sliced

orange mustard dressing

2 tablespoons orange juice

4 tablespoons olive oil

1 teaspoon Dijon mustard

salt and freshly ground black pepper

serves 4

preparation 20 minutes

cooking 1 minute

----

per serving *1972 kilojoules/471 calories, 5 g protein,*
46 g total fat, 8 g saturated fat, 0 mg cholesterol,
11 g carbohydrate, 5 g fibre

1 Peel oranges, remove all the white pith with a sharp knife and segment the flesh.

2 Bring a large saucepan of water to a boil; blanch asparagus 1 minute. Refresh under cold running water.

3 To make orange mustard dressing, whisk orange juice, oil, mustard, salt and pepper in a small bowl until combined.

4 Arrange salad greens on serving plates. Add orange segments, asparagus and avocado slices. Drizzle vinaigrette over the top and add a grinding of pepper.

onion and tropical fruit salad

1 medium red onion, sliced into thin rings

1 large, ripe but firm mango

2 kiwifruit, peeled and thinly sliced
   into rounds

1 small cucumber, thinly sliced

chili lime dressing

1 fresh red chili, seeded and
   finely chopped

2 tablespoons olive oil

2 tablespoons lime juice

1 teaspoon clear honey

2 tablespoons chopped fresh coriander
   (cilantro) leaves

salt and freshly ground black pepper

serves 4

preparation + marinating 45 minutes

per serving *636 kilojoules/152 calories, 2 g protein,*
9 g total fat, 1 g saturated fat, 0 mg cholesterol,
15 g carbohydrate, 3 g fibre

1 Slice onion rings in half. Place in a shallow dish. To make chili lime dressing, combine all the dressing ingredients in a screw-top jar. Shake well to combine. Stir dressing into onion rings; marinate 30 minutes.

2 Slice flesh from mango, cutting down each side of the stone. Peel away skin and cut flesh into thin slices.

3 Add mango, kiwifruit and cucumber to marinated onion and dressing. Combine gently to avoid breaking up the fruit.

mix and match

✱ If you find the taste of coriander (cilantro) too pungent, try using chopped fresh mint.

✱ Add 2 large, ripe, thinly sliced plums to the salad and use 2 large segmented oranges instead of the mango.

citrus salad with goat cheese

citrus salad with goat cheese

Citrus fruits, such as oranges and grapefruit, team well with salad greens and complement crunchy vegetables.

2 small oranges or 2 medium
  mandarins or tangerines
500 g (1 lb) celery stalks, thinly sliced
2 medium carrots, coarsely grated
1 small red onion, finely diced
100 g (4 oz) soft goat cheese
3 tablespoons orange juice
2 tablespoons vegetable oil
1 tablespoon white wine vinegar
1 tablespoon lemon juice
salt and freshly ground black pepper
4 leaves each of treviso radicchio,
  cos (romaine) and iceberg lettuce
½ cup (55 g/2 oz) pecans or walnuts

serves 4
preparation 30 minutes

----

per serving *1277 kilojoules/305 calories, 8 g protein,*
25 g total fat, 5 g saturated fat, 11 mg cholesterol,
12 g carbohydrate, 6 g fibre

1 Peel and segment oranges. Cut in half crosswise. Place in a bowl with celery, carrots and onion. Mix well.

2 Mash goat cheese in a bowl with the orange juice. Stir in oil, vinegar and lemon juice. Add salt and pepper to taste. Spoon dressing over fruit and vegetables; mix gently.

3 To serve, place one leaf of each lettuce variety on each serving plate. Top with salad. Garnish with nuts.

cook's tip

Buy nuts in small quantities and use them as soon as possible. If you have to store them, keep them in an airtight container in the refrigerator or freezer. The oil in nuts quickly turns rancid, particularly in a hot atmosphere.

celery and apples with ricotta dressing

✳ In a serving bowl, combine 500 g (1 lb) finely chopped celery, 2 unpeeled tart red apples cut into cubes and 2 finely sliced spring onions (scallions).

✳ Combine 250 g (8 oz) fresh ricotta, 2 tablespoons olive oil, 1 tablespoon lemon juice, 1 teaspoon horseradish sauce, salt and freshly ground black pepper in a small bowl. Stir into salad. Arrange iceberg lettuce leaves on serving plates and top with salad.

radicchio and fennel salad with oranges

The bitter taste of dark red radicchio complements the aniseed flavour of pale green fennel and the sweetness of oranges.

1 large head treviso radicchio

2 large oranges

1 large or 2 small fennel bulbs (about 1 kg/ 2 lb total) with leafy fronds

2 small white onions

4 tablespoons olive oil

1 tablespoon white wine vinegar

1 tablespoon lemon juice

1 sprig rosemary, leaves finely chopped

salt and freshly ground black pepper

1 cup (120 g/4 oz) pitted black olives

serves 4
preparation 25 minutes

per serving 1141 kilojoules/272 calories, 4 g protein, 19 g total fat, 3 g saturated fat, 0 mg cholesterol, 22 g carbohydrate, 7 g fibre

1 Line individual plates with radicchio leaves. Peel and segment oranges.

2 Using a vegetable peeler, slice fennel bulb into thin strips. Slice onions into thin rings.

3 Whisk oil, vinegar, lemon juice and rosemary in a bowl until combined. Season with salt and pepper to taste.

4 Finely chop a few fennel fronds. Layer fennel, oranges and onions onto radicchio. Drizzle with vinaigrette. Top with fennel fronds and olives.

cook's tip

The salad looks very attractive if the fennel bulbs are cut into thin slices lengthwise using a vegetable peeler. First, trim the stalk so that a small amount remains. This way, the individual layers of fennel will not fall apart during slicing.

sugar-snap peas with grapes and feta

grated peel and juice of 1 small lemon
½ teaspoon caster (superfine) sugar
½ teaspoon Dijon mustard
salt and freshly ground black pepper
1 tablespoon olive oil
300 g (10 oz) sugar-snap peas
250 g (8 oz) seedless black grapes, halved
250 g (8 oz) feta, thinly sliced
50 g (2 oz) rocket (arugula), shredded
175 g (6 oz) baby spinach leaves

serves 4
preparation 15 minutes
cooking 2 minutes

---

per serving 1270 kilojoules/303 calories, 15 g protein,
21 g total fat, 10 g saturated fat, 43 mg cholesterol,
15 g carbohydrate, 3 g fibre

1 Place lemon peel, juice, sugar, mustard and a generous seasoning of salt and pepper in a serving bowl. Whisk until sugar and salt have dissolved completely. Whisk in oil.

2 Cut sugar-snap peas in half crosswise, leaving a few small ones whole. Bring a large saucepan of water to a boil. Add sugar-snaps and bring water back to a boil. Drain sugar-snaps immediately and refresh under cold running water. Add to serving bowl. Turn to coat with dressing.

3 Add grapes, feta, rocket and spinach. Mix again gently to coat with dressing.

sugar-snap peas

Sugar-snap peas, like snow peas (mange-tout) are eaten pods and all. They have a sweet taste and tender texture. They are a good source of dietary fibre and vitamin C.

fruity salad with blue cheese dressing

✳ Crumble or chop 60 g (2 oz) Danish blue cheese in a serving bowl. Mix with 1 tablespoon apple cider vinegar and 2 tablespoons olive oil.

✳ Halve and core 2 ripe but firm pears, then slice thinly. Add to bowl; toss to coat with dressing. Add 250 g (8 oz) halved seedless black grapes and mix well. Add a handful of watercress sprigs, 250 g (8 oz) baby spinach leaves and 2 tablespoons chopped walnuts. Toss to combine.

sugar-snap salad with grapes and feta

red cabbage with citrus

*Teaming red cabbage with sweet ingredients,
as in sweet and sour cabbage with apples,
is a feature of Central European cooking.*

1 small red cabbage (about 750 g/1 lb 10 oz)

1 teaspoon salt

2 medium oranges

3 small mandarins or tangerines

3 tablespoons walnut oil

2 to 3 tablespoons red wine vinegar

freshly ground black pepper

**½ cup (55 g/2 oz) walnuts, coarsely
    chopped**

serves 4

preparation 35 minutes

---

*per serving 1226 kilojoules/293 calories, 7 g protein,
22 g total fat, 2 g saturated fat, 0 mg cholesterol,
16 g carbohydrate, 10 g fibre*

1 Discard thick outer leaves of cabbage. Cut cabbage into quarters. Remove core and slice cabbage thinly. Place in a serving bowl.

2 Sprinkle cabbage with salt. Knead firmly by hand for about 5 minutes; the cabbage will soften slightly and become milder in flavour. Leave 15 minutes. Place in a colander. Rinse under cold running water; drain.

3 Peel and segment oranges and mandarins. Cut into small pieces over a bowl to catch the juices; discard seeds. Combine fruit and cabbage.

4 Whisk reserved citrus juice, oil, vinegar and pepper until combined. Stir into salad. Top with walnuts.

health guide

*Cabbage is a source of vitamin C,
carotenoids and folate and is high
in fibre. It is thought to reduce
hormone-related cancers. Red
cabbage is higher in vitamin C
than green.*

cook's tip

*Walnut oil has a distinctive flavour
that is delicious with the walnuts
in this recipe. Like nuts, oils made
from nuts quickly turn rancid in
a warm temperature. Buy in small
amounts. Store in a cool place.*

red cabbage with citrus

red cabbage with port vinaigrette

✻ Quarter and thinly slice 1 small red cabbage. Bring 150 ml (5 fl oz) water to a boil in a large saucepan with 3 tablespoons red wine vinegar, 1 teaspoon salt and 2 cloves. Add cabbage, cover and cook for 20 to 25 minutes until crisp–tender, stirring occasionally. Transfer to a colander. Drain and let cool.

✻ Combine 2 tablespoons port, 1 tablespoon red wine vinegar, 1 tablespoon cranberry sauce (jelly), 1 tablespoon orange marmalade, 2 tablespoons walnut oil and a pinch of salt. Stir into cabbage. Chill, covered, 2 hours.

roasted beetroot and orange salad

800 g (1 lb 12 oz) baby beetroot (beets), trimmed and scrubbed

3 cloves garlic, peeled, flattened with the back of a knife

2 tablespoons olive oil

1 large orange

⅔ cup (100 g/4 oz) black olives

1 small red onion, thinly sliced

250 g (8 oz) rocket (arugula)

2 teaspoons red wine vinegar

1 teaspoon whole-grain mustard

salt and freshly ground black pepper

serves 4

preparation 10 minutes

cooking 45 minutes

per serving *758 kilojoules/181 calories, 4 g protein, 10 g total fat, 1 g saturated fat, 0 mg cholesterol, 19 g carbohydrate, 5 g fibre*

1 Preheat oven to 180°C/350°F. Combine beetroot, garlic and oil in a baking dish. Cover with cooking (aluminum) foil and roast 45 minutes or until beetroots are tender. Remove beetroots from dish; reserve pan juices.

2 Cut beetroot into quarters. Peel and segment orange. Place in a serving bowl with the olives, onion and rocket.

3 Combine vinegar, mustard and reserved pan juices in a small bowl. Season to taste with salt and pepper. Stir into salad just before serving.

health guide

Oranges are a low GI food. They are ideal for people with diabetes and for anyone needing an energy boost. They are high in vitamin C, which may reduce the risk of strokes and some cancers.

cook's tip

Purchase fresh beetroot with crisp, bright green leafy tops. Scatter raw leaves on salads or cook them as for spinach. They are rich in beta carotene.

crunchy salad with apples

The radish and apples give this salad a satisfying crunch. There's no need to peel apples; their skin contains useful nutrients.

2 tablespoons sunflower seeds

1 small head cos (romaine) lettuce or other crisp lettuce

2 medium tart apples (about 300 g/10 oz)

1 tablespoon lemon juice

1 small black radish or young turnip (about 100 g/4 oz)

alfalfa sprouts or trimmed mustard cress, for garnish

apple cider vinegar dressing

½ cup (125 g/4 oz) sour cream

1 tablespoon apple cider vinegar

2 tablespoons vegetable oil

pinch of sugar

salt and freshly ground black pepper

serves 4

preparation 15 minutes

cooking 2 to 3 minutes

per serving 1225 kilojoules/293 calories, 4 g protein, 25 g total fat, 10 g saturated fat, 41 mg cholesterol, 13 g carbohydrate, 5 g fibre

1 Dry roast sunflower seeds in a heavy pan over medium heat until light brown. Stir constantly, taking care seeds do not burn. Transfer to a plate and leave to cool.

2 Reserve a few whole lettuce leaves and tear or cut the rest into strips. Cut apples into small pieces and place in a bowl with lemon juice to prevent discolouration. Peel radish and grate finely.

3 To make apple cider vinegar dressing, whisk sour cream, vinegar, oil and sugar in a large bowl. Add salt and pepper to taste. Add torn lettuce and apples. Stir gently to combine.

4 Place whole lettuce leaves on serving plate. Top with salad. Sprinkle with sunflower seeds, radish and sprouts.

apples

For apples that are to be used unpeeled, wash and wipe them thoroughly to get rid of any pesticide residues. Biting and chewing an apple stimulates the gums. The sweetness of the apple encourages an increased flow of saliva, which helps to reduce tooth decay by lowering bacteria levels in the mouth.

salad greens with fresh figs

50 g (2 oz) baby spinach leaves

100 g (4 oz) lamb's lettuce (corn salad)

100 g (4 oz) curly endive (frisée)

4 tablespoons coarsely chopped walnuts

4 large fresh figs

blue cheese dressing

50 g (2 oz) soft blue cheese, such as
    Gorgonzola or dolcelatte

2 tablespoons light sour cream

1 tablespoon walnut oil

1½ tablespoons white wine vinegar

2 tablespoons apple juice

pinch of sugar

salt and freshly ground black pepper

serves 4

preparation 25 minutes

---

*per serving 869 kilojoules/208 calories, 6 g protein,
17 g total fat, 5 g saturated fat, 19 mg cholesterol,
8 g carbohydrate, 3 g fibre*

1 Distribute spinach, lamb's lettuce and curly endive among individual serving plates.

2 Trim stem ends from figs. Cut each fig into eight pieces and arrange on top of salad greens.

3 To make blue cheese dressing, mash cheese in a bowl with sour cream. Gradually stir in walnut oil, vinegar, apple juice and sugar until well combined. Add salt and pepper to taste. Spoon over salad and sprinkle with walnuts.

cook's tip

Choose bruise-free figs that are soft but not mushy. Ripe figs may be eaten unpeeled. As they ripen, they become increasingly aromatic and sweet. Figs are a good source of iron, potassium and fibre.

mushroom salad with goat cheese dressing

✳ Prepare salad greens as for main recipe. Slice 250 g (8 oz) large mushrooms. Melt 2 tablespoons butter in a frying pan over medium heat. Add mushrooms. Cook until all the liquid has evaporated, about 10 minutes. Season with salt, pepper and ½ teaspoon dried mixed herbs.

✳ Mix 120 g (4 oz) soft goat cheese or other creamy cheese, 3 tablespoons yogurt, 1 tablespoon olive oil and 1 tablespoon lemon juice. Add salt and pepper to taste. Mix with salad greens. Arrange salad on a serving plate. Top with hot mushrooms.

salad greens with fresh figs

cabbage and nectarines with yogurt chutney

4 tablespoons shelled pumpkin seeds

1 small head Chinese (napa) cabbage
   (about 500 g/1 lb)

1 large head witlof (Belgian endive/chicory)

3 medium fully ripe nectarines

yogurt chutney

juice of 1 medium lemon

2 tablespoons olive oil

$\frac{1}{2}$ cup (125 g/4 oz) yogurt

2 teaspoons mango chutney, plus more
   as needed

salt and freshly ground black pepper

$\frac{1}{4}$ teaspoon mild or hot curry powder,
   plus more as needed

serves 4

preparation 20 minutes

cooking 4 minutes

per serving *999 kilojoules/239 calories, 7 g protein,
16 g total fat, 3 g saturated fat, 5 mg cholesterol,
17 g carbohydrate, 5 g fibre*

1 Dry roast pumpkin seeds in a heavy pan over medium heat for 3 to 4 minutes. Stir constantly, taking care seeds do not burn. Transfer to a plate and leave to cool.

2 Cut cabbage and witlof into thin strips. Use to line a serving platter. Halve nectarines. Slice flesh thinly. Drizzle with a little lemon juice to prevent discolouration.

3 To make yogurt chutney, combine remaining lemon juice, oil, yogurt and chutney. Add salt, pepper and curry powder to taste. Add more chutney to taste.

4 Spoon a little dressing over the salad. Serve the rest separately with a little curry powder sprinkled on top. Place nectarines on top of salad. Sprinkle with pumpkin seeds.

chutney

In India, a chutney is often made to be eaten fresh, using whatever suitable full-flavoured fruit or vegetable ingredients are locally traditional or available. Chutneys are similar to the salsas of Latino cooking and European relishes. They range from mildly spicy to hot, with a variety of seasonings added.

cook's tip

This salad features attractive shades of gold and yellow. Slices of firm ripe peaches or mango may also be used.

cabbage and nectarines with yogurt chutney

spicy chinese cabbage salad

✳ Finely slice 500 g (1 lb) Chinese (napa) cabbage. Slice 3 spring onions (scallions) into rings. Halve 1 red and 1 yellow capsicum (bell pepper), discard seeds and cut into strips. Mix all ingredients in a bowl.

✳ Make a vinaigrette with 3 tablespoons tomato juice, 1 clove crushed garlic, 3 tablespoons olive oil, 2 tablespoons balsamic vinegar, salt, freshly ground black pepper and sambal oelek to taste. Stir into salad. Serve with toasted sourdough bread and wedges of mature, strong-flavoured cheddar.

potato and lentil salad (page 185)

rice, pasta, bean and grain salads

For an easy way to turn a salad into a substantial main course, add some rice, pasta, beans or grains. Versatile and inexpensive, these ingredients with their interesting textures and mild taste team well with many other salad ingredients. They add fibre, protein and starchy carbohydrates to the diet, too.

rice, pasta, beans and grains at a glance

They're versatile, inexpensive and have a long shelf-life. In addition, the numerous varieties of rice, pasta, beans and grains now available in dried or canned form, all add texture to salads and absorb the flavours of other ingredients well. They transform a salad into a substantial main meal and help to make a little go a long way. While these virtues are surely reason enough to include rice, pasta, beans and grains in salad recipes, there's even more to recommend them. They each contain valuable nutrients that aid general health and help to fight specific health problems.

pasta and noodles

Both fresh and dried pasta have the same nutritional benefits. Asian noodles can be used in salads in the same way as Italian pasta. Pasta is low in sodium and fat. Some sauces and dressings used in pasta salads are high in fat and salt. Be judicious in the amount of sauce or dressing used or, where possible, replace ingredients such as full-fat cream, sour cream and other rich dairy products with their low-fat or light counterparts. Salty condiments such as soy sauce can be replaced with a low-sodium variety or herbs.

conchiglie (shells)

farfalle (bow ties)

fettuccine

fusilli (spirals)

penne (quills)

rigatoni

tortellini

rice noodles

rice

Of the many hundreds of different varieties grown, some are used only in their country of origin, while others are widely available. The types used in this book are either long-grain or medium-length grain. Long-grain basmati has a beautiful nutty taste and aroma, while jasmine (or Thai rice) has the aroma of flowering jasmine. The medium-length rice used is the Italian arborio. It absorbs a large volume of liquid during cooking and tastes creamy when cooked, yet still retains its firmness.

Rice is gluten-free, easy to digest and rarely, if ever, causes allergies. It provides complex or starchy carbohydrate and some B vitamins.

Rice can be cooked by boiling (in stock/broth or water), microwaving or steaming. Cooked cold rice is quickly reheated by steaming or microwaving.

'Rice . . . is beautiful when it grows, precision rows of sparkling green stalks shooting up to reach the hot summer sun . . .'

Shizuo Tsuji
Japanese food expert

rice check

* Rice is surprisingly high in kilojoules (calories), so it's best to keep portions small.

* Rice contains only a trace of fat and virtually no sodium.

* Store cooked rice in a sealed container in the refrigerator for a day only. Cooked rice freezes well.

* Wild rice can be expensive. Combine it with other types to minimise cost.

brown rice

Brown rice has a much higher fibre content than white rice and a higher nutrient content. It takes longer to cook than white and has a nutty taste.

long-grain white rice

The milling process removes the bran and germ from brown rice to produce white. Hence, although it is still a source of energy, white rice has less nutritional value and fibre content than brown. The grains remain separate when cooked and the finished result is fairly dry and firm.

wild rice

This is an aquatic grass and not a true rice. Wild rice is high in protein and fibre and several B vitamins. Cooked, it swells to up to four times its original volume. The grain splits to reveal a fluffy white interior. It has a nutty taste and is good combined with fluffy white rice.

beans

Canned and dried beans are rich in health-protecting antioxidants. They provide useful amounts of fibre, protein, iron and zinc. Soluble fibre slows the digestion, leading to a slow, steady blood-sugar rise rather than a spike. The protein does not raise blood sugar levels and it helps the body process carbohydrates in a meal more efficiently. The sodium content of canned beans can be high. Reduce the amount by rinsing the beans in cold water before use.

bean check

* Beans and rice together make a complete protein. On their own, each lacks certain amino acids, the building blocks of protein.

* For dried beans, the soaking and cooking times vary depending on the type used. As a general rule, soak the beans in cold water for 12 hours or overnight. Drain and rinse. Place in a saucepan. Add water or stock (broth) to cover. Simmer for up to 2 hours. Top up the liquid, as needed.

broad (fava) beans

These large, flat, brown beans with an earthy flavour are often used in Mediterranean and Middle Eastern salads. Use them with ingredients that have a robust flavour, such as spices or smoked meat and fish.

cannellini

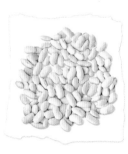

This variety of haricot bean is widely grown in Italy. Cannellini beans have a mild taste that absorbs other flavours well. Use them is Tuscan-style salads that include canned or fresh tuna or hard-boiled eggs or marinated artichoke hearts.

chickpeas

Chickpeas (also known as garbanzo beans) have a nutty taste. They are richer in vitamin E than most other beans. They are often used in East Mediterranean, Indian and North African cooking.

great northern

These large white beans absorb the flavours of other ingredients well. Apart from salads, Great Northern beans are a key ingedient in a robust, classic French cassoulet.

kidney beans

Pink or red kidney-shaped beans have meaty white flesh and a pronounced flavour. They retain their colour on cooking and look most attractive combined with other colourful ingredients in salads. Their flavour and texture work especially well in salads that include white rice.

lentils

Whatever their colour (brown, orange, green or yellow), lentils are rich in protein and high in fibre. Like other grains, they're an excellent meat substitute. Unlike other dried beans, they do not need to be soaked overnight. Lentils feature in Middle Eastern and Central European cuisines and team well with spices.

grains

Like uncooked rice, pasta and beans, grains are best stored in a cool, dry place. They have a long shelf-life; keep an eye on their use-by date. Check unsprayed organic grains regularly because they can attract weevils and other food pests. Whole grains are rich in fibre and complex carbohydrates as well as many vitamins and minerals. They are low in fat and some have the added advantage of being gluten-free.

grain check

✳ Buckwheat, corn (maize), millet and quinoa are gluten-free.

✳ Grains are low in fat. When eaten with canned or dried beans, they are a good source of complete protein.

✳ Research indicates that eating larger quantities of whole grains may significantly reduce the risk of developing type 2 diabetes and heart disease. There is growing evidence that eating whole grains instead of refined varieties can also help to reduce the risk of developing certain types of cancers.

buckwheat

Buckwheat was first grown thousands of years ago in China and Japan. It isn't, in fact, a cereal grain, but is the seed of a plant that belongs to the same family as dock and sorrel. It is also closely related to the rhubarb family. The seeds look like grains and can be cooked in the same way. Buckwheat provides useful amounts of minerals, vitamin B, potassium, phosphorus and dietary fibre. Kasha is the name frequently given to whole buckwheat grains (often cracked) that have been toasted or roasted.

couscous

It is hard to imagine North African cooking without the addition of couscous. Couscous is coarse-ground wheat made into tiny balls and pre-cooked. Preparing 'real' couscous is quite time-consuming but, fortunately, there are some good-quality instant varieties on the market. To prepare them, add boiling water or stock (broth) and then leave to stand for a few minutes before stirring in a little butter and fluffing up the grains with a fork. Couscous is best used in Moroccan and Mediterranean-style salads.

burghul (bulgur wheat)

Originating from the Persian word meaning 'bruised grain', burghul is made of wheat that has been boiled, dried, hulled and shredded. Burghul has a nutty and slightly savoury taste. Although it is often referred to as cracked wheat, it has had the bran removed, which cracked wheat has not. (Cracked wheat is also known as kibbled wheat.) Burghul is available ground to fine, medium or coarse granules. Soak grains in hot water for 15 to 20 minutes, until the water is absorbed and the grains have expanded and become fluffy. With its golden hue and pronounced nutty flavour, burghul is a delicious addition to Middle Eastern dishes. It is best known in tabouleh, a salad containing tomatoes, onions, parsley and mint.

quinoa

Pronounced 'keen-wah', this small grain originally came from the Andes in South America. It can be used like brown rice in salads but has a slightly sweeter taste. The small, round grains contain many valuable nutrients. Used in a salad, boiled quinoa grains taste best with green vegetables and light vinaigrettes, but also team well with capsicum (bell peppers), sweet corn or ham. Quinoa has the added healthy advantage of being gluten-free.

pasta salad with peas and ham

You can use a variety of pasta shapes. Ideally, choose one that holds the mayonnaise well, such as bow-ties or elbow macaroni.

300 g (10 oz) fusilli (spiral pasta)
2 cups (240 g/8 oz) frozen peas
300 g (10 oz) ham, in one piece
10 small gherkins in vinegar, finely diced
3 medium tomatoes, halved and sliced
few sprigs of parsley

yogurt mayonnaise

½ cup (125 g/4 oz) yogurt
½ cup (125 ml/4 fl oz) light mayonnaise
2 tablespoons white wine vinegar
salt and freshly ground black pepper
½ cup (40 g/2 oz) chopped fresh parsley

serves 4
preparation + chilling 1 hour
cooking 15 minutes

----

per serving 2053 kilojoules/490 calories, 27 g protein,
15 g total fat, 3 g saturated fat, 54 mg cholesterol,
61 g carbohydrate, 9 g fibre

1 Cook pasta in plenty of lightly salted boiling water until al dente, following package instructions. Drain, rinse under cold running water and leave to cool. Cook peas in lightly salted water 2 to 3 minutes; leave to cool in cooking water.

2 Strain peas, reserving cooking water. Cut ham into small cubes. Combine pasta, peas, ham and gherkins in a serving bowl; mix well.

3 To make yogurt mayonnaise, whisk yogurt, mayonnaise, 4 tablespoons reserved cooking water and vinegar in a bowl until creamy and well combined. Season generously with salt and pepper. Stir in chopped parsley.

4 Stir dressing into salad. Chill, covered, 30 minutes. Garnish with tomatoes and parsley sprigs.

pasta salad with green vegetables

✳ Cook 300 g (10 oz) farfalle (bow-tie pasta) as for main recipe. Finely dice 2 shallots. Thinly slice 2 zucchini (courgettes).

✳ Heat 3 tablespoons olive oil in nonstick pan. Add shallots; cook until transparent. Add zucchini, 250 g (8 oz) fresh or frozen broad (fava) or lima beans and ½ cup (125 ml/4 fl oz) vegetable stock (broth). Cover; cook over medium heat 10 minutes. Drain; cool. Combine vegetables and pasta in a bowl. Whisk ½ teaspoon cayenne pepper, 1 teaspoon ground cumin and 1 tablespoon lemon juice. Add salt to taste. Stir into salad. Chill.

pasta salad
with peas and ham

asparagus and pasta

If white asparagus is hard to find, you may use green only in this salad. It cooks faster and has a stronger flavour than white.

300 g (10 oz) fettuccine

500 g (1 lb) total of medium to thick green and white asparagus

2 tablespoons olive oil

1 tablespoon lemon-flavoured olive oil

2 tablespoons balsamic vinegar

salt and freshly ground black pepper

150 g (5 oz) fresh ricotta

3 to 4 tablespoons milk

1 tablespoon lemon juice

4 tablespoons freshly grated Parmesan

100 g (4 oz) Parma ham or other prosciutto

fresh basil leaves, for garnish

serves 4

preparation 15 minutes

cooking 15 minutes

----

per serving *1976 kilojoules/472 calories, 21 g protein,*
23 g total fat, 7 g saturated fat, 39 mg cholesterol,
45 g carbohydrate, 4 g fibre

1 Cook pasta in plenty of lightly salted boiling water until al dente, following package instructions. Drain, rinse under cold running water and leave to cool. Trim ends from asparagus spears. Peel white asparagus from the tips to the ends and green asparagus only at the ends.

2 Using a sharp knife or vegetable peeler, slice asparagus lengthwise into thin strips. Place in a steamer basket. Fill a large saucepan with water to a depth equal to the width of two fingers; bring to a boil. Reduce heat to a simmer. Place steamer basket on top of pan. Cover; cook asparagus about 5 minutes or until crisp-tender. Drain, reserving cooking water. Leave to cool.

3 Whisk olive oil, lemon-flavoured olive oil, vinegar and 4 to 5 tablespoons reserved cooking water in a large bowl until combined. Add salt and pepper to taste. Add pasta; stir to coat with dressing. Stir in asparagus.

4 Combine ricotta, milk and lemon juice. Stir in Parmesan; add salt and pepper to taste. Trim fat from ham. Cut ham into narrow strips. Arrange salad in individual bowls. Spoon a little ricotta mixture on each serving. Add ham. Garnish with basil leaves.

health guide

Pasta is low in fat and sodium. Adding salt to the water when cooking pasta is optional; you will still get a good result without it.

farfalle salad with chicken

250 g (8 oz) farfalle (bow-tie pasta)

4 medium zucchini (courgettes) (about 400 g/14 oz)

1 sprig fresh rosemary

1 clove garlic, finely chopped

4 tablespoons olive oil

salt and freshly ground black pepper

175 g (6 oz) rocket (arugula)

175 g (6 oz) cherry tomatoes, cut in half

3 tablespoons balsamic vinegar

3 sprigs each of fresh marjoram, thyme and flat-leaf parsley

2 tablespoons vegetable oil

400 g (14 oz) skinless chicken breast fillets, sliced into thin, even strips

1 tablespoon lemon juice

serves 4

preparation 20 minutes

cooking 20 minutes

----

per serving 2567 kilojoules/613 calories, 39 g protein, 32 g total fat, 5 g saturated fat, 85 mg cholesterol, 39 g carbohydrate, 6 g fibre

1 Cook pasta in plenty of lightly salted boiling water until al dente, following package instructions. Drain, rinse under cold running water and leave to cool. Cut zucchini into rounds. Roughly chop rosemary leaves. Combine zucchini, rosemary, garlic and 2 tablespoons olive oil in a bowl and leave for a few minutes.

2 Heat a nonstick pan over medium heat. Add zucchini mixture and cook until zucchini are golden brown. Sprinkle with salt and pepper and transfer to a large bowl with the pasta. Add rocket and tomatoes. Stir gently to combine.

3 Whisk vinegar, remaining 2 tablespoons oil, salt and pepper in a bowl until combined. Stir into salad.

4 Finely chop leaves of all the herbs. Heat oil in a nonstick pan over high heat and stir-fry chicken until golden brown. Season with salt and pepper.

5 Distribute pasta salad among serving bowls. Top with chicken and herbs and drizzle with lemon juice.

mixed salad with chicken and spicy dressing

✳ Coarsely grate 2 carrots. Roughly chop 3 celery stalks. Finely slice 3 spring onions (scallions). Arrange leaves of 1 head iceberg lettuce on a serving platter and top with vegetables.

✳ Whisk 2 tablespoons lime juice, 4 tablespoons olive oil, 1 tablespoon white wine vinegar, 1 teaspoon ground ginger, 1 teaspoon sugar and salt, pepper and sambal oelek or Chinese chili paste to taste in a small bowl. Stir into salad.

✳ Cut 500 g (1 lb) chicken breast fillets into strips. Stir-fry in vegetable oil until golden brown. Drizzle with 1 tablespoon lime juice. Add to salad.

farfalle salad with chicken

green pasta salad

Pasta is available in many colours, such as green, red and yellow. Green pasta gets its colour either from basil or spinach leaves.

500 g (1 lb) green fettuccine

250 g (8 oz) cherry tomatoes

2 small Lebanese (Mediterranean) or
  pickling cucumbers

250 g (8 oz) rocket (arugula)

1 medium red onion, finely sliced

250 g (8 oz) bocconcini (baby
  mozzarella balls)

black olives for garnish

basil pesto

1 cup (60 g/2 oz) fresh basil leaves

2 cloves garlic, roughly chopped

1 tablespoon pine nuts

4 tablespoons grated pecorino

6 tablespoons olive oil

3 tablespoons lemon juice

2 tablespoons vegetable stock (broth)

salt and freshly ground black pepper

serves 6

preparation 20 minutes

cooking 10 minutes

per serving 2296 kilojoules/548 calories, 19 g protein, 29 g total fat, 8 g saturated fat, 20 mg cholesterol, 52 g carbohydrate, 6 g fibre

1 Cook pasta in plenty of lightly salted boiling water until al dente, following package instructions. Drain, rinse under cold running water and leave to cool. Cut tomatoes in half. Slice cucumbers in half lengthwise and slice thinly.

2 Combine tomatoes, cucumbers, rocket, onion and pasta in a large bowl. Drain bocconcini and mix into the salad.

3 To make basil pesto, clean leaves by wiping them with paper towel; do not wash. Combine basil, garlic, pine nuts and pecorino in a food processor and process finely. Combine oil, lemon juice and stock in a small bowl and add to mixture in a steady stream with the motor running until amalgamated. Add salt and pepper to taste.

4 Stir basil pesto into salad or serve separately. Spoon salad into individual bowls and garnish with olives.

cook's tip

Pesto may be also made with a mixture of equal amounts of basil and fresh parsley leaves. Or, try equal amounts of fresh coriander (cilantro) and parsley leaves.

orecchiette salad with tuna and aioli

350 g (12 oz) orecchiette (little ears pasta)
250 g (8 oz) green asparagus
1 medium zucchini (courgette)
1 medium orange capsicum (bell pepper)
1 can (180 g/7 oz) tuna in water, drained
1 cup (120 g/4 oz) pitted green olives

herb vinaigrette

2 tablespoons red wine vinegar
2 tablespoons sunflower oil
salt and freshly ground black pepper
1 teaspoon dried mixed herbs

aioli

2 cloves garlic
$\frac{1}{2}$ teaspoon salt
1 egg yolk
1 tablespoon white wine vinegar
$\frac{1}{2}$ cup (125 ml/4 fl oz) olive oil
1 tablespoon lemon juice
freshly ground black pepper

serves 4
preparation 20 minutes
cooking 8 minutes

----

*per serving 2855 kilojoules/682 calories, 20 g protein,
41 g total fat, 6 g saturated fat, 64 mg cholesterol,
59 g carbohydrate, 6 g fibre*

1 Cook pasta in plenty of lightly salted boiling water until al dente, following package instructions. Drain, rinse under cold running water and leave to cool. Trim asparagus and cut into small pieces. Place in a steamer basket. Fill a large saucepan with water to a depth equal to the width of two fingers; bring to a boil. Reduce heat to a simmer. Place steamer basket on top of pan. Cover; cook asparagus 6 to 8 minutes. Leave to cool.

2 Slice zucchini into rounds. Cut capsicum in half and chop into small pieces. Separate tuna into flakes with a fork. Finely chop olives.

3 To make herb vinaigrette, whisk all the ingredients in a large bowl until combined. Add pasta, asparagus, zucchini, capsicum and olives.

4 To make aioli, have all ingredients at room temperature to avoid curdling. Grind garlic and salt to a fine paste in a bowl. Using electric beaters or a whisk, beat in egg yolk and $\frac{1}{2}$ tablespoon vinegar until creamy. Add oil, drop by drop at first, then in a steady stream. Beat until mixture is thick and creamy. Season well with remaining $\frac{1}{2}$ tablespoon vinegar, lemon juice and salt and pepper to taste.

5 Distribute salad among serving bowls and add tuna. Spoon a little aioli on top. Serve remainder on the side.

health guide

Buy canned tuna that is packed in water. Tuna packed in oil is higher in kilojoules (calories). If you choose to use it, drain it well to remove as much oil as possible.

pasta vegetable salad in capsicum halves

250 g (8 oz) small elbow pasta

1 medium green capsicum (bell pepper)

2 medium red and 2 medium yellow capsicums (bell peppers)

150 g (5 oz) cheddar or Swiss-style cheese

½ cup (90 g/3 oz) drained canned or frozen and defrosted corn kernels

4 small gherkins in vinegar, finely diced

1 medium white onion, finely diced

½ cup (30 g/1 oz) chopped fresh basil

cream dressing

2 tablespoons olive oil

2 tablespoons white wine vinegar

1 tablespoon lemon juice

½ cup (125 g/4 oz) whipping cream

herb salt and freshly ground black pepper

serves 4

preparation 30 minutes

cooking 10 minutes

per serving *2399 kilojoules/573 calories, 19 g protein, 34 g total fat, 17 g saturated fat, 74 mg cholesterol, 47 g carbohydrate, 5 g fibre*

1 Cook pasta in plenty of lightly salted boiling water until al dente, following package instructions. Drain, rinse under cold running water and leave to cool.

2 Halve green capsicum and cut into small pieces. Halve red and yellow capsicums without removing stalks; discard seeds. Cut cheese into small cubes.

3 To make cream dressing, whisk oil, vinegar, lemon juice and cream in a large bowl until combined. Add herb salt and pepper to taste. Add pasta, corn, gherkins, onion and capsicum pieces and stir to combine. Taste and add more seasoning, as needed. Spoon salad mixture into capsicum halves. Top with cheese. Sprinkle with chopped basil.

raw capsicums

Raw capsicums (bell peppers) are rich in vitamin C. Red ones contain the highest amount. Store in a cool, dark place and use within a few days. The vitamin content declines the longer that the capsicums are kept.

pasta vegetable salad
in capsicum halves

pasta salad with grilled capsicums

✳ Cook 500 g (1 lb) farfalle (bow-tie pasta) as for main recipe. Leave to cool. Roast 6 red capsicums (bell peppers) in a preheated 250°C/500°F oven until skin blisters. Remove from oven, cover with a wet kitchen towel and leave 5 minutes. Peel off skin. Cut capsicums into small pieces.

✳ Whisk 4 tablespoons olive oil, 2 tablespoons white wine vinegar, 2 tablespoons lemon juice, ½ teaspoon Dijon mustard and 1 clove garlic, finely chopped, until combined. Add salt and pepper to taste. Mix all ingredients in a serving bowl. Sprinkle with finely chopped fresh parsley.

farfalle salad with beans and ham

This simple, economical recipe is easily varied. Use smoked chicken or turkey or a combination of spicy cooked chorizo, salami and ham.

300 g (10 oz) farfalle (bow-tie pasta)

400 g (14 oz) fresh butter (yellow wax) beans, trimmed

6 sprigs thyme

1/2 teaspoon salt

250 g (8 oz) ham, in one piece

2 shallots, finely diced

4 large red radishes, cut into quarters, for garnish

paprika sour cream dressing

200 g (7 oz) light sour cream

1 tablespoon vegetable oil

2 tablespoons herb vinegar

salt and freshly ground black pepper

1/4 teaspoon ground sweet paprika

serves 4

preparation + cooling 40 minutes

cooking 10 minutes

---

per serving *1867 kilojoules/446 calories, 22 g protein, 18 g total fat, 8 g saturated fat, 62 mg cholesterol, 47 g carbohydrate, 6 g fibre*

1 Cook pasta in plenty of lightly salted boiling water until al dente, following package instructions. Drain, rinse under cold running water and leave to cool.

2 Place beans, 3 sprigs thyme and 1/2 teaspoon salt in a saucepan and cover with water. Cook, covered, 10 minutes or until crisp-tender. Drain, reserving cooking water. Briefly immerse in iced water and drain again.

3 Trim ham of excess fat and cut into narrow strips. Combine pasta, beans, shallots and ham in a large bowl. Finely chop leaves from remaining 3 sprigs thyme.

4 To make dressing, mix sour cream, 2 tablespoons cooking water, oil, vinegar, salt, pepper, sweet paprika and chopped thyme in a bowl until creamy.

5 Stir dressing into salad. Divide salad among serving bowls and garnish with radishes.

cook's tip

Green beans, purple wax beans or snake or Chinese beans may also be used in this recipe. Don't overcook beans or they will lose their crunch and valuable nutrients. Plunge them into iced water after cooking to stop the cooking process and retain their fresh, bright appearance.

tortellini, carrot and egg salad

300 g (10 oz) carrots
1 tablespoon vegetable oil
1 small onion, finely chopped
½ cup (125 ml/4 fl oz) vegetable
   stock (broth)
500 g (1 lb) fresh tortellini filled with
   spinach and ricotta
1 small head butter (butterhead) lettuce
2 medium eggs, hard-boiled

herb cream

½ cup (125 g/4 oz) whipping cream
½ cup (125 g/4 oz) low-fat yogurt
2 tablespoons lemon juice
½ teaspoon herb mustard
3 tablespoons chopped fresh dill
3 tablespoons chopped fresh parsley
salt and freshly ground black pepper

serves 4
preparation + cooling 30 minutes
cooking 10 minutes

----

per serving 1960 kilojoules/468 calories, 17 g protein,
26 g total fat, 13 g saturated fat, 170 mg cholesterol,
41 g carbohydrate, 6 g fibre

1 Score five narrow grooves lengthwise along each carrot,
Slice carrots into thin rounds to create flower-shaped discs.

2 Heat oil in a nonstick pan and cook onion over medium
heat until transparent. Add carrots and stock. Cover pan
and cook about 5 minutes; carrots should be crisp-tender.
Remove pan from heat. Leave to cool. Cook pasta in plenty
of lightly salted boiling water until al dente, about 4 minutes.
Drain, rinse under cold running water. Leave to cool.

3 To make herb cream, whisk cream, yogurt, lemon juice
and mustard in a large bowl until combined. Stir in herbs.
Season with salt and pepper to taste.

4 Mix carrots and pasta into herb cream. Tear lettuce into
large pieces and distribute among serving plates. Top with
salad. Cut eggs into quarters and place on top.

eggs

Store eggs in the refrigerator because they
will age more in a day at room temperature
than in a week in a refrigerator.
Store them in their
carton so that you will
be reminded of the use-
by or best-before date.

soba noodle salad

¾ cup (185 ml/6 fl oz) chicken stock (broth)

2 cloves garlic, crushed

½ teaspoon ground ginger

¼ teaspoon dried crushed chili

350 g (12 oz) skinless chicken breast fillets

300 g (10 oz) soba (buckwheat) noodles

250 g (8 oz) green beans, cut in halves

2 medium carrots (about 250 g/8 oz), cut into matchsticks

1 tablespoon soft brown sugar

1 tablespoon salt-reduced soy sauce

1 tablespoon peanut or vegetable oil

2 cups (175 g/6 oz) finely shredded green cabbage

serves 4

preparation 20 minutes

cooking 15 minutes

----

per serving *1629 kilojoules/389 calories, 38 g protein,*
8 g total fat, 2 g saturated fat, 74 mg cholesterol,
42 g carbohydrate, 8 g fibre

1 Combine stock, garlic, ginger and chili in a large pan; bring to a boil. Reduce heat to a simmer. Add chicken and cook, covered, 10 minutes, or until cooked through, turning once. Transfer chicken to a plate, reserving cooking liquid. Slice chicken thinly when cool.

2 Cook noodles in plenty of boiling water until al dente, according to package instructions. Add beans and carrots for final minute of cooking time; drain.

3 Whisk brown sugar, soy sauce, oil and reserved cooking liquid in a large bowl. Add chicken, noodles, beans, carrots and cabbage; mix thoroughly. Serve at room temperature.

buckwheat

Buckwheat, from which soba noodles and kasha (roasted buckwheat) are made, is not a true grain; it's the fruit of a rhubarb-like plant. It contains more lysine, an essential amino acid, than grains and is gluten-free.

noodle and squid salad

3 red chilies, seeded and finely chopped

pinch of salt

1 teaspoon freshly ground black pepper

500 g (1 lb) cleaned small squid or calamari, halved

1 tablespoon vegetable oil

100 g (4 oz) rice vermicelli

1 small red onion, finely sliced

2 teaspoons grated fresh ginger

2 teaspoons Asian fish sauce

3 tablespoons salt-reduced soy sauce

2 tablespoons lime juice

3 tablespoons chopped fresh coriander (cilantro)

2 teaspoons soft brown sugar

serves 4

preparation + soaking 10 minutes

cooking 1 minute

per serving 1177 kilojoules/281 calories, 33 g protein, 7 g total fat, 1 g saturated fat, 361 mg cholesterol, 20 g carbohydrate, 1 g fibre

1 Combine chilies, salt and pepper in a medium bowl. Brush squid with oil. Add to bowl and toss to coat with chilies.

2 Pour boiling water over vermicelli; leave 5 minutes or until softened. Drain.

3 Toss vermicelli, onion, ginger, fish sauce, soy sauce, lime juice, coriander and sugar in a serving bowl.

4 Preheat a ridged, iron pan or heavy-based frying pan. Add squid, cook over high heat about 30 seconds on each side. Serve on top of noodles.

noodle and mushroom sweet and sour salad

A symbol of longevity in Asia because of their health-promoting properties, shiitake mushrooms have a rich, smoky taste and a meaty texture.

250 g (8 oz) glass (cellophane) noodles

250 g (8 oz) fresh shiitake mushrooms

250 g (8 oz) Chinese (napa) cabbage

2 medium carrots (about 250 g/8 oz)

3 tablespoons vegetable oil

1 clove garlic, finely chopped

1 tablespoon finely chopped fresh
    ginger root

2 tablespoons soy sauce

2 tablespoons rice vinegar

2 teaspoons soft brown sugar

1 tablespoon lime juice

salt and freshly ground black pepper

2 red chilies, finely sliced

serves 4

preparation + soaking 30 minutes

cooking 10 minutes

----

*per serving 1337 kilojoules/319 calories, 3 g protein,
14 g total fat, 2 g saturated fat, 0 mg cholesterol,
45 g carbohydrate, 6 g fibre*

1 Pour boiling water over noodles; leave 10 minutes. Wipe mushrooms with paper towel, remove stalks and slice large caps in half, leaving others whole.

2 Slice cabbage into quarters and remove core. Slice cabbage thinly. Cut carrots into fine strips. Drain noodles and cut into short lengths.

3 Combine noodles, cabbage and carrots in a bowl. Heat oil in a pan and sauté mushrooms over high heat. Add garlic and ginger and cook another 3 minutes. Stir in soy sauce and 1 tablespoon rice vinegar. Remove from heat. Add brown sugar, lime juice and salt and pepper to taste. Leave to cool.

4 Combine mushroom mixture and noodle mixture. Add remaining 1 tablespoon rice vinegar and season to taste with salt and pepper. Distribute among individual serving dishes. Sprinkle with chilies.

cook's tip

Glass noodles must not be boiled. Soak them in hot water and wait until they are soft before cutting them into shorter sections with kitchen scissors. Glass noodles are available from Asian supermarkets.

salami rice salad

Rice is a versatile, inexpensive ingredient. Its soft texture and mild taste work well with many salad greens and vegetables.

¾ cup (140 g/5 oz) long-grain rice
350 ml (12 fl oz) salt-reduced vegetable
    stock (broth)
500 g (1 lb) broccoli
1 medium yellow capsicum (bell pepper)
250 g (8 oz) spicy salami, in one piece
leaves of 3 sprigs thyme, finely chopped
½ teaspoon ground sweet paprika

dressing

3 tablespoons light mayonnaise
½ cup (125 g/4 oz) yogurt
1 tablespoon olive oil
2 tablespoons white wine vinegar
herb salt
freshly ground black pepper

serves 4
preparation + cooling 30 minutes
cooking 35 minutes

---

*per serving 2208 kilojoules/527 calories, 22 g protein,
32 g total fat, 10 g saturated fat, 73 mg cholesterol,
38 g carbohydrate, 4 g fibre*

1 Place rice and stock in a saucepan, cover and bring to a boil. Reduce heat to low, half cover pan and cook rice 15 to 20 minutes or until cooked. Remove from heat. Let stand, uncovered, until cool, loosening rice occasionally with a fork.

2 Chop broccoli into small pieces. Place in a steamer basket. Fill a large saucepan with water to a depth equal to the width of two fingers; bring to a boil. Reduce heat to a simmer. Place steamer basket on top of pan. Cover; cook broccoli 8 to 12 minutes, or until crisp-tender. Remove from steamer and leave to cool. Reserve cooking liquid.

3 Halve capsicum and cut into small strips. Peel salami and cut into small strips.

4 To make dressing, whisk mayonnaise, yogurt, oil and 1 tablespoon vinegar in a large bowl until well combined. Add herb salt and pepper to taste. Add rice, vegetables and salami and stir to combine. If salad is too dry, mix in 3 to 4 tablespoons of reserved cooking liquid.

5 Mix half the thyme into the salad. Check seasoning, adding remaining 1 tablespoon vinegar and salt and pepper to taste. Sprinkle with paprika and remaining thyme.

cook's tip

Chorizo, a Spanish sausage made from coarsely chopped fatty pork seasoned with smoked paprika, may be used in this recipe. Fry slices until crisp over high heat and drain off fat before using.

spicy brown rice salad with feta

1 cup (200 g/7 oz) brown rice

½ teaspoon salt

300 g (10 oz) mini (Japanese) or large eggplants (aubergines)

5 tablespoons olive oil

1 clove garlic, finely sliced

2 tablespoons ajvar (spicy capsicum and eggplant relish)

3 tablespoons lemon juice

½ to 1 teaspoon dried chili flakes

finely chopped leaves of 4 sprigs mint

salt and freshly ground black pepper

3 large tomatoes, diced

heart of 1 cos (romaine) lettuce

125 g (4 oz) feta cheese, cubed

⅔ cup (100 g/4 oz) kalamata olives

serves 4

preparation 30 minutes (overnight soaking)

cooking 1 hour

---

per serving 2561 kilojoules/612 calories, 15 g protein,
33 g total fat, 8 g saturated fat, 22 mg cholesterol,
64 g carbohydrate, 8 g fibre

1 Mix rice, 2 cups (500 ml/16 fl oz) water and ½ teaspoon salt in a saucepan. Cover and soak overnight. Bring rice to a boil, uncovered. Cook half covered over low heat for 40 minutes. Remove from heat; leave to cool. Loosen rice occasionally with a fork.

2 Leave mini eggplants whole. Dice large ones. Heat 3 tablespoons oil in a nonstick pan over medium heat. Cook eggplants about 10 minutes, turning occasionally.

3 Add garlic and cook 2 minutes. Remove pan from heat, leave to cool.

4 Combine ajvar, 2 tablespoons lemon juice, remaining 2 tablespoons oil, chili flakes and mint in a large bowl; season with salt and pepper to taste. Mix in cooked rice and tomatoes. Season with remaining 1 tablespoon lemon juice and salt and pepper to taste.

5 Line a serving plate with lettuce. Top with salad, eggplants, feta and olives.

rice salad with creamy dressing

❋ Prepare 1 cup (200 g/7 oz) rice as described in main recipe. Leave to cool. Halve and dice 1 red, 1 green and 1 yellow capsicum (bell pepper). Finely chop 1 clove garlic. Combine all ingredients in a serving bowl.

❋ Whisk ½ cup (125 g/4 oz) whipping cream, 2 tablespoons crème fraîche, 2 tablespoons ajvar or another vegetable relish and 1 tablespoon olive oil in a bowl and stir until creamy. Add salt and pepper to taste. Stir dressing into salad. Add a few black and green olives.

spicy brown rice salad with feta

paella with chicken and prawns

3 tablespoons olive oil

1 cup (200 g/7 oz) risotto (arborio) rice

¼ teaspoon ground saffron

3 tablespoons dry white wine

1 cup (500 ml/16 fl oz) salt-reduced chicken stock (broth)

1 bay leaf

1 cup (120 g/4 oz) frozen green peas

100 g (4 oz) frozen green beans

3 tablespoons lemon juice

2 tablespoons sherry vinegar

salt and freshly ground black pepper

1 medium red capsicum (bell pepper)

2 medium tomatoes

heart of 1 cos (romaine) lettuce

chicken and prawns

250 g (8 oz) skinless chicken breast fillets

12 medium-sized uncooked prawns (shrimp)

2 cloves garlic, thinly sliced

2 tablespoons lemon juice

1 tablespoon olive oil

salt and freshly ground black pepper

3 tablespoons olive oil (for frying)

lemon wedges, for garnish

serves 4

preparation + standing 1 hour 30 minutes

cooking 20 minutes

---

per serving 2470 kilojoules/590 calories, 32 g protein, 28 g total fat, 4 g saturated fat, 87 mg cholesterol, 49 g carbohydrate, 6 g fibre

1 Heat 1½ tablespoons oil in a saucepan. Add rice and saffron and cook, stirring, until transparent. Add wine, stock, 4 tablespoons water and bay leaf. Bring to a boil. Add peas and beans and cook until rice has absorbed all the liquid. Remove from heat.

2 Combine rice, peas and beans in a large bowl. Whisk remaining 1½ tablespoons oil, lemon juice and vinegar until combined. Add salt and pepper to taste. Stir into rice mixture. Leave 1 hour in a cool place.

3 Chop capsicum in half and cut into dice. Pour boiling water over tomatoes, leave 2 minutes then plunge into iced water. Peel and dice. Mix capsicum and tomatoes into rice.

4 Cut chicken into thin strips and place in a bowl with half the garlic and 1 tablespoon lemon juice. Peel and clean prawns (*see right*). Place in a bowl with remaining garlic, remaining 1 tablespoon lemon juice, 1 tablespoon olive oil, salt and pepper.

5 Heat 3 tablespoons oil in a heavy pan over high heat. Add chicken mixture; sear chicken quickly on all sides. Add prawn mixture and sear prawns on both sides. Reduce heat to medium. Cook another 5 minutes or until done. Arrange lettuce leaves on a large platter. Top with rice salad and chicken and prawn mixture. Garnish with lemon wedges.

cook's tip

Arborio rice is a creamy textured, medium-grain Italian rice used in making paella and risotto because it remains firm in the centre. It absorbs a large amount of stock (broth) during cooking.

peeling prawns (shrimp)

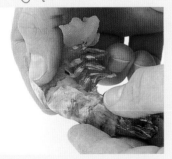

1 If head is still intact, twist it off carefully. Holding tail firmly, push thumb of other hand through shell and remove.

2 Cut along back of prawn with a small, sharp knife. Pull out black intestinal tract with fingertips or a knife. Discard.

3 Rinse prawns under cold running water. Place on paper towel and pat dry.

rice salad with ginger-soy dressing

The Hindi word basmati means fragrant. It refers to the nut-like flavour and aroma of this small, but long-grained rice.

¾ cup (140 g/5 oz) basmati or other fragrant rice

½ teaspoon salt

125 g (4 oz) fresh baby corn (about 10)

150 g (5 oz) snow peas (mange-tout)

1 medium red capsicum (bell pepper)

3 spring onions (scallions), finely chopped

1 can (190 g/7 oz) bamboo shoots, drained

4 tablespoons roasted cashew nuts

ginger-soy dressing

1 tablespoon finely grated fresh ginger root

3 tablespoons rice vinegar

2 tablespoons soy sauce

2 tablespoons sunflower or peanut oil

1 tablespoon medium-hot mango chutney

serves 4

preparation + cooling 1 hour

cooking 20 to 25 minutes

per serving *1386 kilojoules/331 calories, 8 g protein, 16 g total fat, 2 g saturated fat, 0 mg cholesterol, 39 g carbohydrate, 4 g fibre*

1 Combine rice, 1 cup (250 ml/8 fl oz) water and salt in a saucepan and bring to a boil. Half cover rice and cook over low heat 20 to 25 minutes. Remove from heat. Leave to cool. Loosen rice occasionally with a fork.

2 Bring a pan of lightly salted water to a boil. Blanch corn 3 minutes and snow peas 1 minute. Drain, immerse in iced water to arrest cooking. Drain; leave to cool.

3 Halve capsicum and cut into narrow strips. Cut snow peas and corn in half. Mix rice and all the salad vegetables in a large bowl.

4 To make ginger-soy dressing, combine vinegar, soy sauce, oil and chutney in a bowl. (If chutney contains large pieces of mango, break them up with a fork before adding.) Stir to combine.

5 Stir dressing into rice salad. Arrange salad on serving plates and sprinkle with cashew nuts.

cook's tip

Rice is classified by size and shape (long, medium and short grain). Long-grain rice remains separate and dry when cooked and is ideal for use in rice salads.

spicy rice salad with pineapple

1 cup (185 g/7 oz) basmati rice

½ teaspoon salt

1 cup (200 g/7 oz) drained canned pineapple
slices or pieces in natural juice

4 stalks celery

300 g (10 oz) small mushrooms, chopped

2 spring onions (scallions), sliced

4 to 6 large Chinese (napa) cabbage leaves

curry vinaigrette

100 g (4 oz) crème fraîche or sour cream

3 tablespoons milk

2 tablespoons raspberry vinegar

1 tablespoon sunflower oil

¼ teaspoon ground ginger

1 teaspoon mild curry powder

¼ to ½ teaspoon sambal oelek
or Chinese chili paste

serves 4

preparation + cooling 40 minutes

cooking 25 minutes

----

*per serving 1551 kilojoules/370 calories, 8 g protein,
16 g total fat, 9 g saturated fat, 33 mg cholesterol,
47 g carbohydrate, 6 g fibre*

1 Place rice in a saucepan with 400 ml (14 fl oz) water and ½ teaspoon salt. Bring to a boil, uncovered. Cover pan and cook rice over low heat 15 to 20 minutes or until all liquid is absorbed. Rice should be light and fluffy with steam holes on the surface. Turn off heat, let stand, covered, another 5 minutes. Remove from heat, uncover pan and let rice cool. Loosen grains occasionally with a fork.

2 Chop pineapple slices into small pieces. Slice celery into thin strips. Reserve feathery leaves. Combine rice, pineapple, celery and mushrooms in a large bowl. Add spring onions, reserving a few for garnish.

3 To make dressing, whisk crème fraîche, milk, vinegar, oil, ginger, curry and ¼ teaspoon sambal oelek in a bowl until creamy. Add remaining ¼ teaspoon sambal oelek to taste. Stir into salad ingredients.

4 Cut Chinese cabbage leaves into strips. Divide among individual serving plates and top with rice salad. Garnish with celery leaves and reserved spring onion rings.

cook's tip

*Basmati is an aromatic rice native
to Pakistan and India. It is good
for steaming or boiling. The grains
swell lengthwise only when cooked
and stay separate and dry.*

wild rice salad with tomatoes and chilies

Wild rice is not a rice at all, but rather a tall aquatic grass that grows in Japan, China and the Great Lakes region of North America.

1 tablespoon olive oil

1 medium onion, finely diced

²⁄₃ cup (105 g/4 oz) wild rice

½ cup (90 g/3 oz) long-grain rice

400 ml (14 fl oz) salt-reduced vegetable stock (broth)

8 pickled hot green chilies, drained

4 roma (plum) tomatoes, cored and thinly sliced

150 g (5 oz) rocket (arugula)

250 g (8 oz) bocconcini (baby mozzarella balls)

pesto vinaigrette

3 tablespoons olive oil

3 tablespoons red wine vinegar

2 tablespoons red (sun-dried tomato) pesto

salt and freshly ground black pepper

serves 4

preparation + chilling 1 hour

cooking 30 minutes

----

per serving 2166 kilojoules/517 calories, 18 g protein, 31 g total fat, 9 g saturated fat, 22 mg cholesterol, 42 g carbohydrate, 3 g fibre

1 Heat oil in a saucepan and sweat onion until transparent. Stir in wild rice and long-grain rice. Add stock and bring to a boil, uncovered. Cover pan; cook over low heat 15 to 20 minutes or until all liquid is absorbed. The rice should be light and fluffy with steam holes on the surface. Turn off heat, let stand, covered, 5 minutes. Remove pan from heat, uncover and let cool. Loosen grains occasionally with a fork.

2 Remove seeds from 4 chilies; slice into rounds. Keep remaining chilies whole.

3 To make pesto vinaigrette, whisk oil, vinegar, pesto, salt and pepper in a large bowl. Carefully fold in cooked rice, chopped chilies and tomatoes.

4 Divide rocket leaves among plates. Spoon rice salad onto plates. Add bocconcini. Garnish with whole chilies.

health guide

Wild rice contains more protein than rice does and is richer in lysine, the amino acid that is lacking in most grains. Amino acids are essential for human growth and function.

wild rice salad with tomatoes and chilies

wild rice salad with shallots and lettuce

✳ Prepare rice mixture as described in the main recipe, omitting the onion; let cool. Heat 2 tablespoons olive oil in a nonstick pan, add 300 g (10 oz) whole peeled shallots and ½ cup (125 ml/4 fl oz) dry red wine. Cook, covered, 10 minutes. Uncover and cook until wine has almost evaporated.

✳ Stir in 2 tablespoons balsamic vinegar, 2 tablespoons olive oil, 1 teaspoon chopped fresh rosemary leaves and salt and pepper to taste. Let cool. Stir in rice. Line a platter with cos (romaine) lettuce leaves. Top with rice salad.

warm lentil salad

1 cup (190 g/7 oz) brown lentils

1 medium carrot, diced

2 teaspoons fresh thyme leaves

salt and freshly ground black pepper

6 roma (plum) tomatoes, chopped

2 spring onions (scallions), finely sliced

3 teaspoons olive oil

2 tablespoons red wine vinegar

2 teaspoons Dijon mustard

serves 4

preparation 10 minutes

cooking 30 minutes

per serving *881 kilojoules/210 calories, 8 g protein, 14 g total fat, 2 g saturated fat, 0 mg cholesterol, 13 g carbohydrate, 6 g fibre*

1 Place lentils, carrot, thyme and salt and pepper in a large saucepan; cover with water. Bring to a boil. Cover pan; cook, simmering, 25 minutes or until lentils are tender. Drain.

2 Place lentil mixture in a serving bowl with tomatoes and spring onions. Whisk oil, vinegar and mustard and stir in.

health guide

Lentils and other legumes are a good source of copper, a trace mineral that may help lower blood cholesterol. The iron content of lentils is more easily absorbed by the body if they are cooked or served with a food that is rich in vitamin C, such as tomatoes or cabbage.

potato and lentil salad

1 kg (2 lb) waxy potatoes, peeled and cut
  into large chunks
½ cup (125 ml/4 fl oz) olive oil
2 tablespoons red wine vinegar
4 cups (750 g/1 lb 10 oz) cooked brown
  lentils
1 cup (120 g/4 oz) pitted black olives
1 tablespoon capers, chopped
2 cloves garlic, chopped
1 tablespoon lemon juice
⅔ cup (55 g/2 oz) roughly chopped
  flat-leaf parsley
6 spring onions (scallions), sliced diagonally
freshly ground black pepper

serves 6
preparation 15 minutes
cooking 20 minutes

----

per serving *1553 kilojoules/371 calories, 13 g protein,*
20 g total fat, 3 g saturated fat, 0 mg cholesterol,
36 g carbohydrate, 9 g fibre

1 Cook potatoes in a pan of boiling water 20 minutes
or until tender. Drain and transfer to a large bowl.

2 While potatoes are still hot, whisk oil and vinegar and
stir in. Carefully mix in lentils, olives, capers, garlic, lemon
juice, parsley, spring onions and a good grinding of pepper.
Serve while still warm.

cook's tip

Dry salt-cured olives and those
pickled in brine are high in sodium.
Because capers are also salty, this
salad needs no additional salt.

lentil salad with fried onions and rosemary

2 cups (400 g/14 oz) Puy-style
　green lentils

1 small sprig rosemary

1 small dried bay leaf

3 small unpeeled cooked potatoes

2 large tomatoes, cored and diced

2 tablespoons olive oil

2 tablespoons red wine or herb vinegar

1 tablespoon lemon juice

1 teaspoon grated lemon peel

½ teaspoon ground cumin

1 clove garlic, crushed

salt and freshly ground black pepper

2 large white onions, sliced into rings

2 tablespoons olive oil

½ cup (40 g/2 oz) finely chopped
　fresh flat-leaf parsley

serves 4

preparation + chilling 1 hour 35 minutes

cooking 40 minutes to 1 hour

----

per serving *1573 kilojoules/376 calories, 17 g protein,*
19 g total fat, 3 g saturated fat, 0 mg cholesterol,
34 g carbohydrate, 11 g fibre

1 Place lentils, rosemary and bay leaf in a saucepan. Add water to cover; bring to a boil. Cook on medium heat about 40 minutes or until soft. Leave to cool in cooking liquid. Drain, reserving liquid. Discard rosemary and bay leaf.

2 Peel and dice potatoes and place in a large bowl with tomatoes and lentils. Whisk oil, vinegar, lemon juice, peel, cumin, garlic and 3 tablespoons reserved cooking liquid in a small bowl. Add salt and pepper to taste. Stir into salad. Chill salad, covered, 1 hour.

3 Cook onion rings in oil over moderate heat until golden brown. Check salad for seasoning, adding more salt, pepper and vinegar, if needed. Stir in parsley.

4 Distribute salad among individual serving bowls and top with warm onions.

curried lentil salad

❋ Cook lentils as for main recipe and place in a serving bowl. Combine 1 tablespoon mild curry paste, 2 tablespoons mango chutney, 3 tablespoons olive oil, 2 tablespoons lime juice, 2 finely diced spring onions (scallions) and 1 teaspoon finely chopped fresh ginger. Stir into lentils. Chill 1 hour.

❋ Grate 2 carrots. Wash 250 g (8 oz) baby spinach leaves; cook briefly in the water clinging to the leaves. Add carrots and spinach to bowl. Add salt and pepper to taste and toss to combine. Serve with pita bread.

lentil salad with fried onions and rosemary

white bean salad with sesame dressing

white bean salad with sesame dressing

1 cup (200 g/7 oz) dried small white beans

2 medium tomatoes, cored and diced

1 medium red onion, thinly sliced

2 mild light green banana chilies (capsicums), cut in thin strips

4 tablespoons olive oil

4 tablespoons red wine vinegar

salt and freshly ground black pepper

4 tablespoons tahini (sesame paste)

2 tablespoons lemon juice

2 medium eggs, hard-boiled, sliced

⅓ cup (50 g/2 oz) black olives

½ cup (40 g/2 oz) fresh parsley leaves

serves 4
preparation 25 minutes + 12 hours soaking
cooking 45 minutes

----

per serving 2018 kilojoules/482 calories, 19 g protein, 35 g total fat, 5 g saturated fat, 108 mg cholesterol, 23 g carbohydrate, 16 g fibre

1 Soak beans in water overnight. Drain. Place in a pan and cover with water. Bring to a boil; cook 35 minutes or until soft. Let cool in cooking water. Drain.

2 Place beans in a serving bowl. Add tomatoes, onion and chilies. Whisk oil, vinegar, salt and pepper and stir into salad.

3 Combine tahini, lemon juice and about 4 tablespoons water in a bowl; stir until smooth. Add salt to taste. Add eggs, olives and parsley to salad. Spoon on sesame dressing.

health guide

Sesame seeds are a good source of calcium, magnesium, iron and zinc. They also contain two unique substances called sesamin and sesamolin, both of which have been shown to have a cholesterol-lowering effect in humans.

white bean salad with herb dressing

✳ Cook 250 g (8 oz) dried small white beans as for main recipe. Finely slice 3 spring onions (scallions). Dice 2 small cucumbers. Halve and dice 1 yellow capsicum (bell pepper). Combine all ingredients in a serving bowl.

✳ To make herb dressing, combine ½ cup (125 g/4 oz) sour cream and 2 tablespoons olive oil. Add 1 tablespoon finely chopped fresh marjoram, 1 tablespoon finely chopped fresh mint leaves and 1 tablespoon finely chopped fresh parsley. Season generously with salt and black pepper.

✳ Pour dressing over salad and stir in. Serve with toasted focaccia.

buckwheat and artichoke salad with feta

Buckwheat is not a grain or a type of wheat but is used as if it were. The hulled roasted seeds are called groats or kasha. When cooked, they have a nutty taste.

2 cups (500 ml/16 fl oz) salt-reduced vegetable stock (broth)

1 bay leaf

1 cup (180 g/7 oz) whole-grain roasted buckwheat groats (kasha)

2 teaspoons olive oil

1 can (280 g/10 oz) artichoke hearts, drained

1 medium head round radicchio

2 large tomatoes

1 sprig rosemary

4 sprigs marjoram

4 tablespoons olive oil

1 tablespoon balsamic vinegar

3 tablespoons lemon juice

salt and freshly ground black pepper

150 g (5 oz) feta cheese, cubed

serves 4

preparation + cooling 1 hour 30 minutes

cooking 20 to 30 minutes

----

per serving 2118 kilojoules/506 calories, 14 g protein, 34 g total fat, 9 g saturated fat, 26 mg cholesterol, 35 g carbohydrate, 4 g fibre

1 Place stock, bay leaf and buckwheat in a saucepan and bring to a boil, uncovered. Add oil. Reduce heat to very low. Cover pan; simmer 15 minutes. Remove from heat and leave, covered, 10 minutes. Uncover; fluff buckwheat with a fork. Season with salt to taste. Let cool.

2 Chop artichoke hearts into small pieces. Tear radicchio into small pieces. Halve and core tomatoes, remove seeds. Cut flesh into small cubes.

3 Finely chop rosemary and marjoram leaves. Whisk herbs, oil, vinegar and 2 tablespoons lemon juice in a large serving bowl. Add salt and pepper to taste. Add buckwheat, artichokes, radicchio and tomatoes; stir to combine.

4 Leave salad, covered, 1 hour. Just before serving, add salt, pepper and remaining lemon juice to taste. Add feta and stir to combine.

health guide

Buckwheat contains rutin, which is a known cancer fighter. Rutin also helps to strengthen blood vessels, lower cholesterol levels and lower blood pressure.

buckwheat and artichoke salad with feta

roasted buckwheat salad with yogurt dressing

❋ Prepare 1 cup (180 g/7 oz) whole-grain roasted buckwheat groats
(kasha) as for main recipe; let cool. Dice 2 large tomatoes and 1 red and
1 green capsicum (bell pepper). Slice 3 spring onions (scallions) into rings.
Place all ingredients in a serving bowl.

❋ To make yogurt dressing, mash 100 g (4 oz) feta in a bowl with $\frac{2}{3}$ cup
(175 g/6 oz) yogurt. Whisk in 2 tablespoons olive oil, 2 tablespoons lemon
juice and 1 tablespoon white wine vinegar. Add salt and pepper to taste.
Stir into salad. Sprinkle with 2 tablespoons chopped fresh parsley.

couscous salad with chickpeas

couscous salad with chickpeas

1⅓ cups (240 g/8 oz) instant couscous

½ teaspoon salt

4 roma (plum) tomatoes

2 spring onions (scallions)

½ cup (40 g/2 oz) finely chopped
    fresh flat-leaf parsley

1 can (300 g/10 oz) chickpeas (garbanzo
    beans), rinsed and drained

200 g (7 oz) garlic sausage or cabanossi,
    in one piece

vinaigrette

4 tablespoons olive oil

1 tablespoon red wine vinegar

3 tablespoons lemon juice

1 clove garlic, crushed

1 teaspoon ground cumin

1 teaspoon ground sweet paprika

salt and freshly ground black pepper

serves 4

preparation + standing 35 minutes

per serving 1756 kilojoules/420 calories, 13 g protein,
32 g total fat, 8 g saturated fat, 22 mg cholesterol,
20 g carbohydrate, 4 g fibre

health guide

Chickpeas and couscous combined
give this dish a useful protein
content. For a quick meal, instant
couscous is an ideal ingredient.

1 Bring 1 cup (250 ml/8 fl oz) water to a boil in a medium saucepan. Remove from heat. Stir in couscous and salt and leave to absorb liquid 20 minutes. Leave to cool.

2 Halve and core tomatoes and cut into small dice. Slice spring onions into rings.

3 To make vinaigrette, whisk oil, vinegar, 2 tablespoons lemon juice, garlic, cumin and paprika in a large bowl. Add salt and pepper to taste. Stir parsley, couscous, chickpeas, tomatoes and spring onions into vinaigrette.

4 Just before serving, taste salad and season with salt, pepper and remaining 1 tablespoon lemon juice. Slice sausage into small cubes and stir in.

couscous salad with tuna

✳ Prepare 1⅓ cups (240 g/8 oz) couscous as in main recipe. Halve 2 green capsicums (bell peppers) and cut into strips. Finely dice 1 red onion. Cut 2 zucchini (courgettes) into thin strips. Mix all ingredients in a bowl.

✳ Whisk 3 tablespoons olive oil, 3 tablespoons lemon juice, 1 clove garlic, crushed, ½ teaspoon ground sweet paprika and salt and pepper to taste. Stir into couscous salad. Add 1 tablespoon chopped fresh mint leaves. Stir in 150 g (5 oz) drained, canned, finely flaked tuna.

chickpea, spinach and eggplant salad

Chickpeas (or garbanzo beans) are often used in Mediterranean and Middle Eastern dishes. They have a nutty, earthy taste.

2 medium eggplants (aubergines)
(about 500 g/1 lb in total), thinly sliced
1/3 cup (80 ml/3 fl oz) olive oil
150 g (5 oz) baby spinach leaves
1 cup (175 g/6 oz) cooked chickpeas
250 g (8 oz) feta cheese, crumbled
1 small red onion, thinly sliced
3 tablespoons chopped fresh mint leaves
2 tablespoons lemon juice

serves 4
preparation 5 minutes
cooking 6 minutes

per serving 1789 kilojoules/427 calories, 17 g protein,
35 g total fat, 12 g saturated fat, 43 mg cholesterol,
12 g carbohydrate, 6 g fibre

1 Brush eggplant slices with half the oil. Place in a large nonstick pan over medium-high heat. Cook 2 to 3 minutes each side until golden.

2 Place spinach on a serving platter and top with eggplant, chickpeas, feta, onion and mint.

3 Combine remaining oil and lemon juice. Pour over salad. Serve at room temperature.

eggplant

Eggplants (aubergines) with the best flavour are of medium size with thin skins. Larger ones are more likely to be full of seeds and taste bitter. Bitter eggplants may be sprinkled with salt to draw out the flavour. Wash and pat dry before using.

quinoa, avocado and chorizo salad

1 cup (180 g/7 oz) quinoa

2 cups (500 ml/16 fl oz) tomato juice

½ teaspoon salt

1 medium firm avocado

2 tablespoons lemon juice

1 medium red capsicum (bell pepper), halved
and finely diced

1 medium red onion, finely diced

1⅓ cups (250 g/8 oz) drained and rinsed
canned kidney beans

150 g (5 oz) chorizo, in one piece

vinaigrette

3 tablespoons olive oil

2 tablespoons red wine vinegar

1 to 2 tablespoons lime juice

½ teaspoon ground cumin

1 clove garlic, crushed

salt and freshly ground black pepper

serves 4

preparation + chilling 1 hour 30 minutes

cooking 20 minutes

----

per serving 2827 kilojoules/675 calories, 21 g protein,
45 g total fat, 10 g saturated fat, 39 mg cholesterol,
47 g carbohydrate, 9 g fibre

1 Place quinoa, tomato juice and salt in a saucepan. Bring to a boil, uncovered. Cover pan and cook 10 to 15 minutes over low heat. Turn off heat, let stand, covered, 5 minutes. Remove from heat, uncover pan and let cool, occasionally loosening grains with a fork.

2 Dice avocado, place in a bowl and sprinkle with lemon juice to prevent discolouration. Place on a large serving plate with capsicum, onion and kidney beans.

3 To make vinaigrette, whisk oil, vinegar, 1 tablespoon lime juice, ground cumin and garlic in a bowl. Add salt, pepper and remaining 1 tablespoon lime juice to taste.

4 Pour vinaigrette over salad and stir in. Chill salad, covered, 1 hour.

5 Peel chorizo and slice thinly. Heat a nonstick pan over medium heat and fry sausage on both sides until light golden. Drain and add to salad. Serve at once.

quinoa

Quinoa is often classified as a grain but is, in fact, of the same plant family as spinach. While the tops of the plant are edible, it is the seeds that are generally served. Quick cooking brings out the delicate flavour and makes the seeds fluffy. Use as a substitute for rice. Quinoa is high in iron and protein.

quinoa, avocado and chorizo salad

quinoa with sweet and spicy dressing

✳ Prepare 1 cup (180 g/7 oz) quinoa as in main recipe, using water in place of tomato juice. Place in a serving bowl.

✳ Thinly slice 3 red onions and 300 g (10 oz) baby carrots. In a nonstick pan, heat 2 tablespoons peanut (groundnut) oil over medium heat. Add carrots and cook 3 minutes. Add onions; cook 5 minutes. Add 100 g (4 oz) baby spinach leaves. Cook just until wilted. Transfer to serving bowl.

✳ To make dressing, whisk 4 tablespoons dry white wine, 2 tablespoons honey, ½ teaspoon sambal oelek or Chinese chili paste and 1 teaspoon mustard. Stir into salad.

chicken kebab salad with peanut sauce (page 228)

meat and poultry salads

Marinades made with oils, vinegars and fresh herbs and stir-fry sauces that combine spicy Asian flavours enhance the taste of meat and poultry and add a new dimension to salads. Lean meat and poultry provide high-quality protein for growth and cell repair as well as iron and B vitamins.

beef salad in cucumber herb marinade

500 g (1 lb) beef blade or round steak

2 medium onions, roughly chopped

2 celery stalks, roughly chopped

2 medium carrots (about 250 g/8 oz),
 roughly chopped

1 bay leaf

3 teaspoons salt

1 tablespoon whole black peppercorns

1 clove

200 g (7 oz) sweet and sour pickled
 cucumbers (bread and butter
 cucumbers) from a jar

2 medium white onions

1 teaspoon allspice

5 tablespoons liquid from pickle jar

2 tablespoons sunflower or peanut oil

2 tablespoons white wine vinegar

1 tablespoon finely chopped fresh dill

1 tablespoon finely chopped fresh parsley

serves 4

preparation 35 minutes

cooking 2 hours

marinating 12 hours

---

per serving 1312 kilojoules/313 calories, 26 g protein,
15 g total fat, 4 g saturated fat, 60 mg cholesterol,
17 g carbohydrate, 2 g fibre

1 Trim beef of fat. Place beef, roughly chopped vegetables, bay leaf, 2 teaspoons salt, 1 teaspoon peppercorns and the clove in a saucepan. Cover with water; bring to a boil. Skim any fat from surface with a slotted spoon. Continue cooking, partly covered, over low heat 2 hours. Remove pan from heat. Leave meat to cool in cooking liquid.

2 Dice cucumbers and onions and place in a large bowl. Remove meat from pan. Reserve cooking liquid and discard vegetables. Cut meat into small cubes. Add to bowl with remaining peppercorns and allspice and mix well.

3 To make marinade, combine cucumber pickle liquid, oil, 1 tablespoon vinegar and remaining 1 teaspoon salt. Pour marinade over meat mixture. Top up with cooking liquid so that meat mixture is completely covered. Marinate, covered, in refrigerator 12 hours.

4 Remove from refrigerator 30 minutes before serving. Stir in a little of the herbs. Taste and add remaining 1 tablespoon vinegar, if needed. Spoon salad into serving bowls using a slotted spoon. Sprinkle with remaining herbs.

cook's tip

This is a useful recipe to make ahead. It keeps well for 3 days in the refrigerator and the flavours intensify. Trim meat of any excess fat before using.

beef salad in
cucumber herb marinade

beef and potato salad with horseradish dressing

✳ Cook 500 g (1 lb) lean beef as for the main recipe, without the carrots
and celery. Add 2 chopped carrots and 2 chopped celery stalks in the last
10 minutes of cooking; carrots and celery should still be crunchy.

✳ Remove meat, carrots and celery from stock. Let cool; chop into small
pieces. Place in a serving bowl. Dice 1 small red onion and 4 medium
cooked potatoes. Add to bowl and mix well.

✳ To make horseradish dressing, whisk 200 g (7 oz) light sour cream with
2 tablespoons olive oil, 2 tablespoons white wine vinegar and 1 tablespoon
horseradish cream. Add 1 small apple, finely grated, and salt and pepper to
taste. Add 2 tablespoons chopped fresh parsley. Serve with meat salad.

beef salad with lentils

1 tablespoon whole-grain mustard

6 tablespoons olive oil

generous pinch of ground black pepper

2 beef steaks (about 500 g/1 lb in total)

1 cup (200 g/7 oz) Puy-style green lentils

1 small sprig rosemary

300 ml ($\frac{1}{2}$ pint/10 fl oz) salt-reduced beef
   stock (broth)

2 medium carrots (about 250 g/8 oz), diced

$\frac{1}{2}$ teaspoon salt

freshly ground black pepper

3 tablespoons red wine vinegar

1 tablespoon chopped fresh thyme leaves

4 tablespoons whipping cream

2 teaspoons horseradish cream

100 g (4 oz) lamb's lettuce (corn salad)

3 tablespoons finely chopped chives

serves 4

preparation 40 minutes

cooking 40 minutes

per serving 2361 kilojoules/564 calories, 34 g protein,
41 g total fat, 11 g saturated fat, 84 mg cholesterol,
16 g carbohydrate, 6 g fibre

1 Combine mustard, 1 tablespoon oil and pepper. Rub steaks with mixture. Cover and chill until ready to cook. Place lentils, rosemary and stock in a pan. Bring to a boil, uncovered. Cover, cook lentils over low heat 20 minutes. Add carrots; cook another 10 minutes. Remove pan from heat. Leave lentils and carrots to cool in cooking liquid. Remove rosemary. Add $\frac{1}{2}$ teaspoon salt.

2 Heat 1 tablespoon oil in a nonstick frying pan over medium-high heat. Add steaks; cook 3 to 5 minutes each side. Remove from pan, wrap in cooking (aluminum) foil.

3 Whisk remaining 4 tablespoons oil and 2 tablespoons vinegar in a medium bowl. Add salt and pepper to taste. Drain lentils and carrots from pan and add to bowl. Stir in thyme. Whip cream in a small bowl until stiff; fold in the horseradish cream.

4 Slice steaks thinly and add any juices from meat to lentil mixture. Add remaining 1 tablespoon vinegar and salt and pepper to taste. Place lentil mixture on serving plates with lamb's lettuce. Add meat, top with a little horseradish cream mixture and sprinkle with chives. Serve remaining horseradish cream mixture separately.

thai beef salad

500 g (1 lb) beef rump steak
$\frac{1}{2}$ cup salt-reduced soy sauce
2 cloves garlic, crushed
5 tablespoons lime juice
500 g (1 lb) broccoli
$\frac{1}{3}$ cup (20 g/1 oz) fresh mint leaves
$\frac{1}{3}$ cup (20 g/1 oz) fresh basil leaves
$\frac{1}{4}$ cup (15 g/$\frac{1}{2}$ oz) fresh coriander
   (cilantro) leaves
1 small cucumber, halved lengthwise
   and sliced
2 red chilies, thinly sliced
2 teaspoons soft brown sugar

serves 4
preparation 25 minutes
cooking 10 minutes

----

per serving 901 kilojoules/215 calories, 31 g protein,
7 g total fat, 3 g saturated fat, 60 mg cholesterol,
5 g carbohydrate, 4 g fibre

1 Place steak, $\frac{1}{4}$ cup soy sauce, garlic and 2 tablespoons lime juice in a large bowl. Leave 10 minutes.

2 Preheat grill (broiler) to high heat; cook steak 2 minutes each side. Set aside.

3 Place broccoli in a steamer basket. Fill a large pan with boiling water to a depth equal to the width of two fingers; bring to a boil. Reduce heat to a simmer. Place steamer basket on top of pan. Cover, cook broccoli 5 to 6 minutes or until crisp-tender. Leave to cool 10 minutes. Place in a large bowl with mint, basil and coriander. Add cucumber slices.

4 Slice steak and add to salad. Combine chilies, sugar, remaining $\frac{1}{4}$ cup soy sauce and remaining 3 tablespoons lime juice in a bowl. Stir gently into salad. Pile salad onto serving plates.

mexican beef salad

This spicy salad combines iron-rich beef and
a mixture of vegetables packed with vitamins.
It makes a sustaining main meal.

500 g (1 lb) cooked lean beef

2 long red chilies

½ cup (30 g/1 oz) finely chopped fresh
   coriander (cilantro) leaves

4 tablespoons olive oil

3 tablespoons red wine vinegar

2 tablespoons lime juice

¼ teaspoon sweet ground paprika

salt and freshly ground black pepper

1 red and 1 orange capsicum (bell pepper)

8 drained and rinsed canned baby corn
   spears

2 large tomatoes

2 spring onions (scallions), thinly sliced

50 g (2 oz) corn chips

serves 4

preparation 35 minutes

marinating 1 hour

----

per serving *2039 kilojoules/487 calories, 40 g protein,*
31 g total fat, 8 g saturated fat, 88 mg cholesterol,
12 g carbohydrate, 4 g fibre

1 Cut beef into narrow strips; place in a bowl. Chop chilies
finely; discard seeds. Add to bowl. Add coriander, reserving
1 tablespoon for garnish.

2 To make vinaigrette, whisk oil, 2 tablespoons vinegar,
lime juice and paprika in a bowl. Add salt and pepper to
taste. Stir into beef mixture. Chill, covered, 1 hour.

3 Dice capsicums. Cut baby corn spears in half. Halve
tomatoes, remove core and seeds; dice. Add to beef mixture
with spring onions and remaining 1 tablespoon vinegar.

4 Just before serving, add salt and pepper to taste. Divide
salad among serving bowls. Add corn chips and sprinkle with
reserved coriander.

health guide

Beef is a leading source of high-quality
protein, vitamin B12 and vitamin B6. It
also contains such essential minerals as zinc
and iron. Select the leanest cuts of beef; they
are the healthiest.

pastrami and artichoke salad

pastrami and artichoke salad

300 g (10 oz) thinly sliced pastrami
4 tablespoons olive oil
1 tablespoon balsamic vinegar
2 tablespoons lemon juice
salt and freshly ground black pepper
100 g (4 oz) rocket (arugula)
6 marinated artichoke hearts, drained
3 ripe roma (plum) tomatoes, sliced
1 medium red onion, thinly sliced into rings

serves 4
preparation + chilling 1 hour 35 minutes

per serving 1275 kilojoules/305 calories, 19 g protein,
23 g total fat, 5 g saturated fat, 51 mg cholesterol,
4 g carbohydrate, 3 g fibre

1 Place pastrami on a plate. To make vinaigrette, whisk oil, vinegar and lemon juice in a bowl. Add salt and pepper to taste. Drizzle half the vinaigrette over pastrami. Chill, covered, 1 hour.

2 Line serving plates with rocket. Cut artichoke hearts into quarters and arrange on plates with tomatoes. Add pastrami and top with onion rings. Drizzle with remaining vinaigrette.

pastrami salad on potatoes

✳ Marinate 300 g (10 oz) sliced pastrami as for the main recipe.

✳ Thinly slice 4 cooked, large potatoes. Overlap slices on individual serving plates. Sprinkle with a little ground cumin and a little ground paprika. Add salt and pepper to taste. Drizzle on 2 tablespoons olive oil.

✳ Slice 12 cherry tomatoes in half; place on potatoes. Top with pastrami.

pastrami

Pastrami is made from highly seasoned beef. The meat is trimmed of fat and the surface then rubbed with salt and a combination of seasonings such as garlic, ground cinnamon, black pepper, paprika, cloves, coriander seeds and allspice. The meat is dry-cured, smoked and cooked. A Turkish version, pastirma, is also made from beef. This type is dried.

spicy sausage and cheese salad

Most types of German-style sausages (wurst) include pork, spices and peppercorns. Cervelat, with its fine texture, is a good variety for this salad.

400 g (14 oz) German-style cooked
  sausage (wurst) or salami
250 g (8 oz) reduced-fat Swiss-style
  cheese, thinly sliced
150 g (5 oz) small gherkins in vinegar
2 medium red onions
½ cup (30 g/1 oz) finely chopped chives

vinaigrette

2 tablespoons vegetable oil
3 to 4 tablespoons white wine vinegar
4 tablespoons gherkin liquid
4 tablespoons beef stock (broth)
1 teaspoon hot mustard
salt and freshly ground black pepper

serves 4
preparation 20 minutes
marinating 1 hour

---

*per serving 2367 kilojoules/566 calories, 37 g protein,
43 g total fat, 17 g saturated fat, 100 mg cholesterol,
8 g carbohydrate, 3 g fibre*

1 Peel sausage and cut into fine strips. Cut cheese and gherkins into fine strips. Finely dice onions. Combine sausage, cheese, gherkins and onions in a large bowl.

2 To make vinaigrette, whisk oil, vinegar, 2 tablespoons gherkin liquid, stock and mustard in a bowl. Add salt and pepper to taste.

3 Pour vinaigrette over salad and toss to combine. Chill, covered, 1 hour. Add remaining 2 tablespoons gherkin liquid and salt and pepper to taste. Sprinkle with chives.

cook's tip

This salad has a sharp taste and a crunchy texture. Drained pickled cabbage (sauerkraut) may be used in place of gherkins. Alternatively, use mixed pickled vegetables.

veal and mushroom salad with basil

500 g (1 lb) veal or chicken schnitzels, cut thin

5 tablespoons olive oil

1 clove garlic, finely chopped

3 spring onions (scallions), finely sliced

500 g (1 lb) mixed small mushrooms, such as button, Swiss brown (cremini) or shiitake, sliced

salt and freshly ground black pepper

1 cup (60 g/2 oz) basil leaves

50 g (2 oz) Parmesan, in one piece

4 tablespoons beef stock (broth)

2 tablespoons port wine

2 tablespoons balsamic vinegar

150 g (5 oz) cherry tomatoes, cut in half

serves 4

preparation 15 minutes

cooking 15 minutes

----

*per serving 1860 kilojoules/444 calories, 35 g protein,
31 g total fat, 7 g saturated fat, 104 mg cholesterol,
5 g carbohydrate, 4 g fibre*

1 Cut veal into thin, even strips. Heat 3 tablespoons oil in nonstick pan over high heat. Sear veal briefly both sides. Add garlic and spring onions; cook 1 minute. Transfer to a plate and keep warm.

2 Heat remaining 2 tablespoons oil in pan. Fry mushrooms over medium heat 5 minutes. Add salt and pepper to taste. Transfer to a plate. Slice basil finely; keep a few leaves whole for garnish. Use a vegetable peeler to shave Parmesan into thin slices.

3 Place stock and port in pan in which veal was cooked; bring to a boil and cook briefly over high heat, stirring in juices and any crusty pieces from the meat. Transfer to a bowl. Add vinegar and salt and pepper to taste. When cooled completely, mix in two thirds of chopped basil.

4 Combine veal and mushrooms; place on a serving plate. Drizzle on stock mixture. Top with Parmesan. Garnish with remaining chopped basil, whole basil leaves and tomatoes.

veal salad with beans

✳ Slice 250 g (8 oz) green beans and 250 g (8 oz) butter (yellow wax) beans into short lengths. Cook beans with 3 sprigs thyme in lightly salted boiling water over medium heat 5 minutes. Drain; let cool. Discard thyme. Finely slice 3 spring onions (scallions). Cut 8 cherry tomatoes in half. Cut 500 g (1 lb) veal schnitzels into thin strips. Heat 2 tablespoons vegetable oil in nonstick pan. Cook veal over high heat 3 to 4 minutes. Season with salt and pepper.

✳ Whisk 2 tablespoons tarragon vinegar, 1 tablespoon white wine vinegar, 3 tablespoons vegetable oil and a pinch of sugar in a large bowl. Add salt and pepper to taste. Add beans, onions, tomatoes and veal. Add salt and pepper to taste. Garnish with 1 tablespoon finely chopped fresh parsley.

veal and mushroom salad
with basil

spicy pork salad

500 g (1 lb) cooked lean pork

250 g (8 oz) Chinese (napa) cabbage

1 can (190 g/7 oz) bamboo shoots, drained

100 g (4 oz) snow peas (mange-tout)

1 small piece fresh ginger root

1 tablespoon chopped lemon grass

2 tablespoons vegetable oil

½ teaspoon sesame oil

3 tablespoons rice vinegar

2 tablespoons salt-reduced soy sauce

1 teaspoon soft brown sugar

salt, to taste

2 tablespoons sesame seeds

2 tablespoons sour cream

1 teaspoon sambal oelek or Chinese
    chili paste

3 tablespoons finely chopped chives

serves 4

preparation 30 minutes

------

per serving 1711 kilojoules/409 calories, 39 g protein,
25 g total fat, 7 g saturated fat, 128 mg cholesterol,
6 g carbohydrate, 4 g fibre

1 Cut pork into very thin strips and place in a bowl. Finely shred Chinese cabbage. Cut bamboo shoots into thin strips. Cut snow peas into strips. Add all vegetables to bowl.

2 Finely chop ginger. Remove hard outer layers from lemon grass and finely chop tender part (*see below*).

3 To make vinaigrette, whisk vegetable oil, sesame oil, 2 tablespoons rice vinegar, soy sauce and sugar in a bowl. Add ginger and lemon grass; whisk to combine. Check seasoning, adding salt to taste. Stir vinaigrette into salad.

4 Toast sesame seeds in a frying pan over medium heat until golden, stirring occasionally. Transfer to a plate; set aside to cool. Combine sour cream and sambal oelek.

5 Taste salad, adding salt and remaining 1 tablespoon rice vinegar, if necessary. Spoon salad onto serving plates. Top with a little sour cream mixture. Sprinkle with sesame seeds and chives.

to prepare lemon grass

1 Remove outside woody layers from lemon grass and cut off root.

2 Trim woody ends from leaves. Wash lemon grass and pat dry with paper towel.

3 Cut tender leaves crosswise in fine strips or chop finely. Or, grind them to a fine paste.

mixed salad with ham

250 g (8 oz) smoked ham

1²⁄₃ cups (200 g/7 oz) frozen peas

salt

2 medium carrots (about 250 g/8 oz)

2 small cucumbers

½ cup (100 g/4 oz) drained pickled onions

2 large tomatoes, cored and diced

100 g (4 oz) lamb's lettuce (corn salad)

alfalfa or mung bean sprouts or mustard
    cress, for garnish

creamy dressing

3 tablespoons mayonnaise

²⁄₃ cup (170 g/6 oz) Greek-style yogurt

1 teaspoon Dijon mustard

2 tablespoons lemon juice

pinch of sugar

salt and freshly ground black pepper

serves 4

preparation 25 minutes

cooking 5 minutes

----

per serving *1151 kilojoules/275 calories, 19 g protein,*
12 g total fat, 4 g saturated fat, 49 mg cholesterol,
22 g carbohydrate, 7 g fibre

1 Trim excess fat from ham; cut ham into small cubes.
Cook peas in lightly salted boiling water for 5 minutes.
Drain, reserving cooking liquid. Leave peas to cool.

2 Coarsely grate carrots. Quarter cucumbers lengthwise,
scoop out seeds with a small spoon and cut flesh into small
pieces. Cut pickled onions in half. Place carrots, cucumbers,
pickled onions, tomatoes and peas in a bowl.

3 To make creamy dressing, whisk mayonnaise, yogurt,
mustard, lemon juice, sugar and 3 tablespoons reserved
cooking liquid in a bowl. Add salt and pepper to taste.

4 Stir dressing into salad. Distribute among serving bowls.
Add lamb's lettuce and alfalfa sprouts.

cook's tip

If lamb's lettuce (corn salad) is not
available, use 50 g (2 oz) rocket
(arugula) or watercress leaves or
a mixture of the two to give this
salad a distinctive peppery taste.

ham salad with grated vegetables

❋ Dice 250 g (8 oz) lean ham. Grate 3 medium carrots. Peel 1 small
celeriac (celery root) and grate. Cut 1 thin leek in half lengthwise; slice
into narrow strips. Finely dice 4 small gherkins. Place in a serving bowl.

❋ Whisk 100 g (4 oz) whipping cream, 3 tablespoons light sour cream,
1 tablespoon olive oil, 2 tablespoons white wine vinegar, salt and freshly
ground black pepper until combined. Stir into salad. Chill, covered, 2 hours.
Serve sprinkled with 2 tablespoons finely chopped fresh parsley leaves.

mixed salad with ham

ham, egg and asparagus salad

500 g (1 lb) white or green asparagus
1 lemon, cut in half
salt
1 teaspoon sugar
350 g (12 oz) smoked ham, in one piece
3 tablespoons light mayonnaise
²⁄₃ cup (170 g/6 oz) yogurt
1 tablespoon vegetable oil
3 tablespoons chopped fresh chervil
   or flat-leaf parsley
freshly ground black pepper
2 medium eggs, hard-boiled
1 heart cos (romaine) lettuce

serves 4
preparation 40 minutes
cooking 30 minutes

- -

per serving *1211 kilojoules/289 calories, 25 g protein,*
17 g total fat, 5 g saturated fat, 163 mg cholesterol,
9 g carbohydrate, 4 g fibre

1 Trim asparagus and peel (*see below*). Cut into short pieces. Thinly slice one lemon half. Squeeze juice from other half.

2 Bring a large saucepan of salted water to a boil with sugar and lemon slices. Add asparagus. Cook over medium heat, 15 minutes for white and 8 minutes for green, or until crisp-tender. Drain and leave to cool.

3 Trim excess fat from ham. Cut ham into wide strips. Place in a bowl with asparagus.

4 To make dressing, whisk mayonnaise, yogurt, oil and 1 tablespoon lemon juice in a bowl. Add chervil and salt and pepper to taste. Stir dressing into asparagus and ham.

5 Peel eggs and cut into eighths. Arrange lettuce leaves on individual plates. Add asparagus and ham and garnish with egg slices.

to peel asparagus

1 Wash white or green asparagus and trim the ends.

2 Peel white asparagus from the top, just below spear head, down to the base. Peel a very thin layer from the top and a thicker one at the base.

3 Green asparagus is less woody and seldom requires peeling. If you choose to do so, peel only the lower half.

chicken with mixed salad greens

2 skinless chicken breast fillets (about
   300 g/10 oz in total)

1 large clove garlic, crushed

1 head oak leaf lettuce

1 small head curly endive (frisée) lettuce

1 head treviso or round radicchio

2 tablespoons butter

salt and freshly ground black pepper

1 small lemon

3 spring onions (scallions), finely sliced

250 g (8 oz) button mushrooms,
   thinly sliced

dressing

½ cup (125 g/4 oz) light sour cream

½ cup (125 g/4 oz) yogurt

1 tablespoon vegetable oil

1 tablespoon white wine vinegar

1 teaspoon Dijon mustard

salt and freshly ground black pepper

serves 4

preparation + chilling 1 hour 15 minutes

cooking 5 minutes

----

*per serving 1548 kilojoules/370 calories, 31 g protein,
23 g total fat, 11 g saturated fat, 114 mg cholesterol,
8 g carbohydrate, 5 g fibre*

1 Cut chicken into strips. Place chicken and garlic in a bowl. Stir to combine. Chill, covered, 1 hour. Cut or tear oak leaf lettuce, curly endive and radicchio into small pieces. Place in a large bowl.

2 Heat butter in a nonstick pan over medium heat. Cook chicken until golden brown and cooked through, about 5 minutes. Add salt and pepper to taste.

3 To make dressing, whisk sour cream, yogurt, oil, vinegar and mustard in a bowl until combined. Add salt and pepper to taste. Stir dressing into salad greens. Distribute salad greens among serving plates.

4 Peel thin strips of rind from lemon. Place chicken, spring onions, mushrooms and lemon rind on top of salad greens.

cook's tip

*This simple salad is easily varied.
Try adding thin strips of pancetta
cooked over medium heat in a pan
until crisp. Or, sprinkle salad with
pine nuts just before serving.*

tarragon chicken salad

2 skinless chicken breast fillets (about 300 g/10 oz in total)

350 ml (12 fl oz) salt-reduced chicken or vegetable stock (broth)

2 long sprigs tarragon

1 small lemon

3 black peppercorns

2 tablespoons tahini (sesame paste)

salt and freshly ground black pepper

1 medium head witlof (Belgian endive/chicory)

150 g (5 oz) baby spinach leaves

2 large oranges, peeled and segmented

½ cup (45 g/2 oz) flaked almonds, toasted

serves 4

preparation 20 minutes

cooking 20 minutes

----

per serving 1274 kilojoules/304 calories, 30 g protein, 15 g total fat, 2 g saturated fat, 64 mg cholesterol, 10 g carbohydrate, 5 g fibre

1 Place chicken in a single layer in a shallow pan. Cover with stock. Remove leaves from tarragon sprigs; set aside. Lightly crush stalks with a rolling pin, then add to pan. Using a vegetable peeler, remove a wide strip of rind from lemon. Add to pan with peppercorns.

2 Place pan over moderate heat and bring stock to a boil. Reduce heat to a simmer, cover pan and cook 15 minutes, or until chicken is cooked through. Remove chicken from pan with a slotted spoon; leave to cool. Strain stock and reserve. Discard stalks, rind and peppercorns.

3 To make dressing, whisk tahini with 4 tablespoons reserved stock. Add another 1 to 2 tablespoons if mixture is too thick. Squeeze juice from lemon; stir into dressing. Chop enough tarragon leaves to make 1 tablespoon. Add to dressing. Add salt and pepper to taste.

4 Slice witlof diagonally into narrow pieces. Place on a large serving platter with spinach leaves. Add orange segments and toasted almonds. Slice chicken into wide strips and add to salad. Spoon on dressing.

health guide

Chicken is an excellent source of protein and provides many B vitamins. Removing the skin reduces the fat content considerably, as most of the fat in chicken is found directly beneath the skin.

cook's tip

The combination of tarragon and chicken is a classic. Tarragon has a pronounced aniseed taste. If you are not fond of it, try thyme or rosemary instead.

chinese chicken salad

250 g (8 oz) spaghetti or linguine

2 tablespoons soy sauce

1 tablespoon rice vinegar

3 teaspoons sesame oil

1 teaspoon sugar

1 teaspoon ground ginger

pinch of salt

2 cooked skinless chicken breast fillets
(about 300 g/10 oz in total), shredded

2 medium carrots, cut into thin strips

1 medium red capsicum (bell pepper),
cut into thin strips

2 spring onions (scallions), finely sliced

serves 4

preparation 20 minutes

cooking 15 minutes

- -

*per serving 1502 kilojoules/359 calories, 31 g protein,
7 g total fat, 1 g saturated fat, 64 mg cholesterol,
42 g carbohydrate, 5 g fibre*

1 Cook pasta in plenty of lightly salted boiling water until al dente, following package instructions. Drain, rinse under cold running water and leave to cool.

2 Combine soy sauce, vinegar, oil, sugar, ginger and salt in a large bowl. Add chicken, carrots, capsicum and spring onions; toss to combine. Add pasta; stir gently to combine.

cook's tip

*Shredded cooked chicken may be
marinated in the soy sauce mixture
for up to 2 days in the refrigerator.
Alternatively, use cooked skinless
turkey breast.*

chicken salad with avocado

2 shallots, quartered

$\frac{1}{2}$ cup (125 ml/4 fl oz) dry white wine

4 tablespoons lemon juice

4 black peppercorns

pinch of salt

2 skinless chicken breast fillets (about 300 g/10 oz in total)

2 large avocados

2 small celery stalks

1 small Lebanese (Mediterranean) cucumber

$\frac{2}{3}$ cup (170 g/6 oz) light sour cream

1 tablespoon whole-grain mustard

1 tablespoon sunflower or peanut oil

2 teaspoons white wine vinegar

pinch of sugar

salt and freshly ground black pepper

pinch of cayenne pepper

a few sorrel leaves, optional

serves 4

preparation 15 minutes

cooking 20 minutes

----

per serving *2174 kilojoules/519 calories, 28 g protein,*
43 g total fat, 13 g saturated fat, 91 mg cholesterol,
4 g carbohydrate, 2 g fibre

1 Place shallots, wine, 1 tablespoon lemon juice, $\frac{1}{2}$ cup (125 ml/4 fl oz) water, peppercorns and salt in a pan; bring to a boil. Add chicken fillets and return to a boil. Reduce heat to low, cover pan and cook chicken 15 minutes, or until cooked through. Remove pan from heat. Leave chicken to cool in cooking liquid.

2 Halve avocados and remove seeds. Remove 4 teaspoons of flesh from each avocado half. Dice, place in a bowl. Mix with 1 tablespoon lemon juice to prevent browning. Drizzle cut surface of avocado halves with 1 tablespoon lemon juice.

3 Dice celery. Peel cucumber, cut in half lengthwise and remove seeds with a small spoon. Dice cucumber. Drain chicken and cut into small cubes. Add chicken, celery and cucumber to diced avocado and stir gently to combine.

4 To make dressing, whisk sour cream, mustard, oil, vinegar, sugar and remaining 1 tablespoon lemon juice in a small bowl. Add salt and pepper to taste. Stir dressing into chicken and vegetables. Spoon mixture into avocado halves.

5 Dust avocados with a little cayenne pepper. Cut sorrel leaves into thin strips, if using, and scatter over avocados. (Sorrel has a distinctive lemony taste.)

chicken salad with cucumber and watercress

A dressing based on sour cream and yogurt goes well with the fresh taste of crisp slices of cucumber and sprigs of peppery watercress.

1 sprig rosemary

1 clove garlic, roughly chopped

2 skinless chicken breast fillets (about 300 g/10 oz in total)

2 tablespoons lime juice

salt and freshly ground black pepper

3 small Lebanese (Mediterranean) cucumbers

150 g (5 oz) watercress

3 tablespoons finely chopped fresh chervil

3 tablespoons finely chopped fresh dill

3 tablespoons finely chopped chives

2 tablespoons sunflower or peanut oil

mustard and lemon dressing

½ cup (125 g/4 oz) light sour cream

½ cup (125 g/4 oz) yogurt

50 ml (2 fl oz) milk

½ teaspoon tarragon or other herb mustard

1 tablespoon lemon-flavoured olive oil

2 tablespoons lemon juice

salt and freshly ground black pepper

serves 4

preparation + chilling 1 hour 15 minutes

cooking 12 minutes

----

per serving 1504 kilojoules/359 calories, 28 g protein, 24 g total fat, 7 g saturated fat, 89 mg cholesterol, 6 g carbohydrate, 3 g fibre

1 Roughly chop rosemary leaves and combine with garlic in a bowl. Add chicken; turn to coat. Drizzle with lime juice and sprinkle with salt and pepper. Chill, covered, 1 hour.

2 Peel fine strips of skin lengthwise from cucumber. Slice cucumbers thinly. Divide watercress into small sprigs.

3 To make mustard and lemon dressing, whisk sour cream, yogurt, milk, mustard, oil and lemon juice in a large bowl until combined. Add salt and pepper to taste. Add cucumber, watercress and herbs to bowl. Stir to coat completely with dressing.

4 Heat oil in a nonstick frying pan over medium heat. Add chicken and cook, turning occasionally, 8 to 10 minutes, until cooked through. Remove from pan and set aside for a few minutes.

5 Arrange cucumber and watercress salad on individual plates. Cut chicken crosswise into thick slices; add to salad.

chicken and pineapple salad with curry dressing

1 ready-to-cook chicken (about 1.6 kg/3 lb)

2 medium onions, roughly chopped

2 celery stalks, roughly chopped

2 medium carrots (about 250 g/8 oz), roughly chopped

1 bay leaf

2 teaspoons salt

1 teaspoon whole black peppercorns

½ small sweet pineapple (about 500 g/1 lb)

3 mandarins, tangerines or small oranges

2 thin leeks

heart of 1 cos (romaine) lettuce

lemon balm leaves, for garnish

curry dressing

4 tablespoons light mayonnaise

½ cup (125 g/4 oz) yogurt

4 tablespoons orange juice

2 tablespoons lemon juice

2 teaspoons mild curry powder

pinch of ground ginger

pinch of cayenne pepper

salt and freshly ground black pepper

serves 4
preparation 30 minutes
cooking 1 hour 15 minutes

----

per serving 1729 kilojoules/413 calories, 43 g protein, 15 g total fat, 4 g saturated fat, 149 mg cholesterol, 25 g carbohydrate, 7 g fibre

1 Place chicken, chopped vegetables, bay leaf, salt and peppercorns in a large saucepan. Cover with water. Bring to a boil. Skim off surface with a slotted spoon. Cook, partly covered, over low heat 1 hour 15 minutes. Remove pan from heat. Leave chicken to cool in cooking liquid.

2 Separate chicken meat from carcass and chop flesh into small pieces; place in a bowl.

3 Trim pineapple, discard core and cut fruit into small pieces. Peel and segment 2 mandarins. Add pineapple and mandarin pieces to chicken. Cut leeks in half lengthwise and cut into very fine strips. Add to bowl.

4 To make curry dressing, whisk mayonnaise, yogurt, orange juice and lemon juice until combined. Stir in curry powder, ginger and cayenne pepper. Add salt and pepper to taste. Stir dressing into chicken and pineapple mixture.

5 Peel and slice remaining mandarin crosswise. Tear or cut lettuce into wide strips. Distribute among serving bowls and top with chicken salad. Garnish with mandarin slices and lemon balm leaves.

cook's tip

Curry dressing is a versatile recipe. Use 4 tablespoons lime juice in place of orange juice and omit the lemon juice. Or, use a hot curry powder and omit the ginger.

chicken kebab salad with peanut sauce

400 g (14 oz) skinless chicken breast fillets

small piece fresh ginger

1 clove garlic, crushed

3 tablespoons salt-reduced soy sauce

1 tablespoon lemon juice

3 tablespoons sunflower or peanut oil

½ teaspoon sambal oelek or Chinese chili paste

4 small fresh red chilies

1 medium red capsicum (bell pepper)

small head baby bok choy

150 g (5 oz) mung bean sprouts

2 spring onions (scallions), thinly sliced

3 tablespoons lime juice

salt and freshly ground black pepper

peanut sauce

3 tablespoons crunchy or smooth peanut butter

1 teaspoon soft brown sugar

1 can (165 ml/6 fl oz) light coconut milk

1 tablespoon white wine vinegar

2 tablespoons salt-reduced soy sauce

½ teaspoon sambal oelek

serves 4

preparation + chilling 1 hour 30 minutes

cooking 10 minutes

----

per serving *2170 kilojoules/518 calories, 42 g protein, 32 g total fat, 9 g saturated fat, 85 mg cholesterol, 13 g carbohydrate, 6 g fibre*

1 Cut chicken breast fillets into large cubes. Peel ginger and grate finely. Combine ginger, garlic, soy sauce, lemon juice, 1 tablespoon oil and sambal oelek in a bowl. Add chicken and turn to coat. Chill, covered, 1 hour.

2 To make chili flowers, using a sharp knife, make 6 cuts from the stem to the tip of each chili; do not cut through the base (*see below right*). Place chilies in a bowl of iced water until ready to serve.

3 Halve capsicum and cut into thin strips. Cut bok choy into thin strips. Arrange capsicum, bok choy, mung beans and spring onions in serving bowls. Whisk lime juice with remaining 2 tablespoons oil. Add salt and pepper to taste. Drizzle over vegetables.

4 Preheat grill (broiler) or barbecue to medium-high heat. Remove chicken from marinade and thread onto 12 skewers. Cook chicken about 6 minutes, turning occasionally.

5 To make peanut sauce, place all ingredients in a pan over low heat. Cook 5 minutes or until sauce thickens.

6 Place kebabs on top of salad. Coat with peanut sauce, serving remainder separately. Remove chilies from iced water and add to salad.

to make chili flowers

1 Make 6 cuts in each chili, from the stem to the tip; do not cut through the base. The chilies should still be intact.

2 Place chilies in iced water. Gradually, the individual strips will curl outwards.

3 Drain chilies. Remove seeds, if wished. Chili flowers are usually used as a garnish and are not eaten, so the heat of the chilies is not of concern.

chicken liver and apple salad

chicken liver and apple salad

400 g (14 oz) ready-to-cook chicken livers

½ cup (125 ml/4 fl oz) dry red wine

2 tablespoons balsamic vinegar

1 bay leaf

1 sprig thyme

1 small head oak leaf lettuce

3 tablespoons vegetable oil

2 medium onions, sliced into thin rings

2 medium tart apples

1 tablespoon butter

1 tablespoon lemon juice

3 tablespoons dry white wine

pinch of ground aniseed

1 tablespoon sultanas (golden raisins)

salt and freshly ground black pepper

serves 4

preparation + chilling 1 hour 30 minutes

cooking 10 minutes

----

per serving *1611 kilojoules/385 calories, 28 g protein,*
24 g total fat, 6 g saturated fat, 639 mg cholesterol,
13 g carbohydrate, 3 g fibre

1 Place chicken livers in a bowl. Add red wine, 1 tablespoon vinegar, bay leaf and thyme. Chill, covered, 1 hour.

2 Tear lettuce into small pieces and arrange on a serving plates. Heat 2 tablespoons oil in a nonstick pan. Add onions and fry until golden brown. Remove from pan; keep warm.

3 Peel apples and slice thinly. Heat butter in a saucepan over medium heat, add apple slices and cook briefly. Add lemon juice, wine, ground aniseed and sultanas. Cover pan; cook another 3 minutes or until apples have softened but still hold their shape. Remove from heat.

4 Remove chicken livers from bowl with a slotted spoon, reserving marinade. Pat livers dry on paper towel. Heat remaining 1 tablespoon oil in a nonstick pan over high heat and cook chicken livers on all sides, 2 to 3 minutes. Add salt and pepper to taste. Place chicken livers on top of lettuce.

5 Pour reserved marinade into pan and bring to a boil. Add remaining 1 tablespoon vinegar and salt and pepper to taste. Drizzle over salad. Arrange apples and onions on top.

warm chicken livers with green beans and tomatoes

✳ Marinate 400 g (14 oz) chicken livers as in main recipe. Trim 500 g (1 lb) green beans; cut into short lengths. Cook in vegetable stock (broth) to cover, about 10 minutes. Drain and let cool. Dice 1 medium red onion. Drain 8 oil-packed sun-dried tomato halves and chop finely.

✳ Mix beans, onions, tomatoes and 1 tablespoon chopped fresh oregano in a serving bowl. Whisk 2 tablespoons olive oil, 2 tablespoons balsamic vinegar, salt and pepper and pour over salad. Heat 3 tablespoons olive oil in a nonstick pan. Cook chicken livers 2 to 3 minutes. Add to salad.

cheese, sausage and potato salad

2 thick slices gouda cheese
6 frankfurters (hot dogs), thinly sliced
1 orange and 1 red capsicum (bell pepper)
3 medium, unpeeled, cooked potatoes
1 can (420 g/15 oz) corn, drained and rinsed
8 small gherkins in vinegar, thinly sliced
2 tablespoons vegetable oil
2 tablespoons white wine vinegar
2 tablespoons vinegar from jar of gherkins
½ cup (125 g/4 oz) yogurt
pinch of sugar
¼ teaspoon ground sweet paprika
salt and freshly ground black pepper
½ cup (30 g/1 oz) finely chopped chives

serves 4
preparation 35 minutes
marinating 1 hour

------

per serving 2102 *kilojoules/502 calories, 22 g protein,*
32 g total fat, 11 g saturated fat, 67 mg cholesterol,
30 g carbohydrate, 6 g fibre

1 Cut cheese into strips. Place in a bowl with frankfurters. Halve capsicums and cut into small cubes. Peel potatoes and cut into small cubes. Add capsicums, potatoes, corn and gherkins to bowl and mix well.

2 Whisk oil, white wine vinegar and vinegar from gherkins in a bowl. Stir in yogurt, sugar and ground paprika. Add salt and pepper to taste. Stir into salad. Chill, covered, 1 hour.

3 Taste salad just before serving. Add more salt and pepper to taste. Sprinkle with chives.

cook's tip

Try to cook potatoes a day ahead; the flavour will be improved. About 2 cups (380 g/13 oz) cooked rice may be used in this salad in place of the potatoes.

sausage, potato and radish salad

✳ Cut 6 cooked turkey or chicken sausages into thin rounds and place in a serving bowl. Peel and dice 500 g (1 lb) waxy potatoes cooked the previous day (see Cook's Tip). Slice 1 small white onion into thin rings. Cut 12 large red radishes into quarters. Add potatoes, onions and radishes to bowl.

✳ Whisk 3 tablespoons balsamic vinegar, 3 tablespoons vegetable oil, 1 teaspoon whole-grain mustard and salt and pepper to taste. Stir into salad. Add 2 tablespoons finely chopped fresh parsley.

cheese, sausage and potato salad

turkey and mushroom salad

Use turkey or chicken in the following three salads.
We suggest using turkey or chicken tenderloins.
Other cuts can be used but may need longer cooking.

250 g (8 oz) turkey or chicken tenderloins

2 tablespoons butter

salt and freshly ground black pepper

12 large white mushrooms

½ cup (125 ml/4 fl oz) dry white wine

1 bay leaf

1 sprig rosemary

2 tablespoons vegetable oil

3 tablespoons raspberry vinegar

2 tablespoons crème fraîche or
   sour cream

1 head oak leaf lettuce

125 g (4 oz) fresh raspberries

serves 6
preparation 10 minutes
cooking 15 minutes

------

per serving 922 kilojoules/220 calories, 12 g protein,
17 g total fat, 7 g saturated fat, 50 mg cholesterol,
3 g carbohydrate, 3 g fibre

1 Cut turkey into small pieces. Heat 1 tablespoon butter in a nonstick pan over medium heat. Add turkey; cook 2 to 3 minutes or until golden and cooked through. Season with salt and pepper; transfer to a plate.

2 Wipe mushrooms with paper towel. Discard stalks. Heat remaining 1 tablespoon butter in pan over medium heat. Add mushrooms, open side up, and cook 3 minutes. Add wine, bay leaf, rosemary and a generous grinding of pepper. Cook, covered, another 5 minutes.

3 Transfer mushrooms to a plate. Cook pan juices over high heat until reduced to one third their original volume. Discard rosemary and bay leaf. Leave pan juices to cool.

4 Pour pan juices into a large bowl. Whisk in oil, vinegar and crème fraîche. Add salt and pepper to taste. Finely chop 4 lettuce leaves. Add to bowl with turkey; stir to combine.

5 Spread remaining whole lettuce leaves on serving plates. Place mushrooms on top, open sides up, and fill with turkey salad. Garnish with raspberries.

raspberries

Raspberries are an excellent source of vitamin C. They are also high in pectin, a form of soluble fibre that helps control blood cholesterol levels. In addition, they provide bioflavonoids that may protect against cancer.

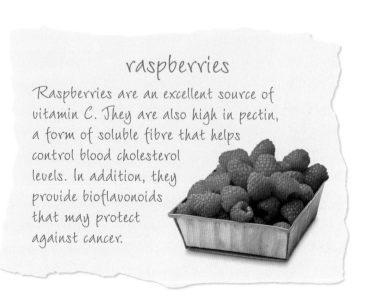

turkey and fruit salad

1 small head iceberg lettuce

1 head treviso or round radicchio

1 small cantaloupe or honeydew melon
  (about 500 g/1 lb)

250 g (8 oz) red seedless grapes

250 g (8 oz) green seedless grapes

1 tablespoon butter

500 g (1 lb) turkey tenderloins or turkey
  breast cutlets, cut into thin strips

salt and freshly ground black pepper

1 tablespoon fresh lemon thyme leaves

¼ cup (25 g/1 oz) walnuts

dressing

2 tablespoons crème fraîche or
  sour cream

2 tablespoons walnut oil

3 tablespoons lemon juice

salt and freshly ground black pepper

serves 4
preparation 20 minutes
cooking 10 minutes

*per serving 2372 kilojoules/567 calories, 39 g protein,
33 g total fat, 10 g saturated fat, 124 mg cholesterol,
29 g carbohydrate, 5 g fibre*

1 Cut or tear iceberg lettuce and radicchio into small pieces. Arrange on individual serving plates.

2 Halve melon and discard seeds. Scoop out flesh with a melon baller. Cut grapes in half. Scatter melon balls and grapes over salad greens.

3 Heat butter in a nonstick pan over medium heat. Cook turkey until browned and cooked through, about 8 minutes. Season with salt and pepper. Stir in lemon thyme.

4 To make dressing, whisk crème fraîche, oil and lemon juice in a bowl. Add salt and pepper to taste. Drizzle over salad greens. Top with turkey and garnish with walnuts.

health guide

Melons contain pectin, a type of soluble fibre that may help keep blood cholesterol levels in check. Melons may also help protect against cardiovascular disease and some cancers.

turkey with fruit and nuts

2 tablespoons grapeseed or vegetable oil

3 shallots, finely sliced

150 g (5 oz) fresh chanterelle or white
  mushrooms, finely sliced

3 tablespoons finely chopped fresh parsley

1 tablespoon lemon juice

salt and freshly ground black pepper

300 g (10 oz) smoked turkey breast, sliced

2 small heads treviso or round radicchio

3 ripe but firm plums (about 200 g/7 oz),
  halved and stoned

$\frac{1}{4}$ cup (25 g/1 oz) walnuts

cheese dressing

100 g (4 oz) creamy goat milk cheese

3 to 4 tablespoons milk

1 tablespoon red wine vinegar

salt and freshly ground black pepper

serves 4
preparation 15 minutes
cooking 10 minutes

------

*per serving 1568 kilojoules/375 calories, 32 g protein,
23 g total fat, 6 g saturated fat, 62 mg cholesterol,
11 g carbohydrate, 4 g fibre*

1 Heat oil in nonstick pan over medium heat. Add shallots;
cook until transparent. Add mushrooms; cook 3 minutes,
stirring. Add parsley and lemon juice. Season to taste with
salt and pepper. Remove from heat. Stir in turkey.

2 Tear or cut radicchio into small pieces and use to line a
serving platter. Top with turkey and mushroom mixture. Cut
plums into thin slices and add to salad.

3 To make cheese dressing, beat cheese, 3 tablespoons
milk and vinegar in a bowl until well combined. If mixture
is not sufficiently runny, add remaining 1 tablespoon milk.
Add salt and pepper to taste. Drizzle dressing over salad.
Garnish with walnuts.

cook's tip

*If plums are not in season, use
fresh fruits, such as apricots or
pears. Pecans, blanched almonds
or pistachios or a mixture of nuts
may be used in place of walnuts.*

tuna and green bean salad (page 247)

fish
and seafood
salads

The crunch of salad greens and the
succulence of shellfish and fresh
or canned fish come together in a
range of colourful salads ranging
from simple to sophisticated. Fish
and seafood need little preparation
and can be quickly steamed, baked,
grilled or poached. They are good
for heart health if eaten regularly.

italian seafood salad

Insalata di mare is a showcase for top-quality seafood. For maximum flavour, use only the freshest produce, not frozen.

4 tablespoons lemon juice

½ cup (125 ml/4 fl oz) white wine vinegar

5 black peppercorns

½ teaspoon fennel seeds

½ teaspoon salt

300 g (10 oz) gutted and cleaned baby squid or calamari

1 kg (2 lb) mussels, scrubbed and debearded

1½ cups (375 ml/13 fl oz) dry white wine

1 bay leaf

300 g (10 oz) medium, cooked prawns (shrimp), peeled and deveined, leaving tails intact

2 celery stalks, thinly sliced

2 roma (plum) tomatoes, finely diced

1 medium red onion, finely diced

2 cloves garlic, finely chopped

3 tablespoons finely chopped fresh flat-leaf parsley

heart of 1 cos (romaine) lettuce

vinaigrette

5 tablespoons olive oil

3 tablespoons lemon juice

pinch of cayenne pepper

salt and freshly ground black pepper

serves 4
preparation 30 minutes
cooking 30 minutes

per serving 2010 kilojoules/480 calories, 48 g protein, 27 g total fat, 4 g saturated fat, 400 mg cholesterol, 10 g carbohydrate, 3 g fibre

1 Bring 2 cups (500 ml/16 fl oz) water to a boil with lemon juice, vinegar, peppercorns, fennel seeds and salt. Add squid and cook over low heat until tender, about 20 minutes. Leave squid in liquid to cool.

2 Leave mussels in a bowl of cold water for 15 minutes, then strain. Discard open mussels. Rinse remaining mussels in cold water until all traces of sand are removed.

3 In a large saucepan, bring white wine and bay leaf to a boil. Add mussels, cover and cook for about 10 minutes until they open. Strain and discard any mussels that remain closed. Remove flesh from open shells. Set aside to let cool.

4 Remove squid from cooking liquid and cut into small pieces. Combine squid, mussels and prawns in a bowl. Mix in celery, tomatoes, onion, garlic and parsley. Place lettuce leaves on individual bowls or plates.

5 To make vinaigrette, whisk oil, lemon juice and cayenne pepper until combined; add salt and pepper to taste. Drizzle over salad, toss lightly and spoon onto lettuce.

mussels

Choose mussels that are firmly closed or that close when tapped sharply or squeezed. Any open mussels must be discarded as they are not fit for eating.

white fish salad with olive vinaigrette

500 g (1 lb) blue-eye cod or other
   firm white fish fillets

1 tablespoon olive oil

½ teaspoon black peppercorns

1 sprig rosemary, 2 sprigs oregano,
   2 sprigs thyme and 1 bay leaf tied in
   a bunch

1 small lemon, thinly sliced

3 large tomatoes

6 marinated artichoke hearts

4 tablespoons finely chopped fresh
   flat-leaf parsley

olive vinaigrette

1 tablespoon olive oil

1 tablespoon balsamic vinegar

1 tablespoon lemon juice

2 cloves garlic, finely chopped

15 pitted green olives and 15 pitted
   black olives, finely chopped

½ teaspoon dried thyme

½ teaspoon dried oregano

salt and freshly ground black pepper

serves 4

preparation 35 minutes

cooking 5 to 8 minutes

*per serving 983 kilojoules/235 calories, 16 g protein,
12 g total fat, 2 g saturated fat, 41 mg cholesterol,
14 g carbohydrate, 4 g fibre*

1 Cut fish fillets into small pieces. Brush a steamer basket with oil and add fish. Place peppercorns, bunch of herbs and lemon slices in a large saucepan.

2 Pour in water to a depth of about two fingers, taking care water does not touch fish in steamer basket. Insert steamer basket and bring water to a boil. Cover fish and cook 5 to 8 minutes, depending on its thickness. Remove steamer basket from saucepan and let fish pieces cool in it.

3 Halve tomatoes, remove seeds and slice into rounds. Cut artichokes into small pieces. Arrange tomatoes, artichokes, parsley and fish pieces on a large platter.

4 To make olive vinaigrette, whisk oil, vinegar, lemon juice and garlic until combined. Fold in olives and herbs; add salt and pepper to taste. Drizzle over salad.

cook's tip

For maximum flavour, marinate the fish pieces in the vinaigrette for up to 2 hours. Then combine with the rest of the ingredients.

white fish salad
with olive vinaigrette

white fish salad with fennel and sun-dried tomatoes

✳ Cut 500 g (1 lb) firm white fish fillets into pieces and cook as for main recipe. Slice 2 small fennel bulbs finely and arrange on a platter. Spread fish on top. Sprinkle with 1 teaspoon fennel seeds.

✳ Drain 8 sun-dried tomato halves in oil, chop finely and sprinkle over salad. Whisk 2 tablespoons lemon juice with 4 tablespoons olive oil and drizzle over salad. Sprinkle with salt and coarsely ground pepper.

tabouleh with fish in lemon dressing

1 cup (180 g/7 oz) burghul (bulgur wheat)

300 g (10 oz) orange roughy or other white fish fillets

1 small lemon, thinly sliced

2 sprigs parsley

5 black peppercorns

1 medium cucumber, seeds removed, diced

4 spring onions (scallions), thinly sliced

250 g (8 oz) cherry tomatoes, halved

2 tablespoons chopped fresh coriander (cilantro)

2 tablespoons chopped fresh mint

2 tablespoons chopped fresh parsley

mint sprigs, for garnish

lemon dressing

2 tablespoons olive oil

2 tablespoons red wine vinegar

2 tablespoons lemon juice

1 tablespoon grated lemon peel

1 teaspoon Dijon mustard

1 clove garlic, crushed

salt and freshly ground black pepper

serves 4

preparation + standing 1 hour

cooking 5 minutes

chilling 1 to 2 hours

per serving 1228 kilojoules/293 calories, 18 g protein, 11 g total fat, 2 g saturated fat, 14 mg cholesterol, 31 g carbohydrate, 8 g fibre

1 Place burghul in a large heatproof bowl and add 2 cups (500 ml/16 fl oz) boiling water. Let stand 45 minutes, or until grains are tender and water has been absorbed.

2 Meanwhile, place fish fillets in a large pan, add lemon slices, parsley sprigs and peppercorns and cold water to cover. Bring to a boil. Reduce heat and simmer, covered, 5 minutes, or until fish is opaque and flakes easily.

3 Remove fish from liquid and set aside to cool. Use a fork to separate fish into large flakes.

4 Place burghul in a serving bowl and add cucumber, spring onions, tomatoes and chopped herbs. Gently mix in fish, taking care not to break it up.

5 To make lemon dressing, whisk all ingredients in a bowl. Pour dressing over salad and mix gently to combine.

6 Chill salad, covered, 1 to 2 hours to allow flavours to develop. Check seasoning before serving and garnish with mint sprigs.

cook's tip

Orange roughy is a white-fleshed fish that is similar to cod. You may substitute any firm white fish for orange roughy, or use drained and flaked tuna canned in water.

vietnamese fish salad

500 g (1 lb) whiting or other white fish fillets, skinned

2 cups (500 ml/16 fl oz) rice vinegar

2 medium onions, finely sliced

1 tablespoon white sugar

1 teaspoon salt

2 tablespoons shelled raw peanuts

2 tablespoons white rice

2 tablespoons finely shredded fresh mint

1 fresh red chili, seeded and finely chopped

extra shredded fresh mint leaves and thin slivers of red chili, for garnish

serves 4

preparation + marinating 1 hour 40 minutes

cooking 5 to 7 minutes

----

per serving 905 kilojoules/216 calories, 28 g protein, 4 g total fat, 1 g saturated fat, 119 mg cholesterol, 14 g carbohydrate, 2 g fibre

1 Remove small bones from fish; cut fillets in half crosswise and slice into long, thin strips. Place in a large bowl with about 300 ml (½ pint/10 fl oz) rice vinegar, making sure fish is covered with liquid. Marinate 1 hour.

2 Place onions, sugar, salt and remaining vinegar in a bowl. Stir until sugar and salt have dissolved. Leave to soak 30 minutes.

3 Crush peanuts finely. Dry-fry in a heavy nonstick pan over low heat 2 to 3 minutes until evenly browned. Remove from pan and set aside.

4 Add rice to pan and toast 3 to 4 minutes until golden brown all over, then crush finely.

5 Remove marinated fish and onion from vinegar. Place in a large bowl and add mint and chili. Toss gently to combine; sprinkle toasted crushed peanuts and rice on top and toss again. Garnish with extra mint and chili.

tuna and green bean salad

3 cloves garlic, peeled

250 g (8 oz) green beans, halved

6 small red potatoes (about 375 g/13 oz), halved

2 tablespoons balsamic or red wine vinegar

2 tablespoons low-fat mayonnaise

1 tablespoon olive oil

pinch of salt

½ cup (30 g/1 oz) fresh basil leaves

250 g (8 oz) cherry tomatoes, halved

1 can (425 g/15 oz) water-packed tuna, drained

6 cos (romaine) lettuce leaves

⅓ cup (50 g/2 oz) black olives, for garnish

serves 4

preparation 15 minutes

cooking 20 minutes

per serving 1094 kilojoules/261 calories, 26 g protein, 9 g total fat, 2 g saturated fat, 48 mg cholesterol, 19 g carbohydrate, 5 g fibre

1 Blanch garlic in a large saucepan of boiling water for 3 minutes. Transfer garlic to a food processor or blender; set aside. Add beans to boiling water and cook 4 minutes, or until crisp-tender. Remove beans, rinse under cold water and drain. Add potatoes to pan and cook 12 minutes, or until tender; drain.

2 Add vinegar, mayonnaise, oil and salt to garlic in food processor and purée. Add basil and 2 tablespoons water and purée again.

3 Transfer dressing to a large bowl. Add tomatoes, beans, potatoes and tuna, tossing to coat. Tear lettuce into small pieces. Add lettuce and toss again. Garnish with olives.

tuna

Remarkably lean for a fish with so much flavour, tuna provides good amounts of healthy omega-3 fatty acids. It is also an excellent source of some B vitamins.

tuna and roasted capsicum salad

tuna and roasted capsicum salad

The richness of the tuna is complemented by the smoky sweetness of roasted capsicum and the crispness of fresh green lettuce.

2 red and 2 yellow capsicums (bell peppers)

1 clove garlic

1 large head green lettuce, such as lollo bionda (green coral)

4 tablespoons olive oil

2 tablespoons white balsamic vinegar

salt and freshly ground black pepper

1 can (180 g/7 oz) tuna in water, drained

1 tablespoon small capers

1 tablespoon lemon juice

½ cup (125 g/4 oz) sour cream

1 tablespoon coarsely chopped fresh parsley, for garnish

serves 4
preparation 30 minutes
cooking 15 minutes

----

per serving 1384 kilojoules/331 calories, 13 g protein, 28 g total fat, 8 g saturated fat, 46 mg cholesterol, 7 g carbohydrate, 3 g fibre

1 Preheat oven to 240°C/475°F. Place whole capsicums on cooking (aluminum) foil on baking tray. Roast 15 minutes, turning halfway through, or until blackened and blistered.

2 Remove capsicums from oven. Place cloth towel soaked in cold water on top. Leave 5 minutes. Peel away skin. Cut into broad strips.

3 Cut garlic in half horizontally and rub cut surface over inside of salad bowl. Tear lettuce into small pieces. Add capsicums and lettuce to bowl.

4 To make vinaigrette, whisk 2 tablespoons oil with vinegar until combined; add salt and pepper to taste.

5 Using a fork, break tuna into small pieces in a bowl. Add capers. Whisk remaining 2 tablespoons oil, lemon juice, sour cream and salt and pepper to taste and stir into tuna.

6 Drizzle vinaigrette on capsicum strips and lettuce. Place on a platter. Add tuna mixture and sprinkle with parsley.

smoked trout and roasted capsicum salad

❋ Prepare capsicums as for main recipe. Mix with vinaigrette and arrange on a platter. Peel 4 large hard-boiled eggs, quarter and add to platter. Cut 200 g (7 oz) smoked trout into strips.

❋ Combine 100 g (4 oz) crème fraîche or light sour cream, 3 tablespoons yogurt, 2 tablespoons lemon juice and herb salt and pepper to taste. Stir in smoked trout and 1 tablespoon finely chopped fresh parsley. Spoon trout mixture over salad.

vegetable salad with tuna

This salad combines frozen and fresh vegetables. Use snow peas (mange-tout) in place of frozen peas, when in season.

1¼ cups (150 g/5 oz) frozen peas

150 g (5 oz) frozen green beans

salt

3 chilled cooked potatoes (waxy variety), unpeeled

1 yellow and 1 green capsicum (bell pepper)

1 medium white onion

2 large tomatoes

⅔ cup (100 g/4 oz) green olives stuffed with pimiento

1 small clove garlic, finely chopped

4 tablespoons mayonnaise

1 tablespoon olive oil

2 tablespoons lemon juice

freshly ground black pepper

1 can (180 g/7 oz) water-packed tuna, drained

lemon wedges, to serve

serves 4

preparation 35 to 40 minutes

cooking 15 minutes

per serving 1227 kilojoules/293 calories, 16 g protein, 14 g total fat, 2 g saturated fat, 24 mg cholesterol, 25 g carbohydrate, 9 g fibre

1 Bring ½ cup (125 ml/4 fl oz) water to a boil in a saucepan with ½ teaspoon salt. Add frozen peas and beans, cover and cook 5 minutes. Pour into strainer, reserving liquid. Drain vegetables and let cool.

2 Peel potatoes and cut into small cubes. Trim capsicums and cut into short strips. Slice onion into rings. Halve tomatoes, remove seeds and cut into eighths.

3 Halve olives if desired. Place olives, peas, beans, capsicum strips, onion rings, tomato wedges and diced potatoes in a serving bowl.

4 Combine garlic, mayonnaise, oil, lemon juice and 3 tablespoons of reserved vegetable cooking water. Stir together until smooth. Add salt and pepper to taste.

5 Pour mayonnaise mixture over vegetables. Flake tuna a little. Arrange on vegetables. Serve with lemon wedges.

green beans

Green beans are low in fat, high in dietary fibre and a good source of B vitamins. If using fresh green beans instead of frozen, remove tops, add to a large saucepan of boiling salted water and cook, uncovered, 4 to 6 minutes, until crisp-tender.

vegetable salad with tuna

diced vegetables with tuna

❋ Dice 1 red and 1 yellow capsicum (bell pepper), 3 large tomatoes, 2 Lebanese (Mediterranean) cucumbers, 2 medium carrots and 2 large celery stalks. Arrange on a platter.

❋ Finely dice 1 medium white onion. Drain and flake 1 can (180 g/7 oz) tuna in water or olive oil. Combine with onion. Whisk 2 tablespoons mayonnaise, $1/2$ cup (125 g/4 oz) yogurt, 1 tablespoon sunflower oil and herb salt and pepper to taste. Stir into tuna and onion mixture. Spoon mixture onto vegetables. Sprinkle with chopped fresh parsley.

tuna and egg salad

tuna and egg salad

Canned tuna and egg are a classic salad combination and the sliced onion adds crunch. Use water-packed tuna, if preferred.

2 medium eggs, hard-boiled

2 medium red capsicums (bell peppers)

⅓ cup (50 g/2 oz) green olives stuffed with pimiento

1 large onion

1 small head butter (butterhead) lettuce

1 can (425 g/15 oz) tuna in oil, drained

few sprigs oregano, for garnish

herb vinaigrette

4 tablespoons olive oil

3 tablespoons sherry vinegar

1 clove garlic, crushed

salt and freshly ground black pepper

1 tablespoon each chopped fresh thyme, oregano and flat-leaf parsley

serves 4

preparation 30 minutes

----

per serving *1494 kilojoules/357 calories, 27 g protein,*
25 g total fat, 5 g saturated fat, 154 mg cholesterol,
6 g carbohydrate, 3 g fibre

1 Peel hard-boiled eggs and slice into rounds. Dice capsicums. Slice olives. Cut onion into thin rings. Separate lettuce leaves and use to line serving plates.

2 Arrange eggs, capsicums, onion rings and olives on lettuce leaves. Flake tuna into chunks and add to salad.

3 To make herb vinaigrette, whisk oil, vinegar, garlic and salt and pepper to taste. Stir in chopped herbs .

4 Drizzle vinaigrette over salad. Garnish salad with oregano sprigs.

tuna salad with peas and onions

✳ Cook 1¼ cups (150 g/5 oz) frozen peas in 150 ml (¼ pint/5 fl oz) vegetable stock (broth). Drain and place in a bowl. Cut 1 medium white onion into small cubes. Drain 1 can (425 g/15 oz) water-packed tuna and flake finely. Add onion, tuna and 2 teaspoons small capers to peas.

✳ To make dressing, stir 4 tablespoons mayonnaise and 3 tablespoons yogurt until smooth. Season with salt, white pepper, 1 teaspoon dried Italian herbs and 1 to 2 tablespoons lemon juice. Mix dressing into salad. Arrange salad in small bowls or pile onto slices of pumpernickel bread.

salmon salad with peas and dill

400 g (14 oz) salmon fillet

1 lemon

200 ml (7 fl oz) fish stock (broth)

½ cup (125 ml/4 fl oz) dry white wine

salt and freshly ground black pepper

1⅔ cups (200 g/7 oz) frozen peas

150 ml (¼ pint/5 fl oz) salt-reduced
vegetable stock (broth)

1 small head iceberg lettuce

½ cup (125 g/4 oz) light mayonnaise

½ cup (125 g/4 oz) sour cream

1 teaspoon medium to hot mustard

pinch of sugar

2 tablespoons finely chopped fresh dill

4 dill sprigs, for garnish

serves 4

preparation 30 minutes

cooking 8 to 12 minutes

per serving 1540 kilojoules/368 calories, 24 g protein,
24 g total fat, 11 g saturated fat, 100 mg cholesterol,
12 g carbohydrate, 5 g fibre

1 Slice salmon into small pieces. Cut 4 thin slices from the lemon. Place fish stock, wine, salt, pepper and lemon slices in a saucepan and bring to a boil.

2 Add fish pieces, cover and cook over low heat 3 to 4 minutes. Remove from pan and let cool. Reserve liquid.

3 Place peas and stock in a small saucepan and bring to a boil. Cook peas 3 to 5 minutes; do not overcook. Drain and let cool.

4 Tear lettuce leaves into small pieces and divide among serving plates. Beat mayonnaise, sour cream, mustard, sugar, salt and pepper with 4 tablespoons fish liquid in a bowl until creamy. Stir in chopped dill.

5 Arrange salmon and peas on lettuce. Drizzle with dressing. Cut remaining lemon into thin slices. Garnish salad with lemon slices and dill sprigs.

cook's tip

When buying salmon fillets, check that the flesh is moist and shiny and bounces back when pressed. It should have a pleasant sea smell with no browning around the edges.

dill

Fresh dill lifts the flavour of salmon and other seafood. It is also a good complement to eggs, cucumber and potatoes.

salmon salad with peas and dill

salmon on lettuce and watercress

✳ Cook 400 g (14 oz) salmon as for main recipe and let cool. Tear leaves of 1 small head of curly endive (frisée) lettuce into pieces. Separate 100 g (4 oz) watercress into sprigs. Distribute among individual serving plates. Add salmon. Finely dice 1 medium red onion and sprinkle on top.

✳ Combine $\frac{1}{2}$ cup (125 g/4 oz) sour cream, 1 tablespoon mayonnaise, 1 teaspoon Dijon mustard and salt and pepper to taste. Fold in 1 tablespoon finely chopped pickled vegetables and spoon over salad.

smoked salmon on mixed salad greens

salmon tartare on vegetable carpaccio

✳ Peel 1 cooked beetroot (beet) and 2 cooked potatoes and slice thinly. Thinly slice 2 large cooked carrots and 2 large tomatoes. Place vegetable slices on individual plates. Sprinkle with salt and pepper, drizzle with 2 tablespoons canola or peanut oil and 2 tablespoons sherry vinegar.

✳ Finely dice 400 g (14 oz) smoked salmon and place in a bowl. Mix in 2 to 3 tablespoons lemon juice, salt, ground white pepper and 2 tablespoons finely chopped fresh dill. Arrange salmon tartare on top of vegetable carpaccio.

smoked salmon on mixed salad greens

The inclusion of red caviar, or salmon roe, adds a salty richness to this dish. For an extra touch of luxury, use beluga caviar.

1 small head treviso or round radicchio

1 small head curly endive (frisée) lettuce heart

2 cups (75 g/3 oz) watercress leaves

3 tablespoons finely chopped fresh flat-leaf parsley

400 g (14 oz) smoked salmon, thinly sliced

2 tablespoons red caviar (salmon roe)

vinaigrette

4 tablespoons olive oil

4 tablespoons lemon juice

2 tablespoons lime juice

salt and freshly ground white pepper

serves 4
preparation 20 minutes

----

per serving *1468 kilojoules/351 calories, 28 g protein, 25 g total fat, 4 g saturated fat, 110 mg cholesterol, 4 g carbohydrate, 3 g fibre*

1 Cut or tear treviso and curly endive leaves into pieces. Arrange salad greens with watercress leaves on individual plates. Sprinkle parsley over the top.

2 Separate salmon slices and cut into small strips. Arrange salmon and caviar on top of salad greens.

3 To make vinaigrette, whisk oil, lemon juice and lime juice until combined; add salt and pepper to taste. Drizzle vinaigrette over salad.

smoked salmon

Smoked salmon has slightly lower amounts of omega-3 fatty acids than fresh salmon but, like other oily fish, it provides a rich source of these essential nutrients.

cook's tip

Ideally, use freshly smoked salmon for the best result, but if you do use salmon that's vacuum-packed, make sure to check the use-by or best-before date.

trout fillets with asparagus and tomato salad

1 kg (2 lb) medium to thick green and
   white asparagus

1 teaspoon sugar

150 g (5 oz) cherry tomatoes, halved

400 g (14 oz) smoked trout fillets

4 small eggs, hard-boiled

4 tablespoons sunflower oil

2 tablespoons herb vinegar

1 tablespoon lemon juice

½ teaspoon grated horseradish, from a jar

salt and freshly ground black pepper

4 tablespoons sour cream

1 tablespoon red caviar (salmon roe)

2 tablespoons chopped fresh chives,
   for garnish

serves 4

preparation 30 minutes

cooking 20 to 25 minutes

----

per serving 2019 kilojoules/482calories, 37 g protein,
35 g total fat, 8 g saturated fat, 295 mg cholesterol,
6 g carbohydrate, 3 g fibre

1 Trim ends from asparagus spears. Peel white asparagus from tips to ends and green asparagus only at ends. Bring plenty of lightly salted water to a boil with sugar. Cook white asparagus 10 minutes; add green asparagus and cook a further 5 to 10 minutes. Drain asparagus; let cool.

2 Arrange asparagus and cherry tomatoes on individual plates. Cut trout fillets into large pieces and add to plates. Peel eggs; cut into quarters.

3 Whisk oil, herb vinegar, lemon juice and horseradish until combined; add salt and pepper to taste. Drizzle over salad and trout.

4 Stir sour cream until creamy, season with salt and pepper. Spoon onto each salad portion. Garnish with caviar, eggs and chives.

japanese-style trout with wasabi and rocket

✳ Finely chop 2 spring onions (scallions). Coarsely grate 200 g (7 oz) white (daikon) radish. Arrange 150 g (5 oz) rocket (arugula) on individual serving plates. Top with spring onions and radish. Whisk 2 tablespoons canola or olive oil and 2 tablespoons lemon juice until combined; add salt and pepper to taste. Drizzle over salad.

✳ Remove bones from 300 g (10 oz) fresh trout fillets and chop finely. Mix 1 pinch powered wasabi (Japanese horseradish) with 1 teaspoon rice vinegar, 1 tablespoon sake (Japanese rice wine) and 1 pinch ground ginger; add salt and pepper to taste. Combine with trout. Add to salad Garnish each serving with a little caviar.

trout fillets with
asparagus and tomato salad

matjes herring salad with citrus fruit

2 large oranges

2 large lemons

3 spring onions (scallions)

250 g (8 oz) matjes herring fillets in oil, drained

fresh lemon balm leaves, for garnish

citrus vinaigrette

3 tablespoons sunflower oil

50 ml (2 fl oz) freshly squeezed orange juice

2 tablespoons lemon juice

1 tablespoon white wine vinegar

salt and freshly ground mixed peppercorns

serves 4

preparation 35 minutes

marinating 2 hours

----

per serving *1319 kilojoules/315 calories, 8 g protein, 25 g total fat, 2 g saturated fat, 42 mg cholesterol, 12 g carbohydrate, 3 g fibre*

1 With a sharp knife, remove skin and white pith from oranges and lemons. Working over a bowl, separate oranges and lemons into segments and set aside. Reserve juice.

2 Thinly slice spring onions. Set aside a few light green rings for garnish.

3 Cut herring fillets into small pieces and arrange on a platter with citrus segments and spring onions.

4 To make citrus vinaigrette, whisk oil, reserved juice, orange juice, lemon juice and vinegar until combined; add salt and pepper to taste. Drizzle over salad. Cover and refrigerate at least 2 hours to allow flavours to develop.

5 Remove salad from refrigerator and stand until at room temperature. Garnish with spring onion rings and lemon balm. Serve with pumpernickel or dark wholegrain bread.

matjes herring

Mostly sold vacuum packed, frozen, or in cans, matjes herring is a richly flavoured oily fish that's full of omega-3 fatty acids. Ready-to-eat matjes herring have been skinned, gutted and filleted.

prawn and mango salad

½ medium telegraph (English) cucumber

1 medium red capsicum (bell pepper), sliced

250 g (8 oz) cherry tomatoes, quartered

2 large mangoes, peeled and sliced

16 cooked king prawns (large shrimp),
    peeled and deveined, leaving tails intact

150 g (5 oz) mixed salad leaves

1 clove garlic, crushed

1 tablespoon chili sauce

2 tablespoons olive oil

4 tablespoons lime juice

3 tablespoons chopped fresh mint

freshly ground black pepper

serves 4

preparation 25 minutes

----

per serving *1022 kilojoules/244 calories, 18 g protein,*
11 g total fat, 2 g saturated fat, 120 mg cholesterol,
19 g carbohydrate, 4 g fibre

1 Slice cucumber into thin rounds, leaving skin on. Combine cucumber, capsicum, tomatoes, mangoes, prawns and salad leaves in a large bowl.

2 To make dressing, combine garlic, chili sauce, oil, lime juice and mint in a small screw-top jar. Shake well. Stir dressing into salad.

3 Pile salad onto individual serving plates. Season with freshly ground pepper to taste.

cook's tip

Mangoes are an excellent source
of the antioxidant, beta carotene.
If fresh mangoes are unavailable,
substitute avocado slices for an
equally nutritious salad.

seafood salad with saffron and parsley

1 red and 1 yellow capsicum (bell pepper)

1 cos (romaine) lettuce

250 g (8 oz) swordfish steaks

2 tablespoons lemon juice

salt and freshly ground black pepper

5 tablespoons olive oil

12 uncooked king prawns (large shrimp), peeled and deveined, tails intact

3 cloves garlic, cut into fine sticks

¼ teaspoon ground saffron

150 ml (¼ pint/5 fl oz) dry white wine

2 tablespoons sherry vinegar

4 sprigs curly-leaf parsley, for garnish

serves 4
preparation 30 minutes
cooking 10 minutes

per serving 1642 kilojoules/392 calories, 30 g protein, 27 g total fat, 4 g saturated fat, 121 mg cholesterol, 5 g carbohydrate, 3 g fibre

1 Cut capsicums into strips. Cut or tear lettuce leaves into strips. Place lettuce and capsicum on individual plates.

2 Cut swordfish into small pieces. Drizzle with lemon juice; sprinkle with salt and pepper.

3 Heat 3 tablespoons oil in a nonstick frying pan. Sear fish pieces and prawns on all sides over medium-high heat. Add garlic and saffron and fry briefly. Add wine. Cook, uncovered, until wine is reduced by half.

4 Using a slotted spoon, lift fish and prawns from liquid and place on salad. Remove pan from heat and season pan juices with salt, pepper and sherry vinegar. Drizzle over salad.

5 Heat remaining 2 tablespoons oil in a small, heavy pan. Lightly brown parsley over medium heat. Remove, drain briefly on paper towel and arrange on salad.

crisp seafood salad with yogurt dressing

Crisp, crunchy iceberg lettuce with creamy yogurt and sweet tiny prawns (shrimp) make an ideal combination for a summertime salad.

1 medium head iceberg lettuce
50 g (2 oz) sorrel or baby spinach leaves
250 g (8 oz) cherry tomatoes
150 g (5 oz) cooked and peeled prawns
   (shrimp), thawed if frozen
4 sprigs dill, for garnish
4 thin lemon slices, for garnish

vinaigrette

2 tablespoons canola or olive oil
2 tablespoons lemon juice
salt and ground white pepper

yogurt dressing

1 cup (250 g/8 oz) yogurt
2 tablespoons mayonnaise
1 teaspoon dry vermouth
1 tablespoon lime juice
salt and ground white pepper
pinch of cayenne pepper

serves 4
preparation 30 minutes

per serving 930 kilojoules/222 calories, 13 g protein,
15 g total fat, 3 g saturated fat, 84 mg cholesterol,
7 g carbohydrate, 4 g fibre

1 Cut lettuce into strips. Tear larger sorrel leaves into pieces. Arrange lettuce and sorrel on serving plates. Cut tomatoes into quarters and add to salad.

2 To make vinaigrette, whisk oil and lemon juice until combined; add salt and pepper to taste. Drizzle over lettuce.

3 To make yogurt dressing, stir yogurt, mayonnaise, vermouth and lime juice until creamy. Season well with salt, white pepper and cayenne pepper.

4 Spoon yogurt dressing and prawns on to salad. Garnish with dill and lemon slices.

cook's tip

In place of dry vermouth in the yogurt dressing, use 1 teaspoon dry white wine or 1 teaspoon orange juice. Dry vermouth has a slightly 'herby' taste and aroma.

crisp seafood salad
with yogurt dressing

iceberg lettuce with salmon

✻ Finely shred 1 medium head iceberg lettuce. Slice 3 celery stalks into thin strips and finely grate 2 medium carrots. Combine in a serving bowl.

✻ Whisk 2 tablespoons olive oil, 3 tablespoons lemon juice, 1 teaspoon whole-grain mustard, $\frac{1}{4}$ teaspoon sugar until combined; add salt and white pepper to taste. Pour over salad and stir to combine.

✻ Cut 100 g (4 oz) smoked salmon into strips and place on top of salad. Garnish with lemon slices and celery leaves.

crab and grapefruit salad

White crabmeat is sweet and succulent
with a flaky texture. Buying pre-picked
crabmeat will save a lot of preparation time.

4 medium grapefruit

2 tablespoons mayonnaise

1 tablespoon finely chopped mango chutney

2 teaspoons Dijon mustard

1 teaspoon sesame oil

salt and freshly ground black pepper

400 g (14 oz) crabmeat, picked over to
 remove any pieces of shell or cartilage

1 head witlof (Belgian endive/chicory), cut
 crosswise into thin strips

100 g (4 oz) watercress, tough stems
 trimmed

1 head lettuce, such as mignonette,
 separated into leaves, for serving

serves 4

preparation 25 minutes

---

per serving 765 kilojoules/183 calories, 16 g protein,
5 g total fat, 1 g saturated fat, 87 mg cholesterol,
16 g carbohydrate, 3 g fibre

1 Remove skin and white pith from grapefruit with a paring
knife. Working over a bowl, separate grapefruit segments
from membranes; reserve juice.

2 Whisk mayonnaise, chutney, mustard, sesame oil, a pinch
of salt and pepper and 3 tablespoons reserved grapefruit
juice in a medium bowl.

3 Dice crab and stir into mayonnaise mixture. Add witlof,
watercress and grapefruit segments and toss to combine.
Serve crab salad on a bed of lettuce leaves.

grapefruit

Chemical compounds in
this citrus fruit cause
the body to absorb more
of certain drugs, which
can result in receiving a
larger dose than intended.
This effect is not seen with other
citrus juices. Avoid taking any medication
with grapefruit juice. Grapefruit is rich in
pectin, a type of dietary fibre that seems
to reduce low-density lipoprotein cholesterol.

crab salad with papaya

Fresh crab has a rich flavour that works well with the taste of papaya. Select whole papaya with a fragrant aroma.

4 medium cooked crabs (400 g/14 oz each)

2 spring onions (scallions)

150 g (5 oz) drained canned hearts of palm

2 celery stalks

1 medium ripe papaya or pawpaw

3 tablespoons sunflower oil

3 tablespoons lime juice

3 tablespoons fish stock

2 teaspoons Dijon mustard

salt and freshly ground black pepper

pinch of soft brown sugar

pinch of cayenne pepper

3 tablespoons finely chopped fresh flat-leaf parsley

2 sprigs mint

lime slices, for garnish

serves 4

preparation 40 minutes

----

per serving 918 kilojoules/219 calories, 16 g protein, 15 g total fat, 2 g saturated fat, 95 mg cholesterol, 6 g carbohydrate, 2 g fibre

1 Remove crabmeat from the pincers (claws) and legs of crabs, then remove meat and entrails from the bodies. Discard entrails, keeping only the livers.

2 Cut crabmeat and livers into pieces. Cut undersides of shells along the curved join and break off. Rinse out shells with warm water and let dry.

3 Thinly slice spring onions. Cut hearts of palm into small cubes. Cut celery stalks into small cubes. Halve papaya and scrape out seeds; peel and cut flesh into small cubes. Mix crab pieces and salad ingredients together in a bowl.

4 To make vinaigrette, whisk oil, 2 tablespoons lime juice, fish stock, mustard, salt, pepper, sugar and cayenne pepper until combined. Finely chop mint leaves. Add mint and parsley.

5 Drizzle vinaigrette on salad ingredients. Season with salt, cayenne pepper and remaining 1 tablespoon lime juice. Spoon into crab shells. Garnish with lime slices.

hearts of palm

Mostly sold in cans, hearts of palm or 'palmitos', are the edible buds and tips of a palm tree. Cylindrically shaped with rings like an onion, creamy white palm hearts have a delicate flavour similar to that of artichokes.

breaking open and shelling crabs

1 First carefully twist the pincers (claws) and legs of the crab away from the shells and break off.

2 Using lobster shears, crack open the pincers. Remove meat by pulling it out of the legs using a lobster fork.

3 Lift the tail plates on the undersides of the crab; remove with a twisting movement. Lift out the meat and entrails.

lobster salad with celery and tomatoes

1 small light yellow bunch celery
(celery heart)

6 tablespoons white wine vinegar

1 tablespoon salt

2 ready-to-cook lobster tails (total
600 g/1 lb 8 oz), thawed if frozen

2 fully ripe medium tomatoes

5 spring onions (scallions)

1 clove garlic, finely chopped

4 tablespoons finely chopped flat-leaf
parsley

6 tablespoons olive oil

salt and freshly ground black pepper

serves 4

preparation 50 minutes

cooking 15 minutes

----

*per serving 1437 kilojoules/343 calories, 19 g protein,
28 g total fat, 4 g saturated fat, 90 mg cholesterol,
4 g carbohydrate, 3 g fibre*

1 Remove leaves from celery and set aside. Cut 3 stalks celery into thick pieces and place in a large saucepan. Add 2 litres (3½ pints) water, 3 tablespoons vinegar and 1 tablespoon salt. Bring to a boil. Place lobster tails in saucepan, cover and cook over low heat 15 minutes. Leave in liquid to cool.

2 Thinly slice remaining celery stalks. Halve tomatoes, remove seeds and dice. Slice spring onions. Finely chop celery leaves. Combine celery leaves and stalks, tomatoes, spring onions, garlic and parsley in a bowl.

3 Whisk olive oil and remaining 3 tablespoons vinegar until combined; add salt and pepper to taste. Remove lobster tails from liquid and remove flesh. Discard shells and cooked celery.

4 Cut lobster flesh into small slices. Place in a bowl. Pour 4 to 5 tablespoons cooking liquid over lobster and toss to coat lobster. Arrange salad on individual plates, drizzle with vinaigrette and top with lobster pieces.

mussel salad with croutons

2 kg (4 lb) mussels, scrubbed and debearded

2 cups (500 ml/16 fl oz) dry white wine

1 teaspoon black peppercorns

1 clove

1 bay leaf

3 medium tomatoes

1 medium yellow capsicum (bell pepper)

2 small zucchini (courgettes)

2 shallots

150 g (5 oz) rocket (arugula)

4 tablespoons olive oil

3 to 4 tablespoons lemon juice

4 tablespoons tomato juice

$\frac{1}{4}$ teaspoon dried chili flakes

pinch of sugar

salt and freshly ground black pepper

2 slices black bread or dark rye

1 tablespoon butter

serves 4

preparation 40 minutes

cooking 10 minutes

----

per serving *2089 kilojoules/499 calories, 34 g protein,*
28 g total fat, 6 g saturated fat, 111 mg cholesterol,
28 g carbohydrate, 4 g fibre

1 Leave mussels in a bowl of cold water for 15 minutes, then strain. Discard open mussels. Rinse remaining mussels in cold water until all traces of sand are removed.

2 Place wine, peppercorns, clove and bay leaf in a large saucepan and bring to a boil. Add mussels, cover and cook 5 to 10 minutes until they open. Strain; discard any closed mussels. Remove mussel flesh from open shells and allow to cool completely.

3 Halve tomatoes, remove seeds and cut into small strips. Cut yellow capsicum into small cubes. Thinly slice zucchini. Peel shallots and slice. Remove hard stems from rocket and chop leaves. Place mussels and all prepared salad ingredients except rocket in a bowl and mix together.

4 To make vinaigrette, whisk oil, lemon juice, tomato juice, dried chili flakes and sugar until combined; add salt and pepper to taste. Drizzle vinaigrette over salad.

5 To make croutons, cut bread into cubes. Heat butter in a nonstick pan and lightly fry bread cubes over medium heat, turning often and taking care that they do not burn. Spoon salad into bowls, top with rocket and croutons.

scallops and grapefruit with mustard vinaigrette

Scallops, like most seafood, need light, gentle cooking. Their delicate flavour is offset by the not-too-sweet, not-too-sour flavour of grapefruit.

1 medium red onion
½ head curly endive (frisée) lettuce
100 g (4 oz) rocket (arugula)
2 medium pink grapefruit
12 shelled scallops with coral
2 tablespoons lemon juice
salt and freshly ground black pepper
1 tablespoon butter
2 tablespoons dry vermouth

mustard vinaigrette

3 tablespoons olive oil
2 tablespoons red wine vinegar
1 teaspoon whole-grain mustard
1 teaspoon honey
salt and freshly ground black pepper

serves 4
preparation 20 minutes
cooking 5 minutes

per serving *1083 kilojoules/259 calories, 10 g protein, 19 g total fat, 5 g saturated fat, 34 mg cholesterol, 9 g carbohydrate, 2 g fibre*

1 Finely dice onion. Tear lettuce into bite-sized pieces. Remove hard stems from rocket.

2 With a sharp knife, remove skin and white pith from grapefruit. Separate grapefruit into segments.

3 Drizzle scallops with lemon juice and sprinkle with salt and pepper. Heat butter in a nonstick pan and cook scallops about 2 minutes on each side; add vermouth and cook another 1 to 2 minutes. Remove from heat.

4 To make vinaigrette, whisk oil, vinegar, mustard and honey, until thickened slightly; add salt and pepper to taste.

5 Arrange lettuce leaves on individual plates and drizzle with vinaigrette. Top with diced onion and grapefruit segments. Arrange scallops on top.

scallops

The muscle from the large white scallop shells is particularly firm, but still tender. It has a mild, slightly sweet taste. A scallop shell also contains a roe sack, the orange-red coral, that is prized by gourmets. Scallops are a good source of zinc and provide iron.

barbecued calamari with tomato vinaigrette

Champagne vinegar is a light, mildly flavoured vinegar. It is sold in gourmet food stores. If not available, substitute white wine vinegar.

500 g (1 lb) calamari or squid rings
2 cloves garlic, crushed
4 tablespoons finely chopped fresh
   flat-leaf parsley
2 tablespoons olive oil
4 tablespoons white wine
salt and freshly ground black pepper
1 small head cos (romaine) lettuce

tomato vinaigrette

2 large tomatoes
2 tablespoons olive oil
1 tablespoon champagne vinegar
2 tablespoons lemon juice
4 sprigs fresh thyme, finely chopped
salt and freshly ground pepper

serves 4
preparation + marinating 2 hours 30 minutes
cooking 3 minutes

----

per serving 1218 kilojoules/290 calories, 32 g protein,
16 g total fat, 3 g saturated fat, 361 mg cholesterol,
3 g carbohydrate, 3 g fibre

1 Place calamari, garlic and parsley in a bowl. Add oil, wine, salt and pepper. Mix together, cover and marinate in refrigerator about 2 hours.

2 Tear lettuce into pieces and arrange on individual plates. Halve tomatoes, remove seeds and finely dice.

3 To make tomato vinaigrette, whisk oil, champagne vinegar, lemon juice and thyme until combined; add salt and pepper to taste. Add diced tomatoes and mix together. Drizzle vinaigrette over lettuce leaves.

4 Heat barbecue or preheat grill (broiler) to medium heat. Cook calamari on barbecue or under grill about 3 minutes, turning occasionally. Place on salad and serve while hot.

cook's tip

Calamari is delicious when cooked on the barbecue. Sear until just cooked through and make sure the rings don't turn black or the flesh will taste bitter.

barbecued calamari with tomato vinaigrette

barbecued calamari salad

❋ Marinate and barbecue 500 g (1 lb) calamari or squid rings as for main recipe. Tear 1 lollo rossa (red coral) lettuce into bite-sized pieces. Thinly slice 1 medium red onion. Arrange lettuce leaves and onion rings on a platter.

❋ Finely chop 3 red capsicums (bell peppers) and 2 cloves garlic. In a blender, purée capsicums and garlic; blend in 3 tablespoons olive oil, 2 tablespoons lemon juice, salt, pepper and cayenne pepper. Pour over salad. Arrange calamari on top.

spiced seasonal fruit salad (page 296)

dessert fruit salads

Fresh fruit salads, with their refreshing flavours and vibrant colours, make the perfect end to a meal. In winter, dried fruit and canned fruit are useful options. Keep salads simple or indulge a little with toppings such as fruit purées, chopped nuts, praline and cream or chocolate sauces.

fruit and berries at a glance

Fruit and berries are not only the central ingredient of fruit salads, but also often add a certain something to savoury salads. Eat at least two servings of fresh fruit every day for daily well-being and long-term good health.

shopping

Generally, the heavier the fruit, the juicier it is and the better it will taste. The stronger the scent of a fruit, the riper it will be. The flesh of a ripe, perfect piece of fruit should yield to a light touch. Spots or signs of mould indicate that the fruit is spoiled. Buy fruit in season and buy only as much fresh fruit as you will eat in the next two days. Fully ripe fruit can only be stored for a limited time. Buy quick-ripening fruit, such as pears or bananas, at different levels of ripeness so they don't all have to be eaten at the same time.

storing

Wash fruit thoroughly just before eating. Store any delicate varieties, such as melons, berries, apricots and peaches, in the vegetable crisper of the refrigerator. Apples, hard pears, citrus fruit, firm peaches and nectarines can be stored at room temperature as they are harvested unripe and continue to ripen during storage. Berries and grapes, on the other hand, should be eaten quickly, because they are harvested when ripe and soon become rotten. They keep for a few days in the refrigerator. Do not squash berries as bruising leads to the delicate fruit rapidly spoiling. Note that unripe fruit ripens more quickly if a ripe piece of fruit is stored with it or if the fruit is stored in a brown paper bag at room temperature.

nutrition

Most fruit is fat-free, has a high water content and contains few kilojoules (calories). Depending on the type, fresh fruit contains abundant vitamins, such as vitamin C and folic acid, as well as numerous minerals and trace elements. Fruit and berries are also rich in carotenoids as well as bioflavonoids, phytochemicals and fibre. Apples and pears should not be peeled or only peeled thinly, because the vitamin C and other nutrients are found in and under the skin.

bananas

Bananas don't grow on trees but on giant herbs related to the Lily and Orchid family. They continue to ripen after picking. When buying, select a range at different stages of ripeness so they won't all ripen at once. Look for shiny yellow skins, either unblemished or with few brown spots. Bananas are high in vitamin C. They contain a mix of carbohydrates to provide sustained energy, and are a good source of dietary fibre, potassium and vitamin B6.

berries

Smaller berries often have more flavour than large ones. Always rinse berries briefly in cold water, then trim only if necessary. Delicate varieties such as raspberries, strawberries and blackberries should be used on the day they are picked, if possible. The more robust varieties will keep in the refrigerator for up to 2 days. The simplest of berry dessert salads can be made by adding sugar to berries and serving them with yogurt or, for something special, zabaglione.

grapes

Classed as berries, most varieties of purple/red and green grapes grown for eating are sweet and juicy with a high glucose and fructose content. Select plump, well-coloured grapes, firmly attached to their stems. Avoid soft or wrinkled fruit and those browning around the stem. Grapes are generally picked when ripe and sweet, to be eaten fresh. Store grapes, unwashed, in the refrigerator in a sealed container or plastic bag. Use within 2 to 3 days.

mangoes

The orange-coloured flesh of the mango is sweet, fragrant and succulent. Fibrous, but edible, strands, surround the very large seed. Select firm, bright mangoes that have a distinct pleasant aroma. Let ripen at room temperature. Store ripe fruit in the vegetable crisper or in a plastic bag in the refrigerator. Use within 3 days.

melons

Ripe watermelons have firm red flesh and brown seeds. When buying watermelons, test them for ripeness by tapping the melon and listening carefully. If it sounds firm and echoes, it is ripe. If it sounds dull, it has been picked for some time or is unripe. Melons such as galia melons, muskmelons, cantaloupes and rockmelons should smell aromatic without any hint of acetone. They should have no soft spots or cracks and certainly no mould formation. Ripe specimens yield slightly to pressure at the stems. They do not ripen further after harvesting and will only get softer. Store uncut melons at room temperature. Once cut, cover and refrigerate. Melons add a refreshing note to summer salads.

pineapples

Pineapple flesh contains a protein-splitting enzyme, so fresh pineapple tastes sour with milk products and prevents gelatine from setting. This enzyme is destroyed by heating and it can tenderise meat if used in a marinade. Select plump pineapples with a sweet, pleasant aroma and fresh-looking skin and leaves. Pineapples do not ripen further after picking. They become juicier, but not sweeter, once harvested. Store in a cool place. Once cut, cover and refrigerate. Use within 2 days.

stone fruits

Fully ripe plums and peaches are juicy and sweet and the stones (pits) are easy to remove. Firm, less ripe plums and peaches are often tart and are just as suitable for salads or eating raw. The flesh of ripe peaches and plums yields to gentle pressure. Purée ripe, juicy peaches and serve as a fruit sauce with fruit salad.

how much per person?

For fruit salad, allow 150 g (5 oz) to 250 g (8 oz) of peeled, trimmed fruit per serving, depending on the dressing. Allow a little more fruit for light yogurts, dressings or marinades. For richer cream dressings, 150 g (5 oz) is enough. A small, hollowed-out melon or pineapple half filled with fruit salad is enough for one serving.

berry salad with mascarpone cream

250 g (8 oz) each blueberries, blackberries
 and redcurrants

250 g (8 oz) strawberries

4 tablespoons icing (confectioners') sugar

2 tablespoons lemon juice

10 lady finger (sponge finger) biscuits

mascarpone cream

200 g (7 oz) mascarpone

2 tablespoons milk

2 tablespoons orange liqueur or orange
 juice

1 tablespoon sugar

icing (confectioners') sugar, for dusting

serves 4

preparation 20 minutes

----

*per serving 2305 kilojoules/550 calories, 7 g protein,
31 g total fat, 20 g saturated fat, 147 mg cholesterol,
61 g carbohydrate, 9 g fibre*

1 Combine all the berries in a bowl. Mix icing sugar and lemon juice and pour over berries. Stir carefully to combine.

2 Place lady fingers in a freezer bag. Seal and place on a flat surface. Crush with a rolling pin to make coarse crumbs. Spread crumbs on dessert plates. Top with berries.

3 To make mascarpone cream, whisk mascarpone, milk, orange liqueur and sugar in a bowl until thick and well combined. Spoon a little mascarpone cream onto each serving. Dust with a little icing sugar.

cook's tip

Try a combination of peaches, apricots, plums and mangoes and flavour the mascarpone cream with almond liqueur instead of orange.

berry salad with pistachio cream

✳ Mix 250 g (8 oz) blueberries, 250 g (8 oz) raspberries and 250 g (8 oz) redcurrants in a large bowl. Cut 350 g (12 oz) strawberries into halves and add to bowl. Combine 4 tablespoons crème de cassis liqueur, 1 tablespoon lemon juice and 3 tablespoons icing (confectioner's) sugar. Pour over berries and stir gently to combine. Spoon into dessert bowls.

✳ To make pistachio cream, whip ½ cup (125 g/4 oz) whipping cream with 1 tablespoon vanilla sugar until thickened. Finely grind 3 tablespoons chopped pistachios in a food processor. Fold into cream. Serve with berries.

berry salad with mascarpone cream

kiwifruit and blueberry salad

½ cup (55 g/2 oz) slivered almonds

8 kiwifruit

½ cup (125 ml/4 fl oz) port or red wine

few small strips lemon peel

250 g (8 oz) blueberries

icing (confectioners') sugar, for garnish

raspberry cream

150 g (5 oz) frozen raspberries, thawed

4 tablespoons icing (confectioners') sugar

2 teaspoons vanilla sugar

2 tablespoons raspberry liqueur (schnapps)
   or almond liqueur

½ cup (125 g/4 oz) double (heavy) cream

serves 4

preparation 15 minutes

cooking 5 minutes

per serving *2074 kilojoules/495 calories, 6 g protein,*
25 g total fat, 11 g saturated fat, 50 mg cholesterol,
49 g carbohydrate, 10 g fibre

1 Dry roast slivered almonds in a pan over medium heat until golden, tossing to prevent burning. Transfer to a plate and leave to cool. Peel kiwifruit and slice crosswise.

2 Place port and lemon peel in a pan. Bring to a boil; add kiwifruit. Reduce heat to low. Poach fruit 1 minute. Remove pan from heat. Remove fruit with a slotted spoon, discarding lemon peel, and leave to cool. Arrange on serving plates with blueberries.

3 To make raspberry cream, place raspberries in a fine sieve over a bowl. Press berries with the back of a spoon to make a fine purée without any seeds. Reserve a little purée for decoration. Stir icing sugar, vanilla sugar and raspberry liqueur into purée. Fold in cream.

4 Dust kiwifruit and blueberries with icing sugar. Spoon a little raspberry cream onto plates. Using a teaspoon, swirl in a little reserved purée. Scatter on roasted slivered almonds.

blackberry and lychee salad with yogurt

2 tablespoons flaked almonds

2 ripe peaches

1 tablespoon lemon juice

250 g (8 oz) blackberries

1 can (560 g/1 lb 4 oz) lychees, drained

½ cup (125 ml/4 fl oz) freshly squeezed
  orange juice

3 tablespoons dry marsala or sherry

pinch of ground mace

2 teaspoons icing (confectioners') sugar

50 g (2 oz) small amaretti biscuits
  (small almond macaroons)

1 cup (250 g/8 oz) yogurt

2 teaspoons vanilla sugar

mint or lemon balm leaves, for garnish

serves 4

preparation 20 minutes

*per serving 1092 kilojoules/261 calories, 7 g protein,
6 g total fat, 2 g saturated fat, 12 mg cholesterol,
40 g carbohydrate, 7 g fibre*

1 Dry roast flaked almonds in a pan over medium heat until golden, tossing to prevent burning. Transfer to a plate.

2 Halve peaches and cut into slices. Place in a bowl; drizzle with lemon juice to prevent discolouration. Add blackberries and lychees. Combine orange juice, marsala, ground mace and icing sugar in a bowl. Drizzle mixture over fruit. Place mixture in serving bowls.

3 Place amaretti biscuits in a freezer bag. Seal, place on a flat surface and crush with a rolling pin to make fine crumbs. Combine yogurt, vanilla sugar and amaretti crumbs. Spoon over fruit. Add flaked almonds and mint leaves.

cook's tip

To make vanilla sugar, push a dried vanilla bean into a jar of sugar. After about two weeks, take it out. The vanilla flavour and aroma will have permeated the sugar.

mixed fruit salad in melon halves

Cantaloupe melons get their name because they were first cultivated near Cantalupo in Italy, during the mid–18th century.

250 g (8 oz) sweet cherries

1 medium banana

4 apricots

250 g (8 oz) damsons or other blue plums

3 tablespoons lemon juice

4 tablespoons liquid honey

3 sprigs mint

2 small cantaloupe (muskmelon) or
   honeydew melons

$\frac{1}{2}$ cup (125 g/4 oz) whipping cream

mint leaves, for garnish

serves 4

preparation 30 minutes

----

per serving 1487 kilojoules/355 calories, 4 g protein,
12 g total fat, 8 g saturated fat, 36 mg cholesterol,
58 g carbohydrate, 7 g fibre

1 Remove pits from cherries. Slice banana, apricots and plums. Combine fruit in a bowl.

2 Mix lemon juice and honey and pour over fruit. Remove mint leaves from sprigs. Cut into fine strips. Stir into salad.

3 Halve melons and scrape out seeds. Use a melon baller to scoop out flesh, leaving a rim of flesh about 1 cm ($\frac{1}{2}$ inch) thick. Add melon balls to bowl.

4 Whip cream until stiff. Spoon fruit salad into melon halves. Garnish with cream rosettes and mint leaves.

cook's tip

Prepare the melons ahead of time and keep covered in the refrigerator. Any mixture of seasonal fruit may be used in this recipe.

cherries

The flavour and low-kilojoule (low-calorie) content of the various sweet cherry varieties (more than 1000 worldwide) make cherries an ideal snack. Sour cherries are more nutritious than the sweet types. They are often used in jams and jellies.

melon salad with yogurt lime sauce

¼ small watermelon (1 kg/2 lb), cubed

½ cantaloupe (muskmelon), cubed (about 2½ cups)

¼ honeydew melon, cubed (2 cups)

1 cup (175 g/6 oz) seedless red or green grapes

½ small pineapple (500 g/1 lb), cubed

yogurt lime sauce

1 cup (250 g/8 oz) yogurt

2 tablespoons sour cream

2 tablespoons honey

1 tablespoon lime juice

pinch of ground ginger

serves 8

preparation 30 minutes

------

per serving *623 kilojoules/149 calories, 3 g protein, 4 g total fat, 2 g saturated fat, 12 mg cholesterol, 26 g carbohydrate, 3 g fibre*

1 Combine all the melons, grapes and pineapple in a large bowl. Chill, covered, until serving time.

2 To make yogurt lime sauce, combine yogurt, sour cream, honey, lime juice and ginger in a small bowl. Chill, covered, until serving time.

3 Serve fruit salad in individual bowls. Serve yogurt lime sauce on the side.

cook's tip

If fresh pineapple is not available, use 1 cup (200 g/7 oz) drained canned pineapple cubes or pieces. Or, omit the pineapple and use 2 large mangoes, sliced or cubed.

fruit salad in pineapple halves

4 tablespoons flaked almonds

2 small pineapples (each 1 kg/2 lb)

2 medium oranges

1 medium banana

1 tablespoon lemon juice

100 ml (4 fl oz) orange juice

2 tablespoons maple syrup

2 tablespoons brown (amber) rum

$\frac{1}{2}$ cup (180 g/7 oz) chocolate topping (syrup)

serves 4

preparation 35 minutes

per serving 1530 kilojoules/365 calories, 6 g protein, 5 g total fat, 0 g saturated fat, 0 mg cholesterol, 70 g carbohydrate, 9 g fibre

1 Dry roast flaked almonds in a pan over medium heat until golden, tossing to prevent burning. Transfer to a plate to cool. Cut pineapples, including crown, in half lengthwise. Remove flesh with a sharp knife, leaving a rim 2 cm (1 inch) thick. Discard woody core and cut flesh into small pieces.

2 Segment oranges and cut into pieces. Slice bananas. Drizzle bananas with lemon juice to prevent browning. Combine all the fruit in a bowl.

3 Whisk orange juice, maple syrup and rum and stir into salad. Place pineapple halves on dessert plates and fill with fruit salad. Drizzle with chocolate topping and sprinkle roasted flaked almonds on top.

to make caramel

1 Place sugar cubes, lemon juice and water in a heavy-based saucepan with a heat-proof handle. Bring to a boil over high heat until sugar has dissolved.

2 Boil uncovered until large bubbles form and syrup reaches about 140°C (275°F). Do not stir, or the sugar will crystallise and be unsuitable for use. Do not let sugar burn.

3 Push bubbles aside with a wooden spoon, carefully watching colour. As soon as sugar is an amber colour, remove from heat and finish as described in main recipe.

pineapple salad with almond brittle

Use plain yogurt for the yogurt cream. It will derive its citrusy flavour from the orange juice, peel and liqueur.

sunflower oil, for brushing
50 g (2 oz) sugar cubes (about 12 cubes)
1 teaspoon lemon juice
1 to 2 teaspoons ground cinnamon
1 cup (100g/4 oz) slivered almonds
1 medium pineapple (about 2 kg/4 lb)
2 tablespoons brown sugar
orange peel and mint leaves, for garnish

yogurt cream
$\frac{1}{2}$ cup (125 g/4 oz) yogurt
50 ml (2 fl oz) freshly squeezed orange
    juice
$\frac{1}{2}$ teaspoon finely grated orange peel
1 tablespoon orange liqueur
1 teaspoon icing (confectioners') sugar
$\frac{1}{2}$ cup (125 g/4 oz) whipping cream

serves 4
preparation 40 minutes
cooking 8 to 10 minutes

----

per serving 2119 kilojoules/506 calories, 11 g protein, 29 g total fat, 9 g saturated fat, 41 mg cholesterol, 50 g carbohydrate, 9 g fibre

1 To make almond brittle, brush a piece of baking (waxed) paper thinly with oil; set aside. Place sugar cubes, lemon juice and 3 tablespoons water in a heavy saucepan with a heat-proof handle; cook until caramelised (*see opposite*).

2 Remove saucepan from heat. Immediately stir cinnamon and slivered almonds into the caramel; spread mixture onto prepared baking paper, keeping almond slivers as far apart as possible. Let brittle cool.

3 Preheat oven to 220°C/425°F. Peel pineapple and cut into slices. Arrange slices on ovenproof dessert plates and sprinkle with brown sugar. Bake 8 to 10 minutes and remove. Let cool until lukewarm.

4 To make yogurt cream, stir yogurt, orange juice, orange peel, orange liqueur and icing sugar until smooth and creamy. Whip cream until stiff and fold into yogurt mixture.

5 Chop cooled almond brittle or crush coarsely with a rolling pin. Spoon yogurt cream into the centre of each salad portion and sprinkle almond brittle on top. Garnish with orange peel and mint leaves. Serve while lukewarm.

citrus fruit salad with chocolate

50 g (2 oz) white chocolate

50 g (2 oz) bittersweet dark chocolate

3 large pink grapefruit

2 large oranges

4 large mandarins (tangerines)

2 tablespoons lemon juice

1 tablespoon lime juice

2 tablespoons orange liqueur

2 tablespoons agave or maple syrup
   or honey

icing (confectioners') sugar, for dusting

1 teaspoon each of lime and orange peel

serves 4

preparation + marinating 1 hour

---

per serving *1426 kilojoules/340 calories, 6 g protein,*
9 g total fat, 6 g saturated fat, 3 mg cholesterol,
55 g carbohydrate, 6 g fibre

1 Melt white and dark chocolate separately in double-boilers. Pour each into a freezer bag and cut a very tiny corner from each bag. Pipe decorative spirals of white and dark chocolate onto dessert plates and chill in refrigerator.

2 Peel grapefruit, oranges and mandarins, removing white pith. Separate into segments and place on a platter.

3 Mix lemon juice, lime juice, orange liqueur and agave syrup. Pour over fruit, cover and marinate 30 minutes in refrigerator for flavours to develop.

4 Arrange fruit on prepared dessert plates and dust with icing sugar. Top with peel, and serve while still well chilled.

orange and figs with sherry cream

2 medium oranges

2 medium blood oranges

6 ripe figs

3 tablespoons coarsely chopped pistachios

sherry cream

3 tablespoons double (heavy) cream or crème fraîche

4 tablespoons cream sherry

1 tablespoon agave or maple syrup or honey

1 tablespoon lemon juice

1 small pinch of ground cloves

½ cup (125 g/4 oz) whipping cream

serves 4

preparation 20 minutes

per serving 1452 kilojoules/347 calories, 5 g protein, 23 g total fat, 13 g saturated fat, 60 mg cholesterol, 25 g carbohydrate, 5 g fibre

1 Using a zester or sharp knife, slice off thin strips of orange peel; set aside. Peel oranges and blood oranges, removing white pith. Cut into slices and arrange on plates.

2 Thinly peel figs if necessary. Cut into quarters and arrange decoratively on plates.

3 To make sherry cream, combine double cream, sherry, agave syrup and lemon juice in a bowl and beat well. Add ground cloves.

4 Whip cream until stiff. Gently fold into sherry mixture. Spoon dollops of sherry cream over fruit portions. Sprinkle with strips of orange peel and pistachios.

figs

To peel soft ripe figs, cut off the stalk ends and carefully peel off the skin, leaving as much flesh as possible.

mango and papaya salad with cranberries

2 fully ripe mangoes

1 fully ripe papaya or pawpaw

2 tablespoons lime juice

1 medium tart apple

1 medium orange

1 tablespoon unsalted butter

150 g (5 oz) fresh or frozen cranberries

2/3 cup (160 ml/6 fl oz) port or red wine

1 cup (250 ml/8 fl oz) brandy

1 tablespoon honey

2 cloves

1/2 cinnamon stick

serves 4

preparation 20 minutes

cooking 10 minutes

per serving *1523 kilojoules/364 calories, 2 g protein, 4 g total fat, 3 g saturated fat, 12 mg cholesterol, 38 g carbohydrate, 5 g fibre*

1 Peel mangoes and slice. Halve papayas, remove black seeds; peel and slice. Arrange papaya and mango slices alternately on a large platter; drizzle with lime juice.

2 To make cranberry sauce, peel apple and dice. Halve orange. Cut thin strips of orange peel from one half, then squeeze both halves.

3 Heat butter in a saucepan and sauté diced apples until butter begins to brown. Add cranberries, orange peel, port, brandy, orange juice, honey and spices, and bring to a boil. Reduce, uncovered, over medium heat for 5 minutes. Remove from heat.

4 Remove orange peel and spices from sauce. Pour sauce over salad while hot.

orange and pomegranate salad with vanilla cream

6 large juicy oranges

4 tablespoons grenadine syrup

2 tablespoons lime juice

1 pomegranate

¼ teaspoon grated lime peel

½ cup (125 g/4 oz) whipping cream

250 g (8 oz) vanilla ice cream

2 teaspoons rose water

icing (confectioners') sugar, for dusting

serves 4

preparation 30 minutes

per serving 1709 kilojoules/408 calories, 6 g protein,
19 g total fat, 12 g saturated fat, 52 mg cholesterol,
55 g carbohydrate, 6 g fibre

1 Peel oranges, removing white pith. Reserve juice. Separate into segments and arrange on plates.

2 Combine reserved orange juice, grenadine syrup and lime juice and pour over orange segments.

3 Cut out crown of pomegranate, then break pomegranate apart. Take out seeds, removing inner white skins. Sprinkle seeds and grated lime peel over orange segments.

4 Whip cream until stiff. Add ice cream and quickly blend with a hand blender until creamy. Spoon onto each salad portion. Drizzle with rose water. Dust with icing sugar.

warm summer fruit salad with sabayon

Sabayon is like the egg-based Italian dessert zabaglione. It is cooked over simmering water and must not get too hot or it will turn grainy.

1½ cups (375 ml/13 fl oz) apple juice

2 teaspoons caster (superfine) sugar

2 tablespoons brandy

2 large peaches, halved, stoned, thickly sliced

2 large nectarines, halved, stoned, thickly sliced

2 mangoes, peeled, thickly sliced

sabayon sauce

3 egg yolks

4 tablespoons caster (superfine) sugar

½ cup (125 ml/4 fl oz) brandy, rum or orange-flavoured liqueur

serves 6
preparation 10 minutes
cooking 30 minutes

per serving *1040 kilojoules/249 calories, 3 g protein, 3 g total fat, 1 g saturated fat, 106 mg cholesterol, 38 g carbohydrate, 4 g fibre*

1 Pour apple juice into a shallow saucepan or frying pan with a lid. Add caster sugar and brandy. Bring mixture to a boil; reduce heat to medium.

2 Add peaches and nectarines to pan. Cover and poach gently 2 minutes. If skins come off, remove from pan. Add mangoes and poach another 2 minutes. Transfer to a serving bowl, using a slotted spoon.

3 Boil juice mixture 5 to 10 minutes, or until reduced to a slightly heavy syrup. Pour over fruit.

4 To make sabayon sauce, beat egg yolks and caster sugar in top half of a double boiler over gently simmering water, 2 to 3 minutes, until creamy.

5 Beating continuously, add brandy in a thin, steady stream. Continue beating 10 to 12 minutes until sauce is thick. Pour into a jug and serve with poached fruit.

sabayon

You can beat the eggs for a sabayon with water, sweet white wine, champagne, brandy, rum or liqueur. This sauce is usually served warm and foaming. If you want to serve it cold, remove it from the heat after 3 minutes and continue beating for 10 to 12 minutes until creamy.

spiced seasonal fruit salad

This recipe is easily adapted to showcase other summer fruits and berries. Mustard and cayenne pepper add a subtle spicy heat.

1 large mango, peeled and sliced
250 g (8 oz) cherries, pitted
²⁄₃ cup (100 g/4 oz) seedless green grapes
250 g (8 oz) strawberries, hulled
  and cut in half
3 large apricots, halved, stoned, sliced
¾ cup (55 g/2 oz) desiccated (dried)
  coconut
1 tablespoon caster (superfine) sugar
generous pinch of cayenne pepper
generous pinch of mustard powder
pinch of salt

serves 6
preparation 20 minutes
chilling 2 hours or overnight

----

per serving *580 kilojoules/139 calories, 2 g protein,*
6 g total fat, 5 g saturated fat, 0 mg cholesterol,
18 g carbohydrate, 4 g fibre

1 Place all the fruit in a large serving bowl.

2 Finely grind coconut in a spice mill or with a pestle and mortar. Add remaining ingredients and mix well.

3 Add spiced coconut mixture to fruit and stir well to combine. Cover and refrigerate at least 2 hours, preferably overnight to allow the flavours to blend and develop.

mix and match

❋ Replace apricots with 2 large peaches or nectarines or 3 large plums.

❋ If cherries are out of season or expensive, use a mixture of seedless green, black and red grapes. You will need 300 g (10 oz) in total.

❋ Stir 4 or 5 small, very thin pieces of lemon peel into the fruit salad before refrigerating.

cook's tip

Canned fruit may be used in this recipe. Drain thoroughly to remove as much of the syrup as possible and halve the amount of sugar in the spiced coconut mixture.

flambéed apple and walnut salad

6 medium tart apples (such as
   granny smith or boskoop)

2 tablespoons lemon juice

½ cup (125 ml/4 fl oz) dry white wine

1 tablespoon soft brown sugar

2 tablespoons raisins

1 vanilla bean

2 tablespoons crème fraîche or light
   sour cream

½ cup (55 g/2 oz) walnuts

3 tablespoons Calvados (apple brandy),
   cognac or dark rum

serves 4

preparation 20 minutes

cooking 10 minutes

---

per serving *1287 kilojoules/307 calories, 3 g protein,*
14 g total fat, 4 g saturated fat, 13 mg cholesterol,
35 g carbohydrate, 5 g fibre

1 Quarter and peel apples and remove seeds. Cut quarters into large pieces. Place apple pieces, lemon juice, wine, brown sugar and raisins in a saucepan.

2 Slit open vanilla bean and scrape out seeds. Add seeds and bean to pan. Bring mixture to a boil. Cover and cook over low heat 4 to 5 minutes. Apples should be soft but still hold their shape.

3 Remove pan from heat. Remove vanilla bean and drain apples, reserving liquid. Stir crème fraîche into liquid and spoon onto serving plates.

4 Coarsely chop walnuts. Mix with apples and distribute among serving plates. Heat Calvados over low heat, ignite a small amount in a soup or gravy ladle (*see below*), one serving at a time, and pour over fruit salad. Serve at once.

to flambé

1 Heat Calvados over low heat in a small saucepan. Scoop a little into a ladle.

2 Ignite alcohol with a long match, taking care nothing else flammable is within reach.

3 Pour flaming alcohol over salad portion; let flames die out. Flambé a little Calvados for each salad portion.

pear and plum salad with honey cream

sunflower oil, for brushing

50 g (2 oz) sugar cubes (about 12 cubes)

3 tablespoons lemon juice

4 tablespoons pine nuts

2 medium firm williams or bartlett pears

250 g (8 oz) damson or other blue plums

lemon balm leaves, for garnish

honey cream

100 g (4 oz) low-fat quark or light
   sour cream

4 tablespoons honey

¼ teaspoon ground cinnamon

pinch of ground cloves

½ cup (125 g/4 oz) whipping cream

serves 4

preparation 10 minutes

cooking 20 minutes

----

per serving *1959 kilojoules/468 calories, 4 g protein,*
27 g total fat, 12 g saturated fat, 52 mg cholesterol,
54 g carbohydrate, 4 g fibre

1 To make pine nut brittle, lightly brush a piece of baking (waxed) paper with oil. Place sugar, 1 tablespoon lemon juice and 3 tablespoons water in a saucepan with a heat-proof handle. Allow sugar to caramelise until light brown. Remove from heat; stir in pine nuts. Spread mixture on baking paper immediately, as much as possible keeping pine nuts separate from each other. Let brittle cool. Break into pieces.

2 Peel pears, remove seeds and cut into quarters. Cut pear quarters into slices lengthwise. Halve plums; remove stones (pits). Arrange plums and pears on individual plates and drizzle with remaining lemon juice.

3 To make honey cream, stir quark, honey, cinnamon and ground cloves together. Whip cream until stiff and fold into quark mixture. Spoon a little honey cream in the centre of each serving. Sprinkle with pine nut brittle. Garnish with lemon balm leaves.

apple and banana salad with chocolate sauce

50 g (2 oz) bittersweet dark chocolate

½ cup (125 g/4 oz) whipping cream

2 medium green apples

2 tablespoons lemon juice

2 medium ripe bananas

icing (confectioners') sugar for dusting

pinch of ground cinnamon

8 dried dates

2 teaspoons chocolate flakes or shavings

serves 4

preparation + chilling 2 hours 10 minutes

cooking 10 minutes

---

per serving 1245 kilojoules/298 calories, 3 g protein,
17 g total fat, 12 g saturated fat, 37 mg cholesterol,
36 g carbohydrate, 4 g fibre

1 Break dark chocolate into pieces. Place chocolate and cream in top half of a double boiler over gently simmering water. Stir until chocolate melts. Remove and let cool. Chill in refrigerator 2 hours.

2 Peel and quarter apples, removing seeds. Thinly slice apple quarters and place in a bowl; add lemon juice. Peel and slice bananas and combine with apples.

3 Spoon apples and bananas onto dessert plates or bowls and dust with icing sugar and ground cinnamon. Slice dates.

4 Beat chocolate-cream mixture until semi-stiff. Spoon onto salad portions and top with dates and chocolate flakes.

tropical fruit salad

4 tablespoons apricot nectar

2 tablespoons lime juice

3 tablespoons chopped fresh mint leaves

1 large ripe but firm mango, peeled and
    cut into chunks

2 medium slices fresh or canned pineapple,
    cut into wedges

1 large banana, thickly sliced

2 kiwifruit, peeled and cut into chunks

1 medium pawpaw or large papaya, peeled,
    seeded and cut into chunks

serves 4

preparation 30 minutes

per serving *594 kilojoules/142 calories, 3 g protein,*
0 g total fat, 0 g saturated fat, 0 mg cholesterol,
31 g carbohydrate, 7 g fibre

1 Whisk apricot nectar, lime juice and mint in a large bowl. Add mango, pineapple, banana and kiwifruit, tossing to combine. Refrigerate until serving time.

2 To serve, add pawpaw and toss again.

cook's tip

To prepare mangoes, cut from the stem end first. The skin will peel away easily if the fruit is ripe. Slice flesh from mango by cutting down each flat side of the stone (pit).

prickly pears with star fruit

100 g (4 oz) bittersweet dark chocolate

4 Cape gooseberries (physalis/ground cherries/husk tomatoes) in their husks

50 g (2 oz) sugar cubes (about 12 cubes)

1 tablespoon lemon juice

½ cup (125 g/4 oz) whipping cream

4 prickly pears

4 star fruit (carambola), thinly sliced

2 tablespoons lime juice

1 teaspoon icing (confectioners') sugar

icing (confectioners') sugar, for dusting

serves 4

preparation 15 minutes

cooking 20 minutes

----

per serving *1506 kilojoules/360 calories, 3 g protein,*
20 g total fat, 15 g saturated fat, 37 mg cholesterol,
44 g carbohydrate, 6 g fibre

1 Break chocolate into pieces and melt in top half of a double boiler over gently simmering water. Pull back husks from Cape gooseberries. Dip halves into melted chocolate; place on baking (waxed) paper. Leave until chocolate sets.

2 To make caramel sauce, place sugar cubes, lemon juice and 3 tablespoons water in a saucepan with a heat-proof handle. Boil rapidly until sugar turns golden.

3 Remove from heat and stir cream into caramelised sugar, taking care not to let it splatter. Immediately pour sauce into a bowl and let cool.

4 Peel prickly pears, avoiding fine prickles. Cut flesh into thin slices. Arrange prickly pears and star fruit on a platter.

5 Stir lime juice and icing sugar together and drizzle over fruit. Dust with icing sugar. Drizzle caramel sauce over fruit and garnish with chocolate-dipped Cape gooseberries.

vanilla rhubarb with strawberries

800 g (1 lb 12 oz) thin rhubarb stalks

1 vanilla bean

$^2/_3$ cup (160 ml/6 fl oz) dry white wine

3 to 4 tablespoons granulated sugar

500 g (1 lb) strawberries

2 tablespoons orange liqueur

1 tablespoon icing (confectioners') sugar

serves 4

preparation + chilling 1 hour 10 minutes

cooking 10 minutes

- -

per serving 655 kilojoules/157 calories, 4 g protein,
0 g total fat, 0 g saturated fat, 0 mg cholesterol,
29 g carbohydrate, 6 g fibre

1 Peel rhubarb stalks and cut into small pieces.

2 Split open vanilla bean lengthwise and scrape out seeds. Cut in half crosswise. Place rhubarb, vanilla pod, vanilla seeds, wine and sugar in a saucepan and bring to a boil.

3 Cook rhubarb, covered, over low heat 4 to 5 minutes. The pieces should still hold their shape and not become very soft. Remove from heat, let rhubarb cool. Refrigerate 1 hour.

4 Remove vanilla bean and spoon rhubarb into small bowls. Cut about two-thirds of the strawberries into pieces and place in food processor with orange liqueur and icing sugar. Purée until a strawberry froth forms on the surface.

5 Pour puréed strawberries over rhubarb pieces. Garnish with remaining strawberries.

dried fruit salad

1¼ cups (225 g/8 oz) pitted prunes

1 cup (135 g/5 oz) dried apricots

¾ cup (125 g/4 oz) dried peaches or pears, halved

⅓ cup (55 g/2 oz) sultanas (golden raisins)

few thin strips orange peel

1 vanilla bean, halved

½ cup (100 g/4 oz) sugar

2 tablespoons orange flower water or rose water

1 cup (250 g/8 oz) low-fat yogurt, to serve

serves 6

preparation + chilling 1 hour

cooking 25 minutes

per serving 1143 kilojoules/273 calories, 6 g protein, 0.5 g total fat, 0 g saturated fat, 2 mg cholesterol, 62 g carbohydrate, 7 g fibre

1 Place prunes, apricots, peaches, sultanas and orange peel strips in a large saucepan with 4 cups (1 litre/2 pints) water. Scrape seeds from vanilla bean; add seeds and bean to pan. Partly cover and bring slowly to a boil.

2 Cover and simmer 5 minutes. Add sugar and stir until dissolved. Cover and simmer over low heat a further 15 minutes; allow to cool.

3 Drain, transfer to a serving bowl with a little juice from the pan. Stir in orange flower water. Refrigerate, covered, 1 hour. Serve with yogurt on the side.

orange flower water

Orange flower water is a natural extract made from the distillation of orange blossoms. It has a delicate fragrance and an intense flavour. It is used in Middle Eastern and Mediterranean dishes, particularly desserts.

index Page numbers in *italics* refer to feature boxes and tips

a

Aioli, *22*, 160
almonds
  Blackberry and lychee salad with yogurt, 283
  Fruit salad in pineapple halves, 287
  Kiwifruit and blueberry salad, 282
  Pineapple salad with almond brittle, 289
  Tarragon chicken salad, 221
American potato salad, 36
Anchovy dressing, 26
apple cider vinegar, *19*
  Apple cider vinegar dressing, 141
apples, *141*, *278*
  Apple and banana salad with chocolate sauce, 301
  Celery and apples with ricotta dressing, 131
  Chicken liver and apple salad, 231
  Crunchy salad with apples, 141
  Flambéed apple and walnut salad, 298
  Fruity coleslaw, 39
  Mango and papaya salad with cranberries, 292
  Waldorf salad, 28
apricots
  Dried fruit salad, 305
  Mixed fruit salad in melon halves, 284
  Spiced seasonal fruit salad, 297
artichokes, *90*, *112*
  Artichoke and herb salad with white beans, 90
  Artichoke and radicchio salad, 112
  Buckwheat and artichoke salad with feta, 190
  Pastrami and artichoke salad, 207
  White fish salad with olive vinaigrette, 242
arugula *see* rocket
Asian bean sprout salad, 122

Asian chicken salad, 58
asparagus, *101*
  Asparagus and pasta, 155
  Asparagus salad with lemon and garlic mayonnaise, 101
  Ham, egg and asparagus salad, 217
  Orange and asparagus salad, 128
  Orecchiette salad with tuna and aioli, 160
  Trout fillets with asparagus and tomato salad, 258
aubergines *see* eggplant
avocado, *77*
  Chicken salad with avocado, 223
  Cobb salad, 31
  Mixed salad greens with avocado, 77
  Orange and asparagus salad, 128
  Quinoa, avocado and chorizo salad, 196
  Stuffed avocado salad, 33
  Tex Mex salad, 43

b

baby spinach, *15*
  Chickpea, spinach and eggplant salad, 194
  Curried lentil salad, 186
  Fruity salad with blue cheese dressing, 134
  Light potato salad with baby spinach, 89
  Quinoa with sweet and spicy dressing, 197
  Salad greens with fresh figs, 142
  Spinach, roasted garlic and Parmesan, 32
  Tarragon chicken salad, 221
  Watercress and baby spinach with goat cheese, 118
bacon, *37*
  Bacon and potato salad, 37

Bavarian cabbage salad, 116
  Cobb salad, 31
  Curly lettuce salad with eggs and crisp bacon, 68
  Golden yellow salad with crisp bacon, 95
balsamic vinegar, *19*
bamboo shoots
  Rice salad with ginger-soy dressing, 179
  Spicy pork salad, 213
bananas, *278*
  Apple and banana salad with chocolate sauce, 301
  Fruit salad in pineapple halves, 287
  Mixed fruit salad in melon halves, 284
  Tropical fruit salad, 302
Barbecued calamari salad, 275
Barbecued calamari with tomato vinaigrette, 274
basil, *12*
  Basil pesto, 159
  Bocconcini, basil and tomato, 46
  Italian bread salad, 48
  Veal and mushroom salad with basil, 210
Bavarian cabbage salad, 116
Bean salad with cream dressing, 93
Bean salad with paprika vinaigrette, 93
bean sprouts
  Asian bean sprout salad, 122
  Chicken kebab salad with peanut sauce, 228
  Gado gado, 63
  Sprouts salad with mushrooms and celery, 123
beans, *47*
  Chickpea, spinach and eggplant salad, 194
  Couscous salad with chickpeas, 193
  dried, 148

Farfalle salad with beans and
ham, 165
Quinoa, avocado and chorizo
salad, 196
Three bean salad Tuscan-style, 34
Tuscan white bean salad with tuna,
47
types of, 148, 150
White bean salad with herb
dressing, 189
White bean salad with sesame
dressing, 189
see also broad beans; butter
beans; green beans;
kidney beans
beef, *204*
Beef and potato salad with
horseradish dressing, 201
Beef salad in cucumber herb
marinade, 200
Beef salad with lentils, 202
Mexican beef salad, 204
Pastrami and artichoke salad, 207
Pastrami salad on potatoes, 207
Spicy beef salad with capsicum
and corn, 60
Thai beef salad, 203
Thai beef salad with peanuts, 60
beetroot, *51, 138*
Fresh beetroot salad with yogurt,
73
Roasted beetroot and orange
salad, 138
Root vegetable salad with spicy
vinaigrette, 87
Russian salad, 51
Salmon tartare on vegetable
carpaccio, 256
Belgian endive *see* witlof
bell pepper *see* capsicum
berries
Berry salad with mascarpone
cream, 280
Berry salad with pistachio cream,
280
Blackberry and lychee salad with
yogurt, 283
Kiwifruit and blueberry salad, 282

blackberries
Berry salad with mascarpone
cream, 280
Blackberry and lychee salad with
yogurt, 283
blue cheese
Blue cheese dressing, 134, 142
Cobb salad, 31
Fruity salad with blue cheese
dressing, 134
Salad greens with fresh figs, 142
Tossed salad with pears and blue
cheese, 126
blue-eye cod
White fish salad with olive
vinaigrette, 242
blueberries
Berry salad with mascarpone
cream, 280
Berry salad with pistachio cream,
280
Kiwifruit and blueberry salad, 282
bocconcini, *46*
Bocconcini, basil and tomato, 46
Green pasta salad, 159
Wild rice salad with tomatoes and
chilies, 182
bok choy, 15
Bok choy with pan-fried tofu and
peanuts, 121
Chicken kebab salad with peanut
sauce, 228
bread salad
Bread salad with roasted
capsicums, 49
Italian bread salad, 48
Middle Eastern bread salad, 55
broad beans, 150
Bean salad with cream dressing, 93
Bean salad with paprika vinaigrette,
93
Pasta salad with green vegetables,
152
broccoli
Marinated vegetable salad, 82
Salami rice salad, 173
Thai beef salad, 203
buckwheat, 151, *168, 190*

Buckwheat and artichoke salad
with feta, 190
Roasted buckwheat salad with
yogurt dressing, 191
Soba noodle salad, 168
burghul, *57, 151*
Tabouleh, 57
Tabouleh with fish in lemon
dressing, 245
butter beans
Farfalle salad with beans and ham,
165
Golden yellow salad with crisp
bacon, 95
Mixed bean salad with spicy cream
dressing, 94
Three bean salad Tuscan-style, 34
Veal salad with beans, 210
butter lettuce, 15
Tortellini, carrot and egg salad, 166
Tossed salad with pears and blue
cheese, 126
Tuna and egg salad, 253

C

cabanossi
Couscous salad with chickpeas, 193
cabbage, *136*
Bavarian cabbage salad, 116
Cabbage and nectarines with
yogurt chutney, 144
Classic cabbage coleslaw, 39
Soba noodle salad, 168
see also Chinese cabbage
Caesar salad, 26
calamari, *274*
Barbecued calamari with tomato
vinaigrette, 274
Barbecued calamari salad, 275
Italian seafood salad, 241
Noodle and squid salad, 169
canned fruit, *297*
cannellini beans, 150
Tuscan white bean salad with tuna,
47
canola oil, 18, *104*

cantaloupe, 279
  Melon salad with yogurt lime
    sauce, 286
  Mixed fruit salad in melon halves,
    284
  Turkey and fruit salad, 236
cape gooseberries
  Prickly pears with star fruit, 303
caperberries, *88*
  Mixed salad with caperberries, 88
capers
  Russian salad with potato and
    capers, 84
capsicum, *111, 162*
  Barbecued calamari salad, 275
  Bean salad with paprika
    vinaigrette, 93
  Bread salad with roasted
    capsicums, 49
  Cheese, sausage and potato
    salad, 232
  Chicken kebab salad with peanut
    sauce, 228
  Chinese chicken salad, 222
  Diced vegetables with tuna, 251
  Greek salad, 59
  Green summer salad, 111
  Multi-layered salad with yogurt
    mayonnaise, 80
  Mussel salad with croutons,
    271
  Orecchiette salad with tuna and
    aioli, 160
  Paella with chicken and prawns,
    176
  Pasta salad with grilled capsicums,
    163
  Pasta vegetable salad in capsicum
    halves, 162
  Prawn and mango salad, 262
  Quinoa, avocado and chorizo
    salad, 196
  Rice salad with creamy dressing,
    174
  Rice salad with ginger-soy
    dressing, 179
  Roasted buckwheat salad with
    yogurt dressing, 191

Russian salad with potato and
    capers, 84
Salad niçoise, 45
Salami rice salad, 173
Seafood salad with saffron and
    parsley, 263
Smoked trout and roasted
    capsicum salad, 249
Spicy beef salad with capsicum
    and corn, 60
Spicy Chinese cabbage salad, 145
Tuna and egg salad, 253
Tuna and roasted capsicum salad,
    249
Vegetable salad with tuna, 250
Warm grilled mixed vegetable
    salad, 107
White bean salad with herb
    dressing, 189
carambola *see* star fruit
Caramel, 288
carrots
  Carrot salad, 74
  Chicken and pineapple salad with
    curry dressing, 227
  Citrus salad with goat cheese, 131
  Ham salad with grated vegetables,
    214
  Lettuce, carrot and fennel salad
    with vinaigrette, 71
  Marinated vegetable salad, 82
  Mixed salad with ham, 214
  Moroccan-style carrot salad, 75
  Noodle and mushroom sweet and
    sour salad, 171
  Quinoa with sweet and spicy
    dressing, 197
  Russian salad with potato and
    capers, 84
  Soba noodle salad, 168
  Tortellini, carrot and egg salad,
    166
  Turkish carrot salad with garlic
    yogurt, 72
cashew nuts
  Rice salad with ginger-soy dressing,
    179
cauliflower, *82*

Marinated vegetable salad, 82
caviar
  Smoked salmon on mixed salad
    greens, 257
  Trout fillets with asparagus and
    tomato salad, 258
celeriac
  Ham salad with grated vegetables,
    214
  Waldorf salad, 28
celery, *97*
  Asian bean sprout salad, 122
  Celery and apples with ricotta
    dressing, 131
  Chicken and pineapple salad with
    curry dressing, 227
  Chicken salad with avocado, 223
  Citrus salad with goat cheese, 131
  Crab salad with papaya, 268
  Lobster salad with celery and
    tomatoes, 270
  Marinated vegetable salad, 82
  Spicy rice salad with pineapple, 181
  Sprouts salad with mushrooms
    and celery, 123
Champagne vinaigrette, 76
champagne vinegar, 19
cheddar cheese
  Pasta vegetable salad in capsicum
    halves, 162
cheese, *49*
  Cheese, sausage and potato salad,
    232
  Pasta vegetable salad in capsicum
    halves, 162
  see also blue cheese; bocconcini;
    feta cheese; goat cheese;
    gouda cheese; mozzarella
    cheese; Parmesan cheese;
    ricotta
Cheese dressing, 237
Chef's salad, 29
cherries, *284*
  Mixed fruit salad in melon halves,
    284
  Spiced seasonal fruit salad, 297
cherry tomatoes
  Bocconcini, basil and tomato, 46

Crisp seafood salad with yogurt dressing, 264
Farfalle salad with chicken 156
Green pasta salad, 159
Herring salad with radish and rocket, 52
Marinated vegetable salad, 82
Mixed bean salad with spicy cream dressing, 94
Mixed salad with caperberries, 88
Pastrami salad on potatoes, 207
Prawn and mango salad, 262
Rocket and radicchio salad with tomatoes, 115
Tabouleh with fish in lemon dressing, 245
Trout fillets with asparagus and tomato salad, 258
Veal salad with beans, 210
chicken, *221*, *222*
Asian chicken salad, 58
Chef's salad, 29
Chicken and pineapple salad with curry dressing, 227
Chicken kebab salad with peanut sauce, 228
Chicken salad with avocado, 223
Chicken salad with cucumber and watercress, 224
Chicken with salad greens, 218
Chinese chicken salad 222
Cobb salad, 31
Farfalle salad with chicken, 156
Mixed salad with chicken and spicy dressing, 156
Paella with chicken and prawns, 176
Soba noodle salad, 168
Tarragon chicken salad, 221
Tex Mex salad, 43
Veal and mushroom salad with basil, 210
chicken livers
Chicken liver and apple salad, 231
Warm chicken livers with green beans and tomatoes, 231
chicken sausage
Sausage, potato and radish salad, 232

chickpeas, 150, *193*
Chickpea, spinach and eggplant salad, 194
Couscous salad with chickpeas, 193
chicory *see* witlof
chili flowers, *224*
chilies
Asian chicken salad, 58
Chicken kebab salad with peanut sauce, 228
Chili lime dressing, 129
Eggplant salad with chilies and cumin, 99
Fresh tomato salad, 117
Gado gado, 63
Greek salad, 59
Mexican beef salad, 204
Noodle and squid salad, 169
Pico de gallo, 43
Spicy beef salad with capsicum and corn, 60
Thai beef salad, 203
Thai beef salad with peanuts, 60
Vietnamese fish salad, 246
White bean salad with sesame dressing, 189
Wild rice salad with tomatoes and chilies, 182
Chinese beans, *165*
Chinese cabbage
Cabbage and nectarines with yogurt chutney, 144
Gado gado, 63
Noodle and mushroom sweet and sour salad, 171
Spicy Chinese cabbage salad, 145
Spicy pork salad, 213
Chinese chicken salad, 222
chives, 12
Creamy chive yogurt, 66
Spicy pork salad, 213
Spicy sausage and cheese salad, 209
chocolate
Apple and banana salad with chocolate sauce, 301
Citrus fruit salad with chocolate, 290

Fruit salad in pineapple halves, 287
Prickly pears with star fruit, 303
chorizo, *173*
Quinoa, avocado and chorizo salad, 196
chutney, *144*
Yogurt, 144
ciabatta, *48*
Italian bread salad, 48
Citrus fruit salad with chocolate, 290
Citrus salad with goat cheese, 131
Citrus vinaigrette, 261
Classic herb vinaigrette, 21
Classic mayonnaise, 23
Cobb salad, 31
Coleslaw, 39
cod
White fish salad with olive vinaigrette, 242
coleslaw, *39*
Coleslaw, 39
Crunchy nut, 39
Fruity, 39
Mixed cabbage, 39
coriander, 12
Asian chicken salad, 58
Mexican beef salad, 204
Pico de gallo, 43
corn
Cheese, sausage and potato salad 232
Mexican beef salad, 204
Multi-layered salad with yogurt mayonnaise, 80
Rice salad with ginger-soy dressing, 179
Spicy beef salad with capsicum and corn, 60
corn salad *see* lamb's lettuce
cos lettuce, 15
Asian chicken salad, 59
Barbecued calamari with tomato vinaigrette, 274
Caesar salad, 26
Chef's salad, 29

Chicken and pineapple salad with
    curry dressing, 227
Crunchy salad with apples, 141
Green salad with creamy chive
    yogurt, 66
Ham, egg and asparagus salad,
    217
Italian seafood salad, 241
Paella with chicken and prawns, 176
Salad niçoise, 45
Seafood salad with saffron and
    parsley, 263
Spicy brown rice salad with feta,
    174
Tabouleh, 57
Tex Mex salad, 43
Wild rice salad with shallots and
    lettuce, 183
couscous, 151, *193*
    Couscous salad with chickpeas, 193
    Couscous salad with tuna, 193
    Tabouleh, 57
crab, *269*
    Crab and grapefruit salad, 267
    Crab salad with papaya, 268
cranberries, *45*
    Mango and papaya salad with
        cranberries, 292
    Salad with camembert, 44
cress, 15
Crisp seafood salad with yogurt
    dressing, 264
croutons, 66
Crunchy nut coleslaw, 39
Crunchy salad with apples, 141
cucumber, *103*
    Bean salad with paprika
        vinaigrette, 93
    Cucumber salad, 103
    Cucumbers with dill and sour
        cream dressing, 40
    Gado gado, 63
    Greek salad, 59
    Italian bread salad, 48
    Middle Eastern bread salad, 55
    Mixed salad with ham, 214
    Onion and tropical fruit salad, 129
    Potato salad with cucumber, 85

Prawn and mango salad, 262
Radish and cucumber salad, 102
Salad with celery and mint
    dressing, 83
Tabouleh, 57
Tabouleh with fish in lemon
    dressing, 245
Thai beef salad, 203
Thai beef salad with peanuts, 60
Tzatziki, 40
cucumber (pickled)
    Beef salad in cucumber herb
        marinade, 200
    Russian salad, 51
curly endive, 15
    Chicken with mixed salad
        greens, 218
    Curly lettuce salad with eggs and
        crisp bacon, 68
    Egg and radish salad, 104
    Salad greens with fresh figs, 142
    Salad with camembert, 44
    Salmon on lettuce and watercress,
        255
    Scallops and grapefruit with
        mustard vinaigrette, 272
    Smoked salmon on mixed salad
        greens, 257
    see also Lebanese cucumber
Curly lettuce salad with eggs and
    crisp bacon, 68
Curried lentil salad, 186
Curry dressing, 227, *227*
Curry vinaigrette, 181

d

dandelion leaves
    Salad with camembert, 44
dates
    Apple and banana salad with
        chocolate sauce, 301
    Dried fruit salad, 305
Diced vegetables with tuna, 251
dill, 12, *254*
    Cucumbers with dill and sour
        cream dressing, 40

Dill dressing, 33
Salmon salad with peas and dill,
    254
dressing, 20-1
    Anchovy, 26
    Apple cider vinegar, 141
    Blue cheese, 134, 142
    Cheese, 237
    Chili lime, 129
    Classic mayonnaise, 23
    Cream, 162
    Creamy, 214
    Curry, 227
    Dill, 33
    Ginger-soy, 179
    Horseradish, 201
    Lemon, 245
    Mustard and lemon, 224
    Orange mustard, 128
    Paprika sour cream, 165
    Roquefort, 22
    Sour cream, 40, 103
    Spicy cream, 94
    Spicy fruit, 122
    Thousand island, 23
    Yogurt, 191, 264
    see also vinaigrette
Dried fruit salad, 305

e

eggplant, *98, 194*
    Chickpea, spinach and eggplant
        salad, 194
    Eggplant salad with chilies and
        cumin, 99
    Eggplant salad with tahini, 98
    Spicy brown rice salad with feta,
        174
    Warm grilled mixed vegetable
        salad, 107
eggs, *166*
    Aïoli, 22, 160
    American potato salad, 36
    Bacon and potato salad, 37
    Chef's salad, 29
    Cobb salad, 31

Curly lettuce salad with eggs and crisp bacon, 68
Egg and radish salad, 104
Gado gado, 63
Ham, egg and asparagus salad, 217
Red and green salad with champagne vinaigrette, 76
Remoulade, 23
Russian salad with potato and capers, 84
Salad niçoise, 45
Salad with egg vinaigrette, 69
Smoked trout and roasted capsicum salad, 249
Tortellini, carrot and egg salad, 166
Trout fillets with asparagus and tomato salad, 258
Tuna and egg salad, 253
Warm summer fruit salad with sabayon, 294
White bean salad with sesame dressing, 189
English cucumber *see* telegraph cucumber
equipment, 11

f

Farfalle salad with beans and ham, 165
Farfalle salad with chicken, 156
Fattoush *see* Middle Eastern bread salad
fava beans *see* broad beans
fennel, *71*, *132*
    Fennel and green bean salad, 97
    Lettuce, carrot and fennel salad with vinaigrette, 71
    Radicchio and fennel salad with oranges, 132
    White fish salad with fennel and sun-dried tomatoes, 243
feta cheese
    Bread salad with roasted capsicums, 49
    Buckwheat and artichoke salad with feta, 190

Chickpea, spinach and eggplant salad, 194
Greek salad, 59
Roasted buckwheat salad with yogurt dressing, 191
Spicy brown rice salad with feta, 174
Sugar-snap peas with grapes and feta, 134
field greens *see* mesclun
field salad *see* lamb's lettuce
figs, *142*, *291*
    Orange and figs with sherry cream, 291
    Salad greens with fresh figs, 142
fish and seafood *see* seafood and fish
flageolet beans
    Fennel and green bean salad, 97
Flambéed apple and walnut salad, 298
frankfurters
    Cheese, sausage and potato salad, 232
Fresh beetroot salad with yogurt, 73
Fresh tomato salad, 117
fruit salad
    Apple and banana salad with chocolate sauce, 301
    Berry salad with mascarpone cream, 280
    Berry salad with pistachio cream, 280
    Blackberry and lychee salad with yogurt, 283
    Citrus fruit salad with chocolate, 290
    Dried fruit salad, 305
    Flambéed apple and walnut salad, 298
    Fruit salad in pineapple halves, 287
    Kiwifruit with blueberry salad, 282
    Mango and papaya salad with cranberries, 292
    Melon salad with yogurt lime sauce, 286
    Mixed fruit salad in melon halves, 284
    Onion and tropical fruit salad, 129

Orange and figs with sherry cream, 291
Orange and pomegranate salad with vanilla cream, 293
Pear and plum salad with honey cream, 300
Pineapple salad with almond brittle, 289
Prickly pears with star fruit, 303
serve size, 279
Spiced seasonal fruit salad, 297
Tropical fruit salad, 302
Vanilla rhubarb with strawberries, 304
Warm summer fruit salad with sabayon, 294
Fruity coleslaw, 39
Fruity salad with blue cheese dressing, 134

g

Gado gado, 63
galia melon, 279
garbanzo beans *see* chickpeas
garlic
    Asian chicken salad, 58
    Garlic sauce, 22
    Spinach, roasted garlic and Parmesan, 32
garlic sausage
    Couscous salad with chickpeas, 193
gherkins
    Cheese, sausage and potato salad, 232
    Ham salad with grated vegetables, 214
    Spicy sausage and cheese salad, 209
ginger
    Chicken kebab salad with peanut sauce, 228
    Spicy pork salad, 213
Ginger-soy dressing, 179
globe artichokes, *90*
    Artichoke and herb salad with white beans, 90

Artichoke and radicchio salad, 112
goat cheese, *118*
Cheese dressing, 237
Citrus salad with goat cheese, 131
Mushroom salad with goat cheese
dressing, 142
Watercress and baby spinach with
goat cheese, 118
Golden yellow salad with crisp bacon,
95
gouda cheese
Cheese, sausage and potato salad,
232
Multi-layered salad with yogurt
mayonnaise, 80
grains, 14
Buckwheat and artichoke salad
with feta, 190
Couscous salad with chickpeas, 193
Couscous salad with tuna, 193
Quinoa, avocado and chorizo salad,
196
Quinoa with sweet and spicy
dressing, 197
Roasted buckwheat salad with
yogurt dressing, 191
types of, 148, 151
Wild rice salad with shallots and
lettuce, 183
Wild rice salad with tomatoes and
chilies, 182
grapefruit, *267*
Citrus fruit salad with chocolate,
290
Crab and grapefruit salad, 267
Scallops and grapefruit with
mustard vinaigrette, 272
grapes, 278, 279
Melon salad with yogurt lime
sauce, 286
Spiced seasonal fruit salad, 297
Sugar-snap peas with grapes
and feta, 134
Turkey and fruit salad, 236
Waldorf salad, 28
grapeseed oil, 18
Greek salad, 59
green beans, *165, 250*

Fennel and green bean salad, 97
Gado gado, 63
Mixed bean salad with spicy
cream dressing, 94
Paella with chicken and prawns, 176
Russian salad with potato and
capers, 84
Salad niçoise, 45
Soba noodle salad, 168
Three bean salad Tuscan-style, 34
Tuna and green bean salad, 247
Veal salad with beans, 210
Vegetable salad with tuna, 250
Warm chicken livers with green
beans and tomatoes, 231
Green pasta salad, 159
Green salad with creamy chive
yogurt, 66
Green salad with creamy herb
yogurt, 66
Green summer salad, 111
Grilled tomato salad, 108
Grilled tomato salad with cheese, 109
groundnut oil *see* peanut oil

h

ham
Artichoke and herb salad with
white beans, 90
Asparagus and pasta, 155
Asparagus salad with lemon and
garlic mayonnaise, 101
Chef's salad, 29
Farfalle salad with beans and ham,
165
Fennel and green bean salad, 97
Ham, egg and asparagus salad, 217
Ham salad with grated vegetables,
214
Mixed salad with ham, 214
Pasta salad with peas and ham, 152
haricot beans *see* cannellini beans
hazelnut oil, 18
hazelnuts
Carrot salad, 74
hearts of palm, *268*

Crab salad with papaya, 268
herb butters, *66*
Herb cream, 166
herb dressings, 20
Classic herb vinaigrette, 21
Herb vinaigrette, 160, 253
Lemon thyme vinaigrette, 21
Raspberry herb nut
vinaigrette, 20
herbs, 12-13
herrings
Herring and dill salad with
potatoes, 52
Herring salad with radish and
rocket, 52
Matjes herring salad with citrus
fruit, 261
Honey cream, 300
honeydew melon
Melon salad with yogurt lime
sauce, 286
Mixed fruit salad in melon halves,
284
Turkey and fruit salad, 236
Horseradish dressing, 201

i

iceberg lettuce, 16
Asian chicken salad, 59
Caesar salad, 26
Crisp seafood salad with yogurt
dressing, 264
Gado gado, 63
Iceberg lettuce with salmon,
265
Middle Eastern bread salad, 55
Mixed salad with chicken and
spicy dressing, 156
Multi-layered salad with yogurt
mayonnaise, 80
Salmon salad with peas and dill,
254
Turkey and fruit salad, 236
Italian bread salad, 48
Italian seafood salad, 241
Italian-style layered salad, 81

j

Japanese-style trout with wasabi
and rocket, 258
Jarlsberg cheese
Chef's salad, 29

k

kasha *see* buckwheat
kebab salad with peanut sauce,
Chicken, 228
kidney beans, 150
Mixed bean salad with spicy
cream dressing, 94
Quinoa, avocado and chorizo
salad, 196
Tex Mex salad, 43
Three bean salad Tuscan-style, 34
kiwifruit
Kiwifruit and blueberry salad, 282
Onion and tropical fruit salad, 129
Tropical fruit salad, 302

l

lamb's lettuce, 16
Mixed salad with ham, 214
Salad greens with fresh figs, 142
Lebanese cucumber
Chicken salad with avocado, 223
Chicken salad with cucumber and
watercress, 224
Diced vegetables with tuna, 251
Gado gado, 63
Greek salad, 59
Italian bread salad, 48
Tabouleh, 57
Thai beef salad with peanuts, 60
leeks
Chicken and pineapple salad with
curry dressing, 227
legumes *see under name eg* lentils
Lemon and sherry vinaigrette, 71
Lemon dressing, 245
lemon grass, 12, *213*

Spicy pork salad, 213
lemon thyme, 13
Lemon thyme vinaigrette, 21
lemons
Matjes herring salad with citrus
fruit, 261
lentils, *184*
Beef salad with lentils, 202
Curried lentil salad, 186
Lentil salad with fried onions and
rosemary, 186
Potato and lentil salad, 185
Warm lentil salad, 184
lettuce, 14, 15-16, *76*
see also butter lettuce; cos lettuce;
curly endive; iceberg lettuce;
lamb's lettuce; mignonette lettuce
Lettuce, carrot and fennel salad with
vinaigrette, 71
Light potato salad with baby spinach,
89
lima beans
Pasta salad with green vegetables,
152
lobster
Lobster salad with celery and
tomatoes, 270
lollo bionda, 16
Tuna and roasted capsicum salad,
249
lollo rossa lettuce, 16
Barbecued calamari salad, 275
lychees
Blackberry and lychee salad with
yogurt, 283

m

mâche *see* lamb's lettuce
mandarins
Chicken and pineapple salad with
curry dressing, 227
Citrus fruit salad with chocolate,
290
Red cabbage with citrus, 136
mange-tout *see* snow peas
mango, 279, *302*

Asian bean sprout salad, 122
Mango and papaya salad with
cranberries, 292
Onion and tropical fruit salad, 129
Prawn and mango salad, 262
Spiced seasonal fruit salad, 297
Tropical fruit salad, 302
Warm summer fruit salad with
sabayon, 294
marinades, 82
Marinated vegetable salad, 82
marjoram, 12-13
Mascarpone cream, 280
matjes herring, *52, 261*
Herring and dill salad with
potatoes, 52
Herring salad with radish and
rocket, 52
Matjes herring salad with citrus
fruit, 261
mayonnaise, 84, *100*
Aioli, 22, 160
Classic, 23
Lemon and garlic, 101
Yogurt, 80, 152
melons, *236, 279, 284*
Melon salad with yogurt lime
sauce, 286
Mixed fruit salad in melon halves,
284
Turkey and fruit salad, 236
mesclun, *126*
Mexican beef salad, 204
Middle Eastern bread salad, 55
mignonette lettuce, 16
Cobb salad, 31
Crab and grapefruit salad, 267
mint, 13
Asian chicken salad, 59
Tabouleh, 57
Tropical fruit salad, 302
Mixed bean salad with spicy cream
dressing, 94
Mixed cabbage coleslaw, 39
Mixed fruit salad in melon halves, 284
Mixed mushroom salad, 125
Mixed salad greens with avocado, 77
Mixed salad with caperberries, 88

Mixed salad with chicken and spicy
    dressing, 156
Mixed salad with ham, 214
Moroccan-style carrot salad, 75
mozzarella cheese
    Green pasta salad, 159
    Italian-style layered salad, 81
    Wild rice salad with tomatoes and
        chili, 182
Multi-layered salad with yogurt
    mayonnaise, 80
mung bean sprouts
    Asian bean sprout salad, 122
    Chicken kebab salad with peanut
        sauce, 228
    Sprouts salad with mushrooms
        and celery, 123
mushrooms, 107, 125
    Chicken with mixed salad greens,
        218
    Mixed mushroom salad, 125
    Mushroom salad, 70
    Mushroom salad with goat cheese
        dressing, 142
    Noodle and mushroom sweet and
        sour salad, 171
    Spicy rice salad with pineapple, 181
    Sprouts salad with mushrooms
        and celery, 123
    Turkey and mushroom salad with
        basil, 234
    Turkey with fruit and nuts, 237
    Veal and mushroom salad with
        basil, 210
    Warm grilled mixed vegetable
        salad, 107
mussels, 241
    Italian seafood salad, 241
    Mussel salad with croutons, 271
Mustard and lemon dressing, 224
Mustard horseradish vinaigrette, 68
Mustard vinaigrette, 272

N

napa see Chinese cabbage
nasturtium, 16

navy beans
    Fennel and green bean salad, 97
nectarines, 278
    Asian bean sprout salad, 122
    Cabbage and nectarines with
        yogurt chutney, 144
    Warm summer fruit salad with
        sabayon, 294
noodles, 171
    Noodle and mushroom sweet and
        sour salad, 171
    Noodle and squid salad, 169
    Soba noodle salad, 168
    storage of, 148
    types of, 148, 149
nutrition, 148, 278
nuts, 74, 131
    Carrot salad, 74

O

oak leaf lettuce, 16
    Chicken liver and apple salad, 231
    Chicken with mixed salad greens,
        218
    Mushroom salad, 70
    Turkey and mushroom salad, 234
oils, 18
olive oil, 18
olives, 185
    Bocconcini, basil and tomato, 46
    Bread salad with roasted
        capsicums, 49
    Fennel and green bean salad, 97
    Greek salad, 59
    Grilled tomato salad, 108
    Olive vinaigrette, 242
    Orecchiette salad with tuna and
        aioli, 160
    Potato and lentil salad, 185
    Radicchio and fennel salad with
        oranges, 132
    Roasted beetroot and orange
        salad, 138
    Salad niçoise, 45
    Spicy brown rice salad with feta,
        174

Tuna and egg salad, 253
Vegetable salad with tuna, 250
Warm grilled mixed vegetable
    salad, 107
White bean salad with sesame
    dressing, 189
onions
    Chicken and pineapple salad with
        curry dressing, 227
    Chicken liver and apple salad, 231
    Herring and dill salad with
        potatoes, 52
    Lentil salad with fried onions and
        rosemary, 186
    Onion and tropical fruit salad, 129
    Tuna salad with peas and onions,
        253
    see also red onions
orange flower water, 305
orange roughy, 245
    Tabouleh with fish in lemon
        dressing, 245
oranges, 138
    Chicken and pineapple salad with
        curry dressing, 227
    Citrus fruit salad with chocolate,
        290
    Citrus salad with goat cheese, 131
    Fruit salad in pineapple halves, 287
    Mango and papaya salad with
        cranberries, 292
    Matjes herring salad with citrus
        fruit, 261
    Orange and asparagus salad, 128
    Orange and figs with sherry cream,
        291
    Orange and pomegranate salad
        with vanilla cream, 293
    Orange mustard dressing, 128
    Radicchio and fennel salad with
        oranges, 132
    Red cabbage with citrus, 136
    Roasted beetroot and orange
        salad, 138
    Tarragon chicken salad, 221
    see also mandarins
Orecchiette salad with tuna and
    aioli, 160

p

Paella with chicken and prawns, 176
pancetta, *97, 218*
papaya
    Crab salad with papaya, 268
    Mango and papaya salad with
        cranberries, 292
    Tropical fruit salad, 302
Paprika sour cream dressing, 165
Paprika vinaigrette, 93
Parma ham
    Asparagus and pasta, 155
    Fennel and green bean salad, 97
Parmesan cheese
    Caesar salad, 26
    Roast pumpkin and Parmesan
        salad, 114
    Spinach, roasted garlic and
        Parmesan, 32
    Veal and mushroom salad with
        basil, 210
parsley, *12, 57, 93*
    American potato salad, 36
    Bacon and potato salad, 37
    Bocconcini, basil and tomato, 46
    Coleslaw, 39
    Tabouleh, 57
    Three-bean salad Tuscan-style, 34
pasta, *14, 155*
    Asparagus and pasta, 155
    Chinese Chicken salad, 222
    Farfalle salad with beans and
        ham, 165
    Farfalle salad with chicken, 156
    Green pasta salad, 159
    Noodle and mushroom sweet and
        sour salad, 171
    Noodle and squid salad, 169
    Orecchiette salad with tuna and
        aioli, 160
    Pasta salad with green vegetables,
        152
    Pasta salad with grilled capsicums,
        163
    Pasta salad with peas and ham, 152
    Pasta vegetable salad in capsicum
        halves, 162

    Soba noodle salad, 168
    storage of, 148
    Tortellini, carrot and egg salad, 166
    types of, 148, 149
    see also noodles
pastrami, *207*
    Pastrami and artichoke salad, 207
    Pastrami salad on potatoes, 207
pawpaw
    Crab salad with papaya, 268
    Mango and papaya salad with
        cranberries, 292
    Tropical fruit salad, 302
peaches, 278, 279
    Blackberry and lychee salad with
        yogurt, 283
    Dried fruit salad, 305
    Warm fruit salad with sabayon, 294
peanut oil, 18
peanuts
    Asian bean sprout salad, 122
    Bok choy with pan-fried tofu and
        peanuts, 121
    Gado gado, 63
    Peanut sauce, 63, 228
    Thai beef salad with peanuts, 60
    Vietnamese fish salad, 246
pears, 278
    Dried fruit salad, 305
    Fruity salad with blue cheese
        dressing, 134
    Pear and plum salad with honey
        cream, 300
    Tossed salad with pears and blue
        cheese, 126
peas
    Mixed salad with ham, 214
    Paella with chicken and prawns, 176
    Pasta salad with peas and ham, 152
    Russian salad, 51
    Russian salad with potato and
        capers, 84
    Salmon salad with peas and dill,
        254
    Tuna salad with peas and onions,
        253
    Vegetable salad with tuna, 250
    see also snow peas

pecorino
    Artichoke and radicchio salad, 112
pesto, *159*
    Basil, 159
Pesto vinaigrette, 182
Pico de gallo, 43
pine nuts, *218*
    Pear and plum salad with honey
        cream, 300
    Spinach, roasted garlic and
        Parmesan, 32
pineapple, *279, 286*
    Asian bean sprout salad, 122
    Chicken and pineapple salad with
        curry dressing, 227
    Fruit salad in pineapple halves, 287
    Melon salad with yogurt lime
        sauce, 286
    Pineapple salad with almond
        brittle, 289
    Spicy rice salad with pineapple, 181
    Tropical fruit salad, 302
pistachios
    Berry salad with pistachio cream,
        280
    Orange and figs with sherry cream,
        291
pita bread
    Middle Eastern bread salad, 55
plums, 279
    Mixed fruit salad in melon halves,
        284
    Pear and plum salad with honey
        cream, 300
    Turkey with fruit and nuts, 237
    pomegranate salad with vanilla
        cream, Orange and, 293
pork
    Spicy pork salad, 213
    Spicy sausage and cheese salad,
        209
    see also ham
Port vinaigrette, 137
potato salad, *88*
    American potato salad, 36
    Bacon and potato salad, 37
    Light potato salad with baby
        spinach, 89

Mixed salad with caperberries, 88
Potato salad with cucumber, 85
potatoes, 14, *232*
American potato salad, 36
Bacon and potato salad, 37
Beef and potato salad with horseradish dressing, 201
Cheese, sausage and potato salad, 232
Gado gado, 63
Herring and dill salad with potatoes, 52
Lentil salad with fried onions and rosemary, 186
Light potato salad with baby spinach, 89
Mixed salad with caperberries, 88
Pastrami salad on potatoes, 207
Potato and lentil salad, 185
Root vegetable salad with spicy vinaigrette, 87
Russian salad, 51
Russian salad with potato and capers, 84
Salmon tartare on vegetable carpaccio, 256
Sausage, potato and radish salad, 232
Tuna and green bean salad, 247
Vegetable salad with tuna, 250
prawns, *177*
Crisp seafood with yogurt dressing, 264
Italian seafood salad, 241
Paella with chicken and prawns, 176
Prawn and mango salad, 262
Seafood salad with saffron and parsley, 263
Stuffed avocado salad, 33
Prickly pears with star fruit, 303
prosciutto, *97*
Asparagus and pasta, 155
see also Parma ham
pumpkin and Parmesan salad, Roast, 114
prunes
Dried fruit salad, 305
purple waxbeans, *165*

q

quinoa, 151, *196*
Quinoa, avocado and chorizo salad, 196
Quinoa with sweet and spicy dressing, 197

r

radicchio, 17, *115*
Artichoke and radicchio salad, 112
Buckwheat and artichoke salad with feta, 190
Chicken with mixed salad greens, 218
Radicchio and fennel salad with oranges, 132
Rocket and radicchio salad with tomatoes, 115
Smoked salmon on mixed salad greens, 257
Tossed salad with pears and blue cheese, 126
Turkey and fruit salad, 236
Turkey with fruit and nuts, 237
Warm grilled mixed vegetable salad, 107
radishes
Crunchy nut coleslaw, 39
Cucumber salad, 103
Egg and radish salad, 104
Farfalle salad with beans and ham, 165
Herring salad with radish and rocket, 52
Multi-layered salad with yogurt mayonnaise, 80
Radish and cucumber salad, 102
Red and green salad with champagne vinaigrette, 76
Salad with celery and mint dressing, 83
Sausage, potato and radish salad, 232
rapeseed oil, *104*
raspberries, 278, *234*

Berry salad with pistachio cream, 280
Raspberry cream, 282
Turkey and mushroom salad, 234
Raspberry nut herb vinaigrette, 20
Red and green salad with champagne vinaigrette, 76
red cabbage, *136*
Mixed cabbage coleslaw, 39
Red cabbage with citrus, 136
Red cabbage with port vinaigrette, 137
red kidney beans, *34*
Mixed bean salad with spicy cream dressing, 94
Tex Mex salad, 43
Three bean salad Tuscan-style, 34
red onions
American potato salad, 36
Asian chicken salad, 58
Citrus salad with goat cheese, 131
Cucumbers with dill and sour cream dressing, 40
Greek salad, 59
Italian bread salad, 48
Mixed mushroom salad, 125
Mixed salad with caperberries, 88
Onion and tropical fruit salad, 129
Pastrami and artichoke salad, 207
Pico de gallo, 43
Quinoa, avocado and chorizo salad, 196
Quinoa with sweet and spicy dressing, 197
Roasted beetroot and orange salad, 138
Salad niçoise, 45
Scallops and grapefruit with mustard vinaigrette, 272
Spicy beef salad with capsicum and corn, 60
Spicy sausage and cheese salad, 209
Thai beef salad with peanuts, 60
Three bean salad Tuscan-style, 34
Tuscan white bean salad with tuna, 47

Warm grilled mixed vegetable salad, 107

White bean salad with sesame dressing, 189

red vinegar, 19

red wine vinegar, 19

redcurrants

Berry salad with mascarpone cream, 280

Berry salad with pistachio cream, 280

rhubarb with strawberries, Vanilla, 304

rice, 14, *176, 179, 181*

Paella with chicken and prawns, 176

Rice salad with creamy dressing, 174

Rice salad with ginger-soy dressing, 179

Salami rice salad, 173

Spicy brown rice salad with feta, 174

Spicy rice salad with pineapple, 181

storage of, 148

varieties of, 148, 149

Vietnamese fish salad, 246

Wild rice salad with shallots and lettuce, 183

Wild rice salad with tomatoes and chilies, 182

ricotta

Asparagus and pasta, 155

Celery and apples with ricotta dressing, 131

Grilled tomato salad with cheese, 109

Roast pumpkin and Parmesan salad, 114

Roasted beetroot and orange salad, 138

Roasted buckwheat salad with yogurt dressing, 191

rocket, 12, 17, *126*

Artichoke and herb salad with white beans, 90

Farfalle salad with chicken, 156

Green pasta salad, 159

Grilled tomato salad, 108

Herring salad with radish and rocket, 52

Japanese-style trout with wasabi and rocket, 258

Mixed salad with caperberries, 88

Mussel salad with croutons, 271

Pastrami and artichoke salad, 207

Roast pumpkin and Parmesan salad, 114

Rocket and radicchio salad with tomatoes, 115

Salad with camembert, 44

Scallops and grapefruit with mustard vinaigrette, 272

Wild rice salad with tomatoes and chilies, 182

Root vegetable salad with spicy vinaigrette, 87

Roquefort dressing, 22

rosemary, 12

Russian salad, 51

Russian salad with potato and capers, 84

S

Sabayon sauce, 294

safflower oil, 18

salad greens, *10*, 14-17

Chicken with mixed salad greens, 218

Mixed salad greens with avocado, 77

Salad greens with fresh figs, 142

Salad with camembert, 44

Smoked salmon on mixed salad greens, 257

Salad niçoise, 45

Salad with celery and mint dressing, 83

Salad with egg vinaigrette, 69

salami

Salami rice salad, 173

Spicy sausage and cheese salad, 209

salmon, *254*

Iceberg lettuce with salmon, 265

Salmon on lettuce and watercress, 255

Salmon salad with peas and dill, 254

Salmon tartare on vegetable carpaccio, 256

Smoked salmon on mixed salad greens, 257

sambal oelek, *122*

sauces, 22-3

Garlic, 22

Peanut, 63

see also dressing; vinaigrette

sauerkraut, *209*

sausage

Cheese, sausage and potato salad, 232

Sausage, potato and radish salad, 232

Spicy sausage and cheese salad, 209

see also garlic sausage

scallops, *272*

Scallops and grapefruit with mustard vinaigrette, 272

seafood and fish

Barbecued calamari with tomato vinaigrette, 274

Barbecued calamari salad, 275

Couscous salad with tuna, 193

Crab and grapefruit salad, 267

Crab salad with papaya, 268

Crisp seafood salad with yogurt dressing, 264

Diced vegetables with tuna, 251

Herring and dill salad with potatoes, 52

Herring salad with radish and rocket, 52

Iceberg lettuce with salmon, 265

Italian seafood salad, 241

Japanese-style trout with wasabi and rocket, 258

Lobster salad with celery and tomatoes, 270

Matjes herring salad with citrus fruit, 261

Mussel salad with croutons, 271

Noodle and squid salad, 169

Orecchiette salad with tuna and aioli, 160

Paella with chicken and prawns, 176

Prawn and mango salad, 262

Salad niçoise, 45

Salmon on lettuce and watercress, 255

Salmon salad with peas and dill, 254

Salmon tartare on vegetable carpaccio, 256

Scallops and grapefruit with mustard vinaigrette, 272

Seafood salad with saffron and parsley, 263

Smoked salmon on mixed salad greens, 257

Smoked trout and roasted capsicum salad, 249

Stuffed avocado salad, 33

Tabouleh with fish in lemon dressing, 245

Trout fillets with asparagus and tomato salad, 258

Tuna and egg salad, 253

Tuna and green bean salad, 247

Tuna and roasted capsicum salad, 249

Tuna salad with peas and onions, 253

Tuscan white bean salad with tuna, 47

Vegetable salad with tuna, 250

Vietnamese fish salad, 246

White fish salad with fennel and sun-dried tomatoes, 243

White fish salad with olive vinaigrette, 242

sesame dressing, White bean salad with, 189

sesame oil, 18

sesame seeds, *189*

Spicy pork salad, 213

shallots

Wild rice with shallots and lettuce, 183

Sherry cream, 291

shrimp *see* prawns

smoked salmon, *257*

Iceberg lettuce with salmon, 265

Salmon tartare on vegetable carpaccio, 256

Smoked salmon on mixed salad greens, 257

smoked trout

Smoked trout and roasted capsicum salad, 249

snake beans, *165*

snow peas, *79*

Rice salad with ginger-soy dressing, 179

Snow pea and lettuce salad with crunchy croutons, 79

Spicy pork salad, 213

Soba noodle salad, 168

sorrel, 17

Sour cream dressing, 40, 103

soya beans, 150

speck

Bavarian cabbage salad, 116

Spiced seasonal fruit salad, 297

Spicy beef salad with capsicum and corn, 60

Spicy brown rice salad with feta, 174

Spicy Chinese cabbage salad, 145

Spicy fruit dressing, 122

Spicy pork salad, 213

Spicy rice salad with pineapple, 181

Spicy sausage and cheese salad, 209

Spicy vinaigrette, 87

spinach, *118*

Chickpea, spinach and eggplant salad, 194

Curried lentil salad, 186

Fruity salad with blue cheese dressing, 134

Light potato salad with baby spinach, 89

Quinoa with sweet and spicy dressing, 197

Salad greens with fresh figs, 142

Spinach, roasted garlic and Parmesan, 32

Tarragon chicken salad, 221

Watercress and baby spinach with goat cheese, 118

spring onions

Middle Eastern bread salad, 55

Stuffed avocado salad, 33

Tabouleh, 57

Sprouts salad with mushrooms and celery, 123

squash

Marinated vegetable salad, 82

see also pumpkin

squid

Barbecued calamari with tomato vinaigrette, 274

Barbecued calamari salad, 275

Italian seafood salad, 241

Noodle and squid salad, 169

star fruit, Prickly pears with, 303

steaming, *94*

stone fruits, 279

storage, 14, 148, 278, 279

strawberries, 278

Berry salad with mascarpone cream, 280

Berry salad with pistachio cream, 280

Vanilla rhubarb with strawberries, 304

Stuffed avocado salad, 33

sugar-snap peas, *134*

Sugar-snap peas with grapes and feta, 134

sun-dried tomatoes

Warm chicken livers with green beans and tomatoes, 231

White fish salad with fennel and sun-dried tomatoes, 243

sunflower seeds

Crunchy salad with apples, 141

Lettuce, carrot and fennel salad with vinaigrette, 71

sunflower oil, *80*

Swiss-style cheese

Spicy sausage and cheese salad, 209

swordfish

Seafood salad with saffron and parsley, 263

t

Tabouleh, 57
Tabouleh with fish in lemon dressing, 245
tahini, *98*
    Eggplant salad with tahini, 98
tangerines
    Red cabbage with citrus, 136
tarragon, 12, *221*
    Tarragon chicken salad, 221
    Tarragon vinaigrette, 31
telegraph cucumber
    Cucumbers with dill and sour cream dressing, 40
    Middle Eastern bread salad, 55
    Prawn and mango salad, 262
    Tzatziki, 40
Tex Mex salad, 43
Thai beef salad, 203
Thai beef salad with peanuts, 60
Thousand islands dressing, 23
Three bean salad Tuscan-style, 34
thyme, 12
tofu, *121*
    Bok choy with pan-fried tofu and peanuts, 121
    Gado gado, 63
tomatoes, *82, 108*
    Artichoke and herb salad with white beans, 90
    Barbecued calamari with tomato vinaigrette, 274
    Buckwheat and artichoke salad with feta, 190
    Chef's salad, 29
    Cobb salad, 31
    Couscous salad with chickpeas, 193
    Fresh tomato salad, 117
    Greek salad, 59
    Grilled tomato salad, 108
    Grilled tomato salad with cheese, 109
    Lobster salad with celery and tomatoes, 270
    Middle Eastern bread salad, 55
    Mussel salad with croutons, 271
    Pico de gallo, 43

Rocket and radicchio salad with tomatoes, 115
Root vegetable salad with spicy vinaigrette, 87
Spicy brown rice salad with feta, 174
Tabouleh, 57
Warm lentil salad, 184
Wild rice salad with tomatoes and chilies, 182
see also cherry tomatoes; sun-dried tomatoes
Tortellini, carrot and egg salad, 166
Tossed salad with pears and blue cheese, 126
treviso
    Chicken with mixed salad greens, 218
    Smoked salmon on mixed salad greens, 257
    Turkey and fruit salad, 236
    Turkey with fruit and nuts, 237
Tropical fruit salad, 302
trout
    Japanese-style trout with wasabi and rocket, 258
    Smoked trout and roasted capsicum salad, 249
    Trout fillets with asparagus and tomato salad, 258
tuna, *160*
    Couscous salad with tuna, 193
    Diced vegetables with tuna, 251
    Orecchiette salad with tuna and aïoli, 160
    Tuna and egg salad, 253
    Tuna and green bean salad, 247
    Tuna and roasted capsicum salad, 249
    Tuna salad with peas and onions, 253
    Tuscan white bean salad with tuna, 47
    Vegetable salad with tuna, 250
turkey
    Turkey and fruit salad, 236
    Turkey and mushroom salad, 234
    Turkey with fruit and nuts, 237

turkey sausage
    Sausage, potato and radish salad, 232
Turkish carrot salad with garlic yogurt, 72
Tuscan white bean salad with tuna, 47
Tzatziki, 40

u

Vanilla rhubarb with strawberries, 304
vanilla sugar, *283*
veal
    Veal and mushroom salad with basil, 210
    Veal salad with beans, 210
Vegetable salad with tuna, 250
Vietnamese fish salad, 246
vinaigrette, 66
    Caperberry, 88
    Champagne, 76
    Classic herb, 21
    Citrus, 261
    Curry, 181
    Egg, 69
    Herb, 160, 253
    Lemon and sherry, 71
    Lemon thyme, 21
    Mustard, 272
    Mustard horseradish, 68
    Olive, 242
    Paprika, 93
    Pesto, 182
    Port, 137
    Raspberry nut, 20
    Spicy, 87
    Tarragon, 31
    Tomato, 274
    White wine, 29
vinegar, 19, 20

w

Waldorf salad, 28
walnut oil, 18, *136*

walnuts
Flambéed apple and walnut salad, 298
Red cabbage with citrus, 136
Salad greens with fresh figs, 142
Turkey with fruit and nuts, 237
Waldorf salad, 28
Warm chicken livers with green beans and tomatoes, 231
Warm grilled mixed vegetable salad, 107
Warm lentil salad, 184
Warm summer fruit salad with sabayon, 294
wasabi and rocket, Japanese-style trout with, 258
washing salad greens, 14
watercress, 12, *126*
Chicken salad with cucumber and watercress, 224
Crab and grapefruit salad, 267
Green salad with creamy herb yogurt, 66
Salmon on lettuce and watercress, 255
Smoked salmon on mixed salad greens, 257
Tossed salad with pears and blue cheese, 126
Watercress and baby spinach with goat cheese, 118
watermelon, 279
Melon salad with yogurt lime sauce, 286

white beans
Artichoke and herb salad with white beans, 90
Multi-layered salad with yogurt mayonnaise, 80
Tuscan white bean salad with tuna, 47
White bean salad with herb dressing, 189
White bean salad with sesame dressing, 189
white fish
Tabouleh with fish in lemon dressing, 245
Vietnamese fish salad, 246
White fish salad with fennel and sun-dried tomatoes, 243
White fish salad with olive vinaigrette, 242
white radish,
Japanese-style trout with wasabi and rocket, 258
White wine vinaigrette, 29
white wine vinegar, 19
Wild rice salad with shallots and lettuce, 183
Wild rice salad with tomatoes and chilies, 182
witlof, 17
Cabbage and nectarines with yogurt chutney, 144
Egg and radish salad, 104
Tarragon chicken salad, 221
wurst sausage
Spicy sausage and cheese salad, 209

yellow wax beans *see* butter beans
yogurt, *72*
Blackberry and lychee salad with yogurt, 283
Creamy chive, 66
Creamy herb, 66
Fresh beetroot salad with yogurt, 73
Turkish carrot salad with garlic yogurt, 72
Tzatziki, 40
Yogurt chutney, 144
Yogurt cream, 289
Yogurt dressing, 191, 264
Yogurt lime sauce, 286
Yogurt mayonnaise, 80, 152

zucchini
Couscous salad with tuna, 193
Farfalle salad with chicken, 156
Fennel and green bean salad, 97
Marinated vegetable salad, 82
Mussel salad with croutons, 271
Orecchiette salad with tuna and aioli, 160
Pasta salad with green vegetables, 152
Warm grilled mixed vegetable salad, 107

acknowledgments

All photographs not listed below are copyright of Reader's Digest Association.

17 *bottom right* Digital Vision/Getty Images. **138** (orange) C Squared Studios/Photodisc.

Concept code US 4499
Product code 041 3408